Definite, Indefinite, and Partitive Articles

You use articles with nouns to indicate something about those nouns. *Definite articles* refer to something specific, *indefinite articles* are unspecific, and *partitive articles* refer to a part of something. Chapter 2 has a lot more information about French articles.

Gender/Number	Definite (the)	Indefinite (a, an, some)	Partitive (some, any)
masculine singular	le	un	du
feminine singular	la	une	de la
plural	les	des	des

Contractions with À and De

The prepositions **à** (*at, to, in*) and **de** (*of, from*) always contract with the definite articles **le** and **les**:

Article	à + (le/les)	de + (le/les)
le	au	du
les	aux	des

There's no contraction with **à** or **de** plus **la** or **l'**: **à la, à l', de la, de l'**.

À and **de** also contract with the different forms of **lequel** (*which one*):

Form of Lequel	à + (lequel)	de + (lequel)
lequel	auquel	duquel
lesquels	auxquels	desquels
lesquelles	auxquelles	desquelles

There's no contraction with **laquelle: à laquelle, de laquelle.**

Personal Pronouns

Person	Subject Pronoun	Direct Object Pronoun	Indirect Object Pronoun	Reflexive Pronoun
1st person singular	je	me	me	me
2nd person singular	tu	te	te	te
3rd person singular (masc.)	il	le	lui	se
3rd person singular (fem.)	elle	la	lui	se
1st person plural	nous	nous	nous	nous
2nd person plural	vous	vous	vous	vous
3rd person plural	ils, elles	les	leur	se

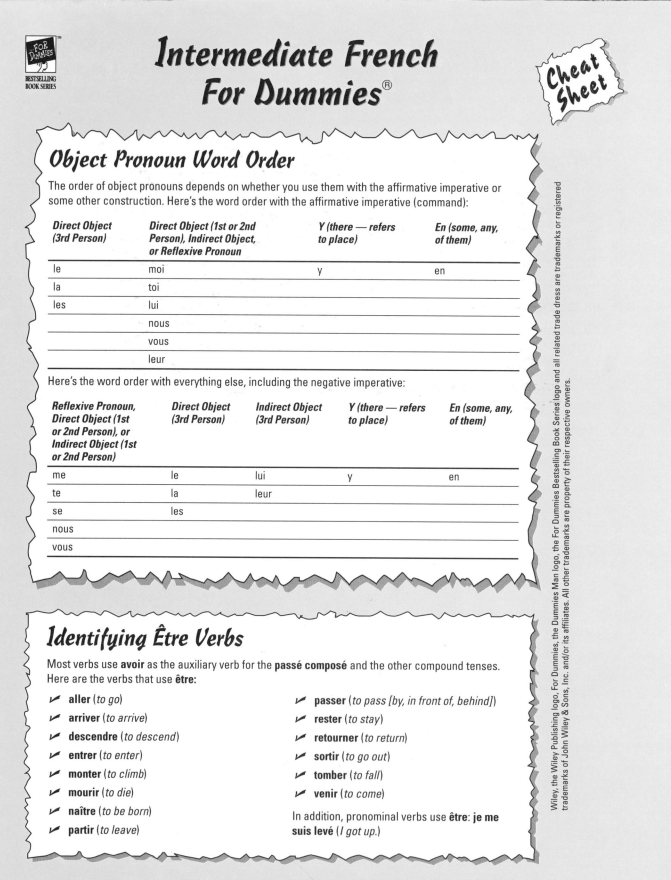

Intermediate French For Dummies®

Object Pronoun Word Order

The order of object pronouns depends on whether you use them with the affirmative imperative or some other construction. Here's the word order with the affirmative imperative (command):

Direct Object (3rd Person)	Direct Object (1st or 2nd Person), Indirect Object, or Reflexive Pronoun	Y (there — refers to place)	En (some, any, of them)
le	moi	y	en
la	toi		
les	lui		
	nous		
	vous		
	leur		

Here's the word order with everything else, including the negative imperative:

Reflexive Pronoun, Direct Object (1st or 2nd Person), or Indirect Object (1st or 2nd Person)	Direct Object (3rd Person)	Indirect Object (3rd Person)	Y (there — refers to place)	En (some, any, of them)
me	le	lui	y	en
te	la	leur		
se	les			
nous				
vous				

Identifying Être Verbs

Most verbs use **avoir** as the auxiliary verb for the **passé composé** and the other compound tenses. Here are the verbs that use **être**:

- **aller** (*to go*)
- **arriver** (*to arrive*)
- **descendre** (*to descend*)
- **entrer** (*to enter*)
- **monter** (*to climb*)
- **mourir** (*to die*)
- **naître** (*to be born*)
- **partir** (*to leave*)
- **passer** (*to pass [by, in front of, behind]*)
- **rester** (*to stay*)
- **retourner** (*to return*)
- **sortir** (*to go out*)
- **tomber** (*to fall*)
- **venir** (*to come*)

In addition, pronominal verbs use **être**: **je me suis levé** (*I got up.*)

For Dummies: Bestselling Book Series for Beginners

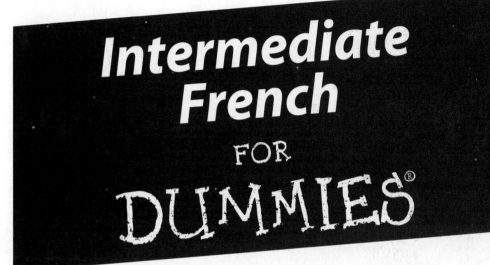

Intermediate French FOR DUMMIES®

by Laura K. Lawless

WILEY

Wiley Publishing, Inc.

Intermediate French For Dummies®

Published by
Wiley Publishing, Inc.
111 River St.
Hoboken, NJ 07030-5774
www.wiley.com

Copyright © 2008 by Wiley Publishing, Inc., Indianapolis, Indiana

Published by Wiley Publishing, Inc., Indianapolis, Indiana

Published simultaneously in Canada

For general information on our other products and services, please contact our Customer Care Department within the U.S. at 800-762-2974, outside the U.S. at 317-572-3993, or fax 317-572-4002.

For technical support, please visit www.wiley.com/techsupport.

Wiley also publishes its books in a variety of electronic formats. Some content that appears in print may not be available in electronic books.

Library of Congress Control Number: 2007943802

ISBN: 978-0-470-18768-5

Manufactured in the United States of America

10 9 8 7 6 5 4 3 2 1

WILEY

About the Author

Laura K. Lawless is a French fanatic. From the day she learned her first French words (the numbers 1–10 at age 10), she has been obsessed with the language of love. Her first trip to France, at 15, further convinced her that French would always be an essential part of her life. Laura has a BA in International Studies from the Monterey Institute of International Studies, and she has done graduate work in French and Spanish translation, interpretation, linguistics, and literature. She also studied French at *Institut de formation internationale* in Mont-St-Aignan, France, and at the *Alliance française* in Toulouse, France.

In 1999, after a year of teaching French and Spanish to adults, Laura became the French Language Guide at About.com (`http://french.about.com`), where she continues to create lessons, quizzes, listening exercises, and games for French students and teachers around the world. Her fascination with all things French guarantees that she will never run out of ideas for her French site or books (this is her fourth). Laura has lived in France, Morocco, and Costa Rica, and after scheming and dreaming for more than half her life, she and her husband will be moving to France in 2008.

Dedication

For O-man, my partner in all but crime.

Author's Acknowledgments

Thanks to my agent, Barb Doyen, who is always on my side, and to my editor Chad Sievers and the rest of the *For Dummies* crew at Wiley Publishing. To all the Francophiles who visit my Web site or read my books, **je vous remercie.** And a big **merci** to my husband, who read everything, even though it was already word perfect — well, almost. **Bisous !**

Publisher's Acknowledgments

We're proud of this book; please send us your comments through our Dummies online registration form located at www.dummies.com/register/.

Some of the people who helped bring this book to market include the following:

Acquisitions, Editorial, and Media Development

Project Editor: Chad R. Sievers

Acquisitions Editor: Michael Lewis

Copy Editor: Danielle Voirol

Editorial Program Coordinator: Erin Calligan Mooney

Technical Editor: Simone Pilon

Editorial Manager: Michelle Hacker

Editorial Assistants: Joe Niesen, Leeann Harney

Cartoons: Rich Tennant (www.the5thwave.com)

Composition Services

Project Coordinator: Patrick Redmond

Layout and Graphics: Alissa D. Ellet, Shane Johnson, Stephanie D. Jumper, Laura Pence, Erin Zeltner

Proofreaders: Caitie Kelly, Susan Moritz, Linda Quigley

Indexer: Broccoli Information Management

Publishing and Editorial for Consumer Dummies

    Diane Graves Steele, Vice President and Publisher, Consumer Dummies

    Joyce Pepple, Acquisitions Director, Consumer Dummies

    Kristin A. Cocks, Product Development Director, Consumer Dummies

    Michael Spring, Vice President and Publisher, Travel

    Kelly Regan, Editorial Director, Travel

Publishing for Technology Dummies

    Andy Cummings, Vice President and Publisher, Dummies Technology/General User

Composition Services

    Gerry Fahey, Vice President of Production Services

    Debbie Stailey, Director of Composition Services

Contents at a Glance

Table of Contents

Introduction

· ·

French is one of the world's great languages. It's a native language on five continents, and it's one of the most common languages in the world. Millions of people in more than 30 countries speak it as a native language, and millions more like you learn it for work, travel, or cultural understanding — or simply because they just love how it sounds.

The French take their language pretty seriously, and the **Académie française** has assumed the role of protecting the language's purity for more than 350 years — though not everyone listens to the **Académie**. French is a working language of many major international organizations, so if you're looking for a job with the United Nations, the International Olympic Committee, the International Red Cross, or Interpol, for example, brushing up on your French skills is a great idea.

Regardless of whether you're planning for business in France or Quebec, prepping for a trip to French-speaking Africa, trying to pass that next exam, or just looking for ways to impress the love of your life, this book can help you speak better, write better, and understand more French.

About This Book

Intermediate French For Dummies is a reference book for intermediate French speakers. It's not a textbook, and you don't have to read it from cover to cover or in any particular order. Just take a look at the Table of Contents or Index to find the grammar point you want to read about or practice and flip to that page. The Cheat Sheet at the beginning and the Appendixes at the end offer quick-reference ways to look up unfamiliar French words, conjugate verbs, and remember details such as which verbs need **être** in the compound tenses.

I divided the book into parts, with each part broken into chapters on related topics. From using the present tense to remembering the past to looking forward to the future, I explain all about French verbs. I also talk about adjectives and adverbs, questions and negation, object and adverbial pronouns . . . everything you need to know to communicate effectively in French.

Not only do you read about French in this book, but you use it as well. The self-contained chapters are divided into sections and include plenty of examples and practice exercises to make sure you understand what you've just read. The Answer Key at the end of each chapter lets you check yourself as you go.

Conventions Used in This Book

To make this book as easy to use as possible, I used certain conventions throughout:

- ✔ I **bold** all the French words so you can spot them immediately, and I always provide English translations for the French in *italics*.

- ✔ In French, the question mark and all other two-part punctuation marks — exclamation points, **guillemets** *(French quotation marks)*, colons, and semicolons — are preceded by a space. (When typing, be sure to use a non-breaking space in front of the punctuation mark to avoid its wrapping to the next line. Or if you set the language of your word-processing software to French, it should add the spaces for you.)

- ✔ In the Answer Key, I provide the *italicized* English translation of French answers so you can better understand each problem. Answers appear in **bold.**

- ✔ When a practice question has more than one correct answer, I provide the most common one. For exercises where you have to make up a sentence, I offer just one possibility so you can compare its grammar to what you wrote.

- ✔ I use the term *mute h* in reference to words like **homme** *(man)* and **habiter** *(to live),* which, for the purposes of contractions and liaisons, act like they start with a vowel. I use the term *aspirate h* to refer to words like **homard** *(lobster)* and **haïr** *(to hate)*, which act like they start with a consonant.

Foolish Assumptions

I wrote this book with the following assumptions about you and your French:

- ✔ You've taken enough French classes to consider yourself an intermediate writer or speaker.

- ✔ You understand basic concepts of English grammar. I define grammar-related terms, so you don't need to have an intimate understanding of sentence structure or to have a grammar guru on speed-dial, but you should be able to recognize the parts of speech and identify parts of a sentence, such as the subject and verb.

- ✔ You want to better your understanding of French grammar, such as verb conjugations and relative pronouns.

- ✔ You use French at work or school and want to improve your writing or speaking skills. Or you're planning a trip to France or another French-speaking country or province to put your French into practice.

If I'm right about these, then this book is for you. If you're not an intermediate French speaker, I recommend that before using this book, you pick up a copy of *French For Dummies*, by Dodi-Katrin Schmidt, Michelle M. Williams, and Dominique Wenzel (Wiley), or take a beginning-level French class.

How This Book Is Organized

I organized *Intermediate French for Dummies* in parts, beginning with the building blocks of French and ending with the Appendixes. Each part has at least two chapters that go into detail about that part's topic. The following sections outline the parts.

Part I: The Building Blocks of French

In this part, I explain the parts of speech and offer tips on using a bilingual dictionary correctly. I introduce the concepts of grammatical gender and number, possessives, and demonstrative adjectives and pronouns (*this, that, these,* and *those*). I also explain numbers, times, and dates.

Part II: The Here and Now: Writing in the Present

In Part II, I show you how to conjugate the present tense of all different kinds of verbs and how to use them. I also explain how to ask questions; make sentences negative; and use the infinitive, present participle, and subjunctive.

Part III: Writing with Panache: Dressing Up Your Sentences

In this part, I explain all about adjectives and adverbs, including how to use them in comparatives and superlatives. I also tell you how to give commands and use pronominal verbs (verbs that need reflexive pronouns). And I discuss prepositions, object and adverbial pronouns, conjunctions, and relative pronouns.

Part IV: That Was Then, and What Will Be, Will Be: The Past and Future Tenses

Part IV tells you all about the past and the four tenses you're likely to need to express it: the **passé composé** and **imparfait** (including how to decide between them), as well as the **plus-que-parfait** (past perfect) and the **passé simple.** I also tell you how to look ahead with the future (what will happen) and the conditional (what would or could happen, assuming a certain condition is met).

Part V: The Part of Tens

Every *For Dummies* book contains this fun, irreverent part with ten-item lists. Here I discuss ten common French mistakes and how to avoid them, provide ten different ways to start a letter, and explain the nuances between ten confusing verb pairs.

Part VI: Appendixes

You can use these Appendixes to conjugate French verbs, find French translations of English words, and discover what French words mean in English.

Icons Used in This Book

Like all *For Dummies* books, this one uses icons to indicate certain kinds of content. You can see them in the left-hand column throughout the book. Here's what they mean:

I use this icon next to a tip on how to use or remember the information provided. Tips save you time and frustration.

This icon points out important concept that you need to store in the back of your mind because you'll use them quite regularly.

Although warnings don't spotlight physical dangers, you should heed this icon because it points out potential pitfalls in the given material.

This icon lets you know about key points of difference between French and English.

This icon pops up at the beginning of every practice exercise so you know it's time to put your skills to the test.

Where to Go from Here

Intermediate French For Dummies is organized to let you read only what you want to read. Take a look at the Table of Contents or Index, pick a topic, and go! Or you may want to start in Chapter 1 to brush up on the parts of speech and get some tips on using a bilingual dictionary more efficiently. Want to talk about the past or future? Then flip to Part IV. It's up to you!

No matter how you choose to read this book, I'm confident that it can help you improve your French writing and speaking skills. Of course, you shouldn't let your practice end with the exercises here. Write to a French pen pal, visit French Web sites and message boards, rent foreign flicks from the library, attempt conversations with your French-speaking friends, or try to translate song lyrics into French while you're stuck in traffic. And when you have a grammar question, come back here and look it up. Pretty soon, the thoughts running through your head may take on a decidedly French flair. **Bonne chance !** (*Good luck!*)

Part I

The Building Blocks
of French

The 5th Wave   By Rich Tennant

"I'm pretty sure I already know the different parts of speech in French. I can speak a number of phrases using sarcasm, boredom, whimsy..."

In this part . . .

Before you get down to the nitty-gritty of verb conjugations and adjective agreement, you need to be familiar with the building blocks of French: the parts of speech. I cover the details in this part, along with tips on using a bilingual dictionary correctly. I also introduce nouns, gender, and number, which provide the foundation for grammatical agreement. Being able to talk about *my book* versus *this book* with possessives and demonstratives makes a big difference in your French skills. I wrap up this part with numbers, times, and dates, which help you express yourself and get to where — and when — you need to go.

Chapter 1

Understanding Parts of Speech and Bilingual Dictionaries

anguage is made up of parts of speech — nouns, verbs, adjectives, and so on. Each of these building blocks has its own function and rules, and understanding them is key to using them correctly, particularly with a foreign language. If you don't know the difference between the parts of speech in English, you probably won't understand them in French, either, which means you're likely to make a lot of mistakes when you write and speak.

Bilingual dictionaries are essential tools for speaking and understanding a new language, but misusing them is easy. You can't accept whatever the dictionary says as gospel — you need to know how to understand the symbols and abbreviations, how to make a choice when given several translations, and how much to trust the answers you get. This chapter explains the basic parts of speech as well as how to get the most out of your bilingual dictionary.

Identifying the Parts of Speech

You're probably already familiar with at least some of the parts of speech, like nouns and verbs, even though you don't necessarily think about them when speaking your native language. Because I use these terms throughout the book, I want to give you an overview of the parts of speech.

To help illustrate the differences between parts of speech, I talk about a sentence that has all eight essential parts of speech in both languages:

> **Je veux vraiment aller en France et visiter les musées célèbres.**
> (*I really want to go to France and visit the famous museums.*)

In the following sections, I bold the part of speech under consideration in my French sentence and English translation.

What's in a name? Nouns

Nouns are people, places, things, and ideas. They're the concrete and abstract things in your sentences, the *who* and the *what* that are doing something or having something done to them. Take a look at the example:

> Je veux vraiment aller en **France** et visiter les **musées** célèbres.
> (*I really want to go to **France** and visit the famous **museums.***)

France is a *proper* noun — a noun that refers to a specific person, place, or thing and that's always capitalized. Other proper nouns are *Laura* (that's me!) and the *Louvre*. *Museums* is a plural noun, which means it's also a *countable* noun because it can be counted: one museum, two museums, three museums, and so on. *Collective* nouns, like *group* and *bunch*, refer to a group of nouns considered a single unit. *Uncountable* nouns, like *beauty* and *fear*, are things that can't be counted.

In French, nouns are also masculine or feminine. Chapter 2 explains French nouns in greater detail. Nouns and verbs (see the upcoming section "Verbs take center stage") are the basic elements of any sentence. Nouns need verbs to tell them what they're doing, and verbs need nouns to explain who or what is acting or being acted upon. You can often replace nouns with pronouns — see "Using Pronouns" later in this chapter.

Underline all the nouns in this section.

> **Q.** *Nouns* are people, places, things, and ideas.

> **A.** *Nouns* are <u>people</u>, <u>places</u>, <u>things</u>, and <u>ideas</u>.

The articles

An article is a very particular part of speech. You can use it only with a noun. French has three kinds of articles:

- ✔ Definite articles: **le, la, les** (*the*)
- ✔ Indefinite articles: **un, une** (*a/an*), **des** (*some*)
- ✔ Partitive articles: **du, de la, des** (*some*)

The *definite article* refers to something specific: **le livre** (*the book*), **les idées** (*the ideas*). An *indefinite article* is unspecific: **un homme** (*a man*), **une chaise** (*a chair*), **des idées** (*some ideas*). *Partitive articles* refer to a part of something: **du pain** (*some bread*), **de la bière** (*some beer*). (***Note:*** In English, *some* is technically considered an adjective, not an article.) Chapter 2 has a lot more information about the French articles.

> Je veux vraiment aller en France et visiter **les** musées célèbres.
> (*I really want to go to France and visit **the** famous museums.*)

Underline the articles in this section.

Q. An article is a very particular part of speech.

A. <u>An</u> article is <u>a</u> very particular part of speech.

Verbs take center stage

Verbs express actions and describe states of being. They tell you what's happening, what the situation is like, and whether any music is pounding in the background during it all.

> Je **veux** vraiment **aller** en France et **visiter** les musées célèbres.
> (*I really **want to go** to France and **visit** the famous museums.*)

Verbs are the most variable part of speech because they have all kinds of different forms, called *conjugations*, which help tell you who or what is doing something, when they're doing it, and how they feel about it. French verbs are classified by how they're conjugated:

- ✔ Regular verbs
  - **-er** verbs
  - **-ir** verbs
  - **-re** verbs
- ✔ Stem-changing verbs
- ✔ Spelling-change verbs
- ✔ Irregular verbs

In addition, verbs have many different forms that give you all kinds of information about their actions:

- ✔ **Tense:** Tense tells you when the verb action takes place — in the present, past, or future — and whether it was completed (*perfect*) or incomplete (*imperfect*).
- ✔ **Mood:** Mood shows how the speaker feels about the verb action — whether it's *indicative, imperative, conditional,* or *subjunctive.*
- ✔ **Voice:** Voice indicates the relationship between the subject and the verb — whether it's *active, passive,* or *reflexive.*

See Chapter 4 for more information about present-tense verb conjugations and Chapters 7, 8, 10, 11, and 15–19 for information about various tenses and moods.

Underline the verbs in this section.

Q. *Verbs* express actions and describe states of being.

A. *Verbs* <u>express</u> actions and <u>describe</u> states of being.

Describing adjectives

Adjectives are flowery, helpful, and exciting words that describe nouns. Adjectives may tell you what color something is, whether it's new or old, or its shape, size, or provenance.

> Je veux vraiment aller en France et visiter les musées **célèbres**.
> (*I really want to go to France and visit the **famous** museums.*)

Adjectives usually aren't essential, the way nouns and verbs are, because they just add some extra information to the basic facts. Compare *My brother has a car* to *My older brother has a red car* — the important information is that your brother has a car; the fact that he's older than you and that the car is red is just window dressing. Adjectives like these are called *descriptive adjectives,* but adjectives come in many other useful varieties:

- Demonstrative adjectives: **ce, cette** (*this, that*), **ces** (*these, those*)
- Indefinite adjectives: **quelques** (*some*), **certain** (*certain*), **plusieurs** (*several*)
- Interrogative adjectives: **quel** (*which*)
- Negative adjectives: **ne . . . aucun, ne . . . nul** (*no, not any*)
- Possessive adjectives: **mon** (*my*), **ton** (*your*), **son** (*his/her*)

Unlike boring old English adjectives, French adjectives have masculine, feminine, singular, and plural forms so that they can agree with nouns. (Chapter 9 tells you lots of other interesting details about adjectives.)

Underline the adjectives in this section.

Q. *Adjectives* are flowery, helpful, and exciting words that describe nouns.

A. *Adjectives* are <u>flowery</u>, <u>helpful</u>, and <u>exciting</u> words that describe nouns.

Using adverbs

Adverbs easily modify verbs, adjectives, and other adverbs. Like adjectives, adverbs aren't always essential, but rather, they add some extra information to the words they're helpfully modifying. In the example sentence, *really* modifies the verb *want*.

> Je veux **vraiment** aller en France et visiter les musées célèbres.
> (*I **really** want to go to France and visit the famous museums.*)

English adverbs often end in *-ly* and indicate how the action of a verb is occurring: happily, quickly, rudely. Most of these words are *adverbs of manner*. The other kinds of adverbs are

- Adverbs of frequency: **jamais** (*never*), **souvent** (*often*)
- Adverbs of place: **ici** (*here*), **partout** (*everywhere*)
- Adverbs of quantity: **très** (*very*), **beaucoup** (*a lot*)

✔ Adverbs of time: **avant** (*before*), **demain** (*tomorrow*)

✔ Interrogative adverbs: **quand** (*when*), **où** (*where*)

✔ Negative adverbs: **ne . . . pas** (*not*), **ne . . . jamais** (*never*)

Read Chapter 9 thoroughly to understand more about French adverbs.

Underline the adverbs in this section.

Q. *Adverbs* easily modify verbs, adjectives, and other adverbs.

A. *Adverbs* <u>easily</u> modify verbs, adjectives, and other adverbs.

Pronouns: They're replacements

Pronouns are easy to understand; they replace nouns. That is, pronouns also refer to people, places, things, and ideas, but they let you avoid repeating the same words over and over.

For example, you could say, "I have a sister. My sister has a cat. The cat has fleas, and the fleas make the cat itch." But hearing those nouns repeated each time gets a little old. A much nicer way to say that would be, "I have a sister. She has a cat. It has fleas, and they make it itch." *I*, *she*, *it*, and *they* are *personal pronouns* because they have different forms for each *grammatical person*. (You can read about grammatical person in Chapter 4.)

> **Je** veux vraiment aller en France et visiter les musées célèbres.
> (***I** really want to go to France and visit the famous museums.*)

French has five types of personal pronouns. The following are all equivalent to *I/me, you,* or *he/him/it:*

✔ Subject pronouns: **je, tu, il**

✔ Direct object pronouns: **me, te, le**

✔ Indirect object pronouns: **me, te, lui**

✔ Reflexive pronouns: **me, te, se**

✔ Stressed pronouns: **moi, toi, lui**

French also has several kinds of *impersonal pronouns*, which doesn't mean they're unkind, just that they don't have different forms for each grammatical person. However, many of them do have different forms for masculine, feminine, singular, and plural. Take a look (***Note:*** I hold off on the definitions for now):

✔ Adverbial pronouns: **y, en**

✔ Demonstrative pronouns: **celui, celle**

✔ Indefinite pronouns: **autre, certain**

✔ Interrogative pronouns: **quel, quelle**

> ✔ Negative pronouns: **aucun, personne**
>
> ✔ Possessive pronouns: **le mien, le tien**
>
> ✔ Relative pronouns: **qui, que, dont**

I explain the different types of pronouns throughout this book: Chapter 2 explains demonstrative and possessive pronouns, Chapter 4 presents subject pronouns, Chapter 5 discusses interrogative ones, and so on.

Underline the pronouns in this section.

Q. *Pronouns* are easy to understand; they replace nouns.

A. *Pronouns* are easy to understand; <u>they</u> replace nouns.

Prepositions: On top of it

A *preposition* is the part of speech you put in front of a noun or pronoun to show the relationship between that word and another word or phrase. When you go to the store, return from vacation, or trip over the shoes you left sitting under a towel lying on the floor, the prepositions tell you how those verbs and nouns fit together. The shoes are *under* the towel, not *on, next to,* or wrapped *in* it. Prepositions may be one word (*to, at, about*) or part of a group of words (*next to, in front of, on top of*).

> Je veux vraiment aller **en** France et visiter les musées célèbres.
> (*I really want to go **to** France and visit the famous museums.*)

Prepositions are difficult to translate, perhaps more so than any other part of speech. The French preposition **à,** for example, usually means *to, at,* or *in,* but also has other meanings in certain expressions:

> ✔ Destination: **Je vais à Paris.** (*I'm going to Paris.*)
>
> ✔ Current location: **Je suis à la banque/à Londres.** (*I'm at the bank/in London.*)
>
> ✔ Function: **un verre à vin** (*a wine glass, a glass for wine*)
>
> ✔ Owner: **C'est à moi.** (*It's mine, It belongs to me.*)

Prepositions are therefore not like a list of vocabulary that you can just memorize, but rather, they're grammatical terms with various functions that you have to study and practice. Chapter 12 explains all about prepositions.

Underline the prepositions in this section.

Q. A *preposition* is the part of speech you put in front of a noun or pronoun to show the relationship between that word and another word or phrase.

A. A *preposition* is the part <u>of</u> speech you put <u>in front of</u> a noun or pronoun to show the relationship <u>between</u> that word and another word or phrase.

Connecting with conjunctions

Conjunctions join two or more words or phrases that are either equal or unequal.

> Je veux vraiment aller en France **et** visiter les musées célèbres.
> (*I really want to go to France **and** visit the famous museums.*)

They come in a couple of varieties:

- ✔ **Coordinating conjunctions:** These words — such as *and, or,* and *but* — bring together equals, as in *I like coffee and tea.* Other examples include *He can't read or write* and *We want to go, but we don't have time.*

  You can tell that a conjunction is coordinating when you can reverse the joined items with little or no difference in meaning. There's no difference between *I like coffee and tea* and *I like tea and coffee.* Likewise, *We want to go, but we don't have time* means pretty much the same thing as *We don't have time, but we want to go.*

- ✔ **Subordinating conjuctions:** Subordinating conjunctions — such as *that, when,* and *as soon as* — combine two *clauses,* or groups of words with a subject and verb. The conjunction tells you that the clause after it is *subordinate,* meaning that clause is dependent on the *main clause,* as in *He thinks that I'm smart* (I may or may not be smart, but he thinks I am), *I don't know when they'll arrive* (They're supposed to arrive, but I don't know when), and *She left as soon as the phone rang* (The phone rang, and then she left).

  If you reverse the clauses in my examples, you end up with either nonsense or a different meaning. *I am smart that he thinks* doesn't make any sense, and *The phone rang as soon as she left* isn't the same thing as *She left as soon as the phone rang* — in fact, it's just the opposite. This test lets you know that these conjunctions are subordinating rather than coordinating. (Chapter 14 examines coordinating and subordinating conjunctions in more detail.)

Underline the conjunctions in this section.

Q. *Conjunctions* join two or more words or phrases that are either equal or unequal.

A. *Conjunctions* join two <u>or</u> more words <u>or</u> phrases <u>that</u> are either equal <u>or</u> unequal.

Correctly Using a Bilingual Dictionary

A bilingual dictionary can be a wonderful tool or a terrible crutch. When you don't know what a word means or how to say something in another language, a bilingual dictionary can give you the answer. But it's not as simple as just looking something up and taking the first thing you see. You have to know what to look up, how to read the information provided, and how much you can depend on the answer you get. This section can help you make a bilingual dictionary a helpful tool and not a hindrance.

Figuring out what to look up

Although dictionaries have thousands of words, you can't find every single word you want just by looking it up. Different versions of words, including plurals, feminines, verb conjugations, comparatives, and superlatives, for example, aren't listed separately, so you need to know where to find these words. You can find them only by looking for the singular, masculine, infinitive, unmodified word.

For example, suppose you see the word **mettez** for the first time and you want to know what it means. You grab your bilingual dictionary and discover there's no entry for **mettez.** Instead of giving up, do a little grammatical analysis. **Mettez** ends in **-ez,** which is a common French verb ending, so conjugate backwards — the infinitive is likely to be **metter, mettir,** or **mettre.** Look those up, and voilà! You discover that **mettre** means *to put.*

Likewise, if you can't find **traductrice,** remove the feminine ending (which Chapter 2 explains) because the word in the dictionary is the default, masculine form **traducteur** (*translator*).

If you're trying to look up an expression, such as **Qui se ressemble s'assemble,** you can start by looking up the first word, **qui,** but you may not have any luck. The dictionary may include the expression under that entry, or it may list it under a different word that the dictionary editors thought was more of a key to the phrase, such as **ressembler.** Check there, and sure enough, you discover that it means *those who resemble each other assemble,* or rather, that it's the French equivalent of the proverb *birds of a feather flock together.*

Note: Pronominal verbs, such as **se ressembler** and **se souvenir,** are listed in the dictionary under the verb, not the reflexive pronoun. So you'd look up **ressembler** and **souvenir,** not **se.** (You can read about pronominal verbs in Chapter 11.)

Choosing the right word based on context and part of speech

Finding the word you want is only half the battle — you also need to think about what it means, which is why you have to understand *context* — the situation in which you're using the word. You may not have any idea what **un avocat** is (check out Figure 1-1), but you need to figure out from the context of the sentence you saw it in whether it's a food or a person; when you look up **avocat,** you find two translations: *avocado* and *lawyer.* The context you're using it in obviously makes a big difference as to which translation is correct (unless, perhaps, you're reading about a lawyer who dressed as guacamole for Halloween!).

Likewise, if you want to know how to say *record* in French, you need to know whether you're looking for the noun, as in *I bought a record,* or the verb, as in *I want to record this song.* When you look up *record* in the dictionary, you see two translations: **un disque** and **enregistrer.** The dictionary doesn't know which one you want — the correct choice depends on context and on your knowing the difference between a noun and a verb.

Figure 1-1:
What the French-English dictionary entry for **avocat** may look like.

AVOCAT
[a vɔ ka] m subst
(person) lawyer,
(fruit) avocado

Some people like to keep a list of words to look up later instead of putting the book or newspaper down every two minutes to look them up right away. If you're one of these, be sure to jot down the phrase or sentence rather than just the word. Otherwise, you'll find when you get the dictionary out that you can't figure out which translation is best, because you have no context to fit it into.

Understanding symbols and terminology

Dictionaries save space by using symbols and abbreviations, and these are not necessarily standard from one dictionary to the next. Your best bet is to check the first few pages of the dictionary — you should see some kind of legend that lists the abbreviations used throughout the book, the pronunciation notation, and symbols that indicate things like word stress, formality or informality, archaic words, silent letters, and so on.

The *International Phonetic Alphabet*, or *IPA,* is a standard system for showing how to pronounce words in any language. Unfortunately, many dictionaries either don't use it or adapt it with their own symbols, so you always need to check your dictionary to see which system they're using to explain pronunciation. The second line in Figure 1-1 shows the IPA spelling for the word **avocat** *(lawyer, avocado).*

The symbols and abbreviations aren't there just to look pretty! If a word is listed as archaic, you don't want to use it (unless you happen to be translating 14th-century poetry). If a term is starred three times, indicating that it's vulgar slang, you definitely don't want to say that to your boss. As I explain in the preceding section, you need to think about how you're using a particular word before you make your selection from the translations offered.

Interpreting figurative language and idioms

When using a bilingual dictionary to determine a word's meaning, you also need to understand whether a term is being used literally or figuratively. French and English are both rich in figurative language, and translating can be tricky. Take the expression *Guy is hot.* Literally, this means that Guy is very warm — he's wearing too many clothes, say, or he has a fever. Figuratively (and informally), it means that Guy is extremely good looking. If you want to translate this sentence into French, you need to figure out which meaning you're after and then make sure to find the correct French translation for that meaning. When you look up the word, in this case, *hot,* the literal meaning(s) is normally listed first, followed by any figurative meaning(s). The latter will have a notation such as *fig.* (short for *figurative*). (For the record, the literal translation of *Guy is hot* is **Guy a chaud,** and the figurative is **Guy est sexy.**)

You may run across figurative language when you translate into English, too. The French expression **connaître la musique** literally means *to know the music,* such as an actual song. Figuratively, it means *to know the routine.* You have to think about which of these English meanings is right for the context in which you saw or heard the French expression.

An *idiom* is an expression that can't be translated literally into another language because one or more words in it are used figuratively. *It's raining cats and dogs* doesn't really mean that household pets are falling from the sky; it just means that it's raining really hard. You absolutely can't look up the individual words to come up with **Il pleut des chats et des chiens** — that makes no sense at all. The French equivalent of *It's raining cats and dogs* is also an idiom: **Il pleut des cordes** (Literally: *It's raining ropes*).

Automated translators, such as online translation Web sites, translate very literally, which is why you should never use them to translate something that you plan to say to someone or write in a letter. All they're good for is helping you get an idea of what something says — translating into a language you understand.

Verifying your findings

After you've found your word or expression and have considered the context you'll be using it in, it's a good idea to verify what you've found. I suggest you use the following ideas to double-check that you're using the right meaning:

✓ **Ask a native.** The best way to verify that you're using the right word is to ask a native speaker. Dictionaries are wonderful tools, but they're not infallible. Language changes — particularly informal language — and dictionaries change constantly. Even if they didn't, they still couldn't tell you that a certain expression or way of using a particular word "just doesn't sound right." Native speakers are the experts. To find a native speaker, ask your professor if he or she knows anyone. If there's a local branch of the Alliance française near you, find out the time of the next meeting. Or you can try an online forum such as http://forums.about.com/ab-french.

✓ **Do a reverse look-up.** One quick and easy way to check whether the word you found is the right one is to do reverse look-up, which is when you look up the translation that the dictionary just gave you. For example, if you've looked up *anger* in the English-French part of the dictionary and found that it means **colère** or **fureur,** you can then look up those two words in the French-English dictionary. You'll see that **colère** says *anger* and **fureur** says *fury,* so that indicates that **colère** is probably the better translation for *anger.*

Another way to confirm a translation is by looking up *anger* in an English dictionary and **colère** in a French dictionary and comparing the definitions.

Answer Key

Nouns:

They're the concrete and abstract <u>things</u> in your <u>sentences</u>, the *who* and the *what* that are doing something or having something done to them. Take a <u>look</u> at the <u>example</u>: Je veux vraiment aller en <u>France</u> et visiter les <u>musées</u> célèbres. (*I really want to go to France and visit the famous museums.*) *France* is a *proper noun* — a <u>noun</u> that refers to a specific <u>person</u>, <u>place</u>, or <u>thing</u> and that's always capitalized. Other proper <u>nouns</u> are *Laura* (that's me!) and the *Louvre*. *Museums* is a plural <u>noun</u>, which means it's also a *countable noun* because it can be counted: one <u>museum</u>, two <u>museums</u>, three <u>museums</u>, and so on. *Collective* <u>nouns</u>, like <u>group</u> and <u>bunch</u>, refer to a <u>group</u> of <u>nouns</u> considered a single <u>unit</u>. *Uncountable* <u>nouns</u>, like <u>beauty</u> and <u>fear</u>, are <u>things</u> that can't be counted. <u>Nouns</u> and <u>verbs</u> (see the upcoming <u>section</u> "Verbs take center <u>stage</u>") are the basic <u>elements</u> of any <u>sentence</u>. <u>Nouns</u> need <u>verbs</u> to tell them what they're doing, and <u>verbs</u> need <u>nouns</u> to explain who or what is acting or being acted upon. You can often replace <u>nouns</u> with <u>pronouns</u> — see "Using <u>Pronouns</u>" later in this <u>chapter</u>. In <u>French</u>, <u>nouns</u> are also masculine or feminine. <u>Chapter</u> 2 explains French <u>nouns</u> in greater <u>detail</u>. Underline all the <u>nouns</u> in this <u>section</u>.

Articles:

You can use it only with <u>a</u> noun. French has three kinds of articles: * Definite articles: <u>le</u>, <u>la</u>, <u>les</u> (*the*) * Indefinite articles: <u>un</u>, <u>une</u> (*a/an*), <u>des</u> (*some*) * Partitive articles: <u>du</u>, <u>de la</u>, <u>des</u> (*some*) The *definite article* refers to something specific: <u>le</u> livre (*the book*), <u>les</u> idées (*the ideas*). An *indefinite article* is unspecific: <u>un</u> homme (*a man*), <u>une</u> chaise (*a chair*), <u>des</u> idées (*some ideas*). *Partitive articles* refer to <u>a</u> part of something: <u>du</u> pain (*some bread*), <u>de la</u> bière (*some beer*). (**Note:** In English, *some* is technically considered <u>an</u> adjective, not <u>an</u> article.) Chapter 2 has <u>a</u> lot more information about <u>the</u> French articles. Je veux vraiment aller en France et visiter <u>les</u> musées célèbres. (*I really want to go to France and visit <u>the</u> famous museums.*) Underline <u>the</u> articles in this section.

Verbs:

They <u>tell</u> you what<u>'s happening</u>, what the situation <u>is</u> like, and whether any music <u>is pounding</u> in the background during it all. Je veux vraiment <u>veux</u> vraiment <u>aller</u> en France et <u>visiter</u> les musées célèbres. (*I really <u>want to go</u> to France and <u>visit</u> the famous museums.*) Verbs <u>are</u> the most variable part of speech because they <u>have</u> all kinds of different forms, called *conjugations*, which <u>help tell</u> you who or what <u>is doing</u> something, when they<u>'re doing</u> it, and how they <u>feel</u> about it. French verbs <u>are classified</u> by how they<u>'re conjugated</u>: * Regular verbs * -er verbs * -ir verbs * -re verbs * Stem-changing verbs * Spelling-change verbs * Irregular verbs In addition, verbs <u>have</u> many different forms that <u>give</u> you all kinds of information about their actions: * Tense: Tense <u>tells</u> you when the verb action <u>takes</u> place — in the present, past, or future — and whether it <u>was</u> <u>completed</u> (*perfect*) or incomplete (*imperfect*). * Mood: Mood <u>shows</u> how the speaker <u>feels</u> about the verb action — whether it<u>'s</u> *indicative*, *imperative*, *conditional*, or *subjunctive*. * Voice: Voice <u>indicates</u> the relationship between the subject and the verb — whether it<u>'s</u> *active*, *passive*, or *reflexive*. <u>See</u> Chapter 4 for more information about present-tense verb conjugations and Chapters 7, 8, 10, 11, and 15–19 for information about various tenses and moods. <u>Underline</u> the verbs in this section.

Adjectives:

Adjectives may tell you <u>what</u> color something is, whether it's <u>new</u> or <u>old</u>, or <u>its</u> shape, size, or provenance. Je veux vraiment aller en France et visiter les musées <u>célèbres</u>. (*I really want to go to France and visit the <u>famous</u> museums.*) Adjectives usually aren't <u>essential</u>, the way nouns and verbs are, because they just add <u>some</u> <u>extra</u> information to the <u>basic</u> facts. Compare *My brother has a car* to *My <u>older</u> brother has a <u>red</u> car* — the <u>important</u> information is that your brother has a car; the fact that he's <u>older</u> than you and that the car is <u>red</u> is just <u>window</u> dressing. Adjectives like these are called *descriptive adjectives,* but adjectives come in <u>many</u> <u>other</u> <u>useful</u> varieties: * <u>Demonstrative</u> adjectives: <u>ce</u>, <u>cette</u> (*this, that*), <u>ces</u> (*these, those*) * <u>Indefinite</u> adjectives: <u>quelques</u> (*some*), <u>certain</u> (*certain*), <u>plusieurs</u> (*several*) * <u>Interrogative</u> adjectives: <u>quel</u> (*which*) * <u>Negative</u> adjectives: <u>ne . . . aucun</u>, <u>ne . . . nul</u> (*no, not any*) * <u>Possessive</u> adjectives: <u>mon</u> (*my*), <u>ton</u> (*your*), <u>son</u> (*his/her*) Unlike <u>boring</u> <u>old</u> <u>English</u> adjectives, <u>French</u> adjectives have <u>masculine</u>, <u>feminine</u>, <u>singular</u>, and <u>plural</u> forms so that they can agree with nouns. (Chapter 9 tells you lots of <u>other</u> <u>interesting</u> details about adjectives.) Underline the adjectives in <u>this</u> section.

Adverbs:

Like adjectives, adverbs aren't <u>always</u> essential, but rather, they add some extra information to the words they're <u>helpfully</u> modifying. In the example sentence, *really* modifies the verb *want*. Je veux vraiment <u>vraiment</u> aller en France et visiter les musées célèbres. (*I <u>really</u> want to go to France and visit the famous museums.*) English adverbs <u>often</u> end in *-ly* and indicate how the action of a verb is occurring: <u>happily</u>, <u>quickly</u>, <u>rudely</u>. Most of these words are *adverbs of manner*. The other kinds of adverbs are * Adverbs of frequency: <u>jamais</u> (*never*), <u>souvent</u> (*often*) * Adverbs of place: <u>ici</u> (*here*), <u>partout</u> (*everywhere*) * Adverbs of quantity: <u>très</u> (*very*), <u>beaucoup</u> (*a lot*) * Adverbs of time: <u>avant</u> (*before*), <u>demain</u> (*tomorrow*) * Interrogative adverbs: <u>quand</u> (*when*), <u>où</u> (*where*) * Negative adverbs: ne . . . <u>pas</u> (*not*), ne . . . <u>jamais</u> (*never*) Read Chapter 9 <u>thoroughly</u> to understand more about French adverbs. Underline the adverbs in this section.

Pronouns:

<u>That</u> is, pronouns also refer to people, places, things, and ideas, but <u>they</u> let you avoid repeating the same words over and over. For example, <u>you</u> could say, "<u>I</u> have a sister. My sister has a cat. The cat has fleas, and the fleas make the cat itch." But hearing those nouns repeated each time gets a little old. A much nicer way to say <u>that</u> would be, "<u>I</u> have a sister. <u>She</u> has a cat. <u>It</u> has fleas, and <u>they</u> make <u>it</u> itch." *<u>I</u>*, *<u>she</u>*, *<u>it</u>*, and *<u>they</u>* are *personal pronouns* because <u>they</u> have different forms for each *grammatical person*. (<u>You</u> can read about grammatical person in Chapter 4.) <u>Je</u> veux vraiment aller en France et visiter les musées célèbres. (*<u>I</u> really want to go to France and visit the famous museums.*) French has five types of personal pronouns. The following are all equivalent to *<u>I/me</u>*, *<u>you</u>*, or *<u>he/him/it</u>*: * Subject pronouns: <u>je</u>, <u>tu</u>, <u>il</u> * Direct object pronouns: <u>me</u>, <u>te</u>, <u>le</u> * Indirect object pronouns: <u>me</u>, <u>te</u>, <u>lui</u> * Reflexive pronouns: <u>me</u>, <u>te</u>, <u>se</u> * Stressed pronouns: <u>moi</u>, <u>toi</u>, <u>lui</u> French also has several kinds of *impersonal pronouns*, <u>which</u> doesn't mean <u>they</u>'re unkind, just that <u>they</u> don't have different forms for each grammatical person. However, <u>many</u> of <u>them</u> do have different forms for masculine, feminine, singular, and plural. Take a look (*Note:* <u>I</u> hold off on the definitions for now): * Adverbial pronouns: <u>y</u>, <u>en</u> * Demonstrative pronouns: <u>celui</u>, <u>celle</u> * Indefinite pronouns: <u>autre</u>, <u>certain</u> * Interrogative pronouns: <u>quel</u>, <u>quelle</u> * Negative pronouns: <u>aucun</u>, <u>personne</u> * Possessive pronouns: <u>le mien</u>, <u>le tien</u> * Relative pronouns: <u>qui</u>, <u>que</u>, <u>dont</u> <u>I</u> explain the different types of pronouns throughout this book: Chapter 2 explains demonstrative and possessive pronouns, Chapter 4 presents subject pronouns, Chapter 5 discusses interrogative <u>ones</u>, and so on. Underline the pronouns in this section.

Prepositions:

When you go <u>to</u> the store, return <u>from</u> vacation, or trip <u>over</u> the shoes you left sitting <u>under</u> a towel lying <u>on</u> the floor, the prepositions tell you how those verbs and nouns fit together. The shoes are *<u>under</u>* the towel, not *<u>on</u>*, *<u>next to</u>*, or wrapped *<u>in</u>* it. Prepositions may be one word (*<u>to</u>*, *<u>at</u>*, *<u>about</u>*) or part <u>of</u> a group <u>of</u> words (*<u>next to</u>*, *<u>in front of</u>*, *<u>on top of</u>*). Je veux vraiment aller <u>en</u> France et visiter les musées célèbres. (*I really want to go <u>to</u> France and visit the famous museums.*) Prepositions are difficult to translate, perhaps more so than any other part <u>of</u> speech. The French preposition <u>à</u>, for example, usually means *<u>to</u>*, *<u>at</u>*, or *<u>in</u>*, but also has other meanings <u>in</u> certain expressions: * Destination: Je vais <u>à</u> Paris. (*I'm going <u>to</u> Paris.*) * Current location: Je suis <u>à</u> la banque/<u>à</u> Londres. (*I'm <u>at</u> the bank/<u>in</u> London.*) * Function: un verre <u>à</u> vin (*a wine glass, a glass <u>for</u> wine*) * Owner: C'est <u>à</u> moi. (*It's mine, It belongs <u>to</u> me.*) Prepositions are therefore not like a list <u>of</u> vocabulary that you can just memorize, but rather, they're grammatical terms <u>with</u> various functions that you have to study and practice. Chapter 12 explains all <u>about</u> prepositions. Underline the prepositions <u>in</u> this section.

Conjunctions:

Je veux vraiment aller en France <u>et</u> visiter les musées célèbres. (*I really want to go to France <u>and</u> visit the famous museums.*) They come in a couple of varieties: * Coordinating conjunctions: These words — such as *<u>and</u>*, *<u>or</u>*, and *<u>but</u>* — bring together equals, as in *I like coffee <u>and</u> tea*. Other examples include *He can't read <u>or</u> write* <u>and</u> *We want to go, <u>but</u> we don't have time.* You can tell that a conjunction is coordinating <u>when</u> you can reverse the joined items with little <u>or</u> no difference in meaning. There's no difference between *I like coffee <u>and</u> tea* <u>and</u> *I like tea <u>and</u> coffee*. Likewise, *We want to go, <u>but</u> we don't have time* means pretty much the same thing as *We don't have time, <u>but</u> we want to go.* * Subordinating conjuctions: Subordinating conjunctions — such as *<u>that</u>*, *<u>when</u>*, and *<u>as soon as</u>* — combine two *clauses*, <u>or</u> groups of words with a subject <u>and</u> verb. The conjunction tells you <u>that</u> the clause after it is *subordinate*, meaning that clause is dependent on the *main clause*, as in *He thinks <u>that</u> I'm smart* (I may <u>or</u> may not be smart, <u>but</u> he thinks I am), *I don't know <u>when</u> they'll arrive* (They're supposed to arrive, <u>but</u> I don't know when), and *She left <u>as soon as</u> the phone rang* (The phone rang, <u>and</u> then she left). If you reverse the clauses in my examples, you end up with <u>either</u> nonsense <u>or</u> a different meaning. *I am smart <u>that</u> he thinks* doesn't make any sense, <u>and</u> *The phone rang <u>as soon as</u> she left* isn't the same thing as *She left <u>as soon as</u> the phone rang* — in fact, it's just the opposite. This test lets you know <u>that</u> these conjunctions are subordinating rather than coordinating. (Chapter 14 examines coordinating <u>and</u> subordinating conjunctions in more detail.) Underline the conjunctions in this section.

Chapter 2

Figuring Out Nouns, Articles, and Possession

*N*ouns are the people, places, and things in your sentences, the *who* and *what* that are doing whatever it is that needs to be done — or that are having something done to them — and the *where* all this excitement is taking place. You're surrounded by nouns — this book, these words, my writing, your thoughts.

Nouns can be specific, general, owned, nearby, or far away. Nouns are either singular or plural, and in French, every noun is masculine or feminine — even tables and chairs! This chapter explains the number and gender of French nouns, plus how to use possessives and demonstratives with them.

Genre Bending: Writing with Masculine and Feminine Nouns

A basic, singular noun refers to just one of something: a book, the cheese, my house. In English, that's about all there is to know about singular nouns. French, however, adds a little more to it: Every noun has a *gender* (**genre**), either masculine or feminine. This section spells out the need-to-know details about gender.

Determining the gender of nouns

In English, only nouns referring to people, certain animals, and some boats have gender. But in French, all nouns have a gender, which makes more of a difference than you can possibly imagine. A noun's gender determines which form of articles, adjectives, pronouns, and sometimes past participles you have to use, so knowing the gender is vital to speaking and writing French. Some words even have different meanings depending on their gender, like **le mari** (*husband*) and **la mari** (*marijuana*). So if you're talking to a police officer, be sure to use the masculine article when telling him that your husband is at home; otherwise, you may just find a search warrant waiting for you when you get there!

Most nouns that refer to people have a logical gender. **Homme** (*man*), **garçon** (*boy*), and **serveur** (*waiter*) are masculine, and **femme** (*woman*), **fille** (*girl*), and **serveuse** (*waitress*) are feminine. Animals and inanimate objects, however, are another kettle (**poissonière** — feminine) of fish (**poisson** — masculine) altogether. The gender of objects and many animals is arbitrary — or at least it seems that way to English speakers. In most cases, there's no way to just look at a word and know what gender it is — you just have to memorize the gender of each word as you learn it.

The best way to remember the gender of nouns is to make sure your vocabulary lists include an article for each noun (see "Understanding Articles and How They Indicate Gender and Number," later in this chapter, for details). If possible, use indefinite articles, because they don't change in front of vowels. Then when you look at your list, the gender of the article tells you the gender of the noun: You can see that **un ordinateur** (*computer*) is masculine, due to the masculine article, and that **une télévision** (*television*) is feminine.

A few word endings tend to indicate whether a noun is masculine or feminine. Words that end in **-age**, as in **message** and **mirage**, and **-eau**, like **manteau** (*coat*) and **chapeau** (*hat*), are usually masculine. On the other hand, most words that end in **-ion**, like **libération** and **possession**, and **-té**, such as **liberté** (*freedom*) and **égalité** (*equality*), are feminine. But there are exceptions to all of these, and thousands of nouns don't end with these letters, so your best bet is to make your vocabulary lists with articles and just learn the articles and nouns together.

Making nouns feminine

Nouns that refer to people often have a masculine "default" form that can be made feminine (see Table 2-1 for examples). Here's how to make the gender switch:

- ✔ To make most of these nouns feminine, just add **-e** to the end. For example, **un étudiant** (*male student*) becomes **une étudiante** (*female student*).

- ✔ If a masculine noun ends in **-en** or **-on,** add **-ne** for the feminine form: **Un pharmacien** (*pharmacist*) becomes **une pharmacienne.**

- ✔ Nouns that end in **-er** change to **-ère** for the feminine.

- ✔ Nouns that end in **-eur** may become feminine with **-euse** or **-rice.**

- ✔ Nouns that end in **-e** in the masculine form have no change for the feminine (other than in the article, which changes to **une, la,** or **de la**).

Table 2-1	Masculine and Feminine Nouns	
English	*Masculine*	*Feminine*
lawyer	un avocat	une avocat**e**
electrician	un électrici**en**	une électrici**enne**
boss	un patr**on**	une patr**onne**
cashier	un caissi**er**	une caissi**ère**
vendor	un vend**eur**	une vend**euse**
translator	un traduct**eur**	une traduct**rice**
tourist	un tourist**e**	une tourist**e**

Nouns that are always masculine or feminine

A number of French nouns have only a masculine or a feminine form, regardless of the gender of the person they refer to. Many of the masculine nouns refer to professions that are stereotypically considered "for men," and the feminist police haven't yet caught up with the language police, at least in France. In Canada and some other French-speaking countries, most nouns that refer to professions have both masculine and feminine forms. However, the **Académie française,** which regulates the "purity" of the French language, doesn't recognize these forms, and thus they're not considered "correct" French.

The following nouns are always masculine:

- **un auteur** (*author*)
- **un charpentier** (*carpenter*)
- **un écrivain** (*writer*)
- **un gouverneur** (*governor*)
- **un ingénieur** (*engineer*)
- **un maire** (*mayor*)
- **un médecin** (*doctor*)
- **un ministre** (*minister*)
- **un peintre** (*painter*)

- **un plombier** (*plumber*)
- **un poète** (*poet*)
- **un policier** (*police officer*)
- **un pompier** (*firefighter*)
- **un président** (*president*)
- **un professeur** (*teacher*)
- **un sculpteur** (*sculptor*)
- **un témoin** (*witness*)

And these nouns are always feminine:

- **une brute** (*boor, lout*)
- **une connaissance** (*acquaintance*)
- **une dupe** (*dupe, sucker*)
- **une idole** (*idol*)
- **une personne** (*person*)
- **une vedette** (*movie star*)
- **une victime** (*victim*)

Time to switch things up. Make each of the masculine nouns feminine and the feminine nouns masculine, but watch out for nouns that can be only one or the other!

Q. un avocat

A. une avocate (*female lawyer*)

1. une boulangère _____

2. un professeur _____

3. une employée _____

4. un étudiant _____

5. une pharmacienne _____

6. un infirmier _____

7. une idole _____

8. un médecin _____

9. une vedette _____

10. un acteur _____

Part Deux: Making Nouns Plural

In addition to masculine and feminine forms, most nouns also have singular and plural forms. Making a noun plural in French is very similar to making a noun plural in English. To make a noun plural, you usually just add an **-s,** as with changing **un homme** (*a man*) to **deux hommes** (*two men*) and **la femme** (*the woman*) to **les femmes** (*the women*). The final **s** is silent, which means that the singular and plural forms of these nouns are pronounced the same way. But you can tell that the noun is plural because the article or number changes.

French often has masculine and feminine words for nouns referring to people, like **un ami** (*male friend*) and **une amie** (*female friend*). However, French is a tad sexist when referring to groups of people. If you have a group of mixed masculine and feminine nouns, you always default to the masculine plural: **des amis.** The only time you can say **des amies** is when you're talking about a group of just girl friends, with not a single male in the bunch. However, if you have 65 girls and just 1 boy, you use **des amis.** (Not very fair, I know.) The same idea applies if you're talking about one person whose gender you don't know, such as *one tourist* — if you don't know whether it's a man or woman, you always default to the masculine: **un touriste.**

This section explains how to form a plural when you can't simply add an **-s.**

Remembering your x's: Other plural patterns

Though most French nouns just add an **-s** for plurals, a few take an **-x,** with or without some other letter changes/additions. These nouns always end in one of the following letter combinations, which let you know that **-x** marks the (plural) spot. See Table 2-2 for some examples.

Table 2-2		Plural Patterns		
English	*French Singular*	*Singular Ending*	*French Plural*	*Plural Ending*
work	le trav**ail**	**-ail**	les trav**aux**	**-aux**
newspaper	le journ**al**	**-al**	les journ**aux**	**-aux**
coat	le mant**eau**	**-eau**	les mant**eaux**	**-eaux**
game	le j**eu**	**-eu**	les j**eux**	**-eux**

Irregular plurals

Some French nouns are irregular because they don't have plural forms. When a noun ends in **-s, -x,** or **-z,** you don't add anything to make the word plural; the singular and plural forms are identical. To tell the difference between the singular and plural, you have to pay special attention to the article (for more on articles, see the following section).

> **le mois** (*the month*) becomes **les mois**
>
> **le prix** (*the price*) becomes **les prix**
>
> **le nez** (*the nose*) becomes **les nez**

A few French nouns have irregular plurals — see Table 2-3 to memorize the most common ones.

Table 2-3		Irregular Plurals
English	*French Singular*	*French Plural*
eye	**un œil**	**des yeux**
ma'am	**madame**	**mesdames**
miss	**mademoiselle**	**mesdemoiselles**
sir	**monsieur**	**messieurs**
sky	**le ciel**	**les cieux**

The plurals of **madame, mademoiselle,** and **monsieur** add an **-s** at the end of the word, which is normal, but they also change from the singular possessive adjective (**mon** or **ma,** which means *my*) at the beginning to the plural possessive adjective. See the section "Working with possessive adjectives" later in this chapter for more info.

Plural practice: Make each of these singular nouns plural.

Q. couteau

A. **couteaux** (*knives*)

11. garçon _____

12. fille _____

13. feu _____

14. pois _____

15. cheval _____

16. monsieur _____

17. ciel _____

18. madame _____

19. gaz _____

20. œil _____

Understanding Articles and How They Indicate Gender and Number

Articles are small words that you can use only with nouns, and they have two purposes:

- ✔ Presenting a noun
- ✔ Indicating the gender and number of a noun

There are three kinds of French articles: definite, indefinite, and partitive. This section describes these three types of articles and identifies when and how you should use them in your French writing and speech.

Grasping the definite articles

Definite articles indicate that the noun they're presenting is specific. In English, the definite article is *the*. French has three different definite articles, which tell you that the noun is masculine, feminine, or plural. If the noun is singular, the article is **le** or **la,** depending on the noun's gender. (**Le** is for masculine nouns, and **la** is for feminine nouns.) If the noun is plural, the article is **les**, no matter what gender the noun is.

If a singular noun begins with a vowel or mute *h,* the definite article **le** or **la** contracts to **l':**

> **l'ami** (*the friend*)
>
> **l'avocate** (*the lawyer*)
>
> **l'homme** (*the man*)

The French definite article is much more common than its English counterpart. In addition to referring to a specific noun, as in **le livre que j'ai acheté** (*the book I bought*), you use the French definite article to talk about the general sense of a noun, as in **J'aime le chocolat** (*I like chocolate*).

Sorting out indefinite articles

Indefinite articles refer to an unspecific noun. The English indefinite articles are *a* and *an*, and the one you use depends on whether the noun that follows begins with a consonant sound or a vowel sound. French has three indefinite articles — **un** (for masculine nouns), **une** (for feminine nouns), and **des** (masculine or feminine plural). The one you use depends on the noun's gender and number.

You use the indefinite article basically the same way in French and English — to refer to an unspecific noun, as in **J'ai acheté une voiture** (*I bought a car*) or **Je veux voir un film** (*I want to see a movie*). Note that **un** and **une** can also mean *one:* **J'ai un frère** (*I have one brother*).

Des is the plural indefinite article, which you use for two or more masculine and/or feminine nouns: **J'ai des idées** (*I have some ideas*), **Nous avons vu des oiseaux** (*We saw some birds*). When you make a sentence with an indefinite article negative, the article changes to **de**, meaning (*not*) *any*.

> **J'ai des questions.** (*I have some questions.*)
>
> **Je n'ai pas de questions.** (*I don't have any questions.*)

See Chapter 6 for more information about negation.

Looking at some partitive articles

Partitive articles are used with things that you take only a part of. They don't exist in English, so the best translation is the word *some*. Like French definite articles, there are three partitive articles, depending on whether the noun is masculine (**du**), feminine (**de la**), or plural (**des**).

You use the partitive article with food, drink, and other uncountable things that you take or use only a part of, like air and money, as well as abstract things, such as intelligence and patience. If you do eat or use all of something, and if it is countable, then you need the definite or indefinite article. Compare the following:

✔ **J'ai acheté du chocolat.** (*I bought some chocolate* — 1 pound.)

 J'ai acheté le chocolat. (*I bought the chocolate* — that you like so much, or that Jacques told me about.)

✔ **Je veux du gâteau.** (*I want some cake* — such as one piece, or the part that's in the bakery display case.)

 Je veux le gâteau. (*I want the cake* —the whole one at the bakery, or that Annette baked yesterday.)

You can see that the feminine partitive article is made up of two words: **de** and the feminine definite article **la**. The masculine partitive article **du** is a contraction of **de** plus the masculine article **le,** and **des** is a contraction of **de** plus the plural definite article **les**.

When a singular noun begins with a vowel or mute *h*, the partitive article **du** or **de la** has to contract to **de l'**:

 de l'oignon (*some onion*)

 de l'eau (*some water*)

 de l'hélium (*some helium*)

Fill in the blanks with the best choice of article. Be sure to consider which type of article works best, as well as which form of that article to use, depending on the gender, number, and first letter of the noun.

Q. Je n'aime pas _____ café.

A. Je n'aime pas **le** café. (*I don't like coffee.*)

21. J'ai acheté _____ oranges.

22. Il a _____ sœur.

23. Avez-vous _____ stylo ?

24. _____ chat qui habite ici est mignon.

25. Je dois avoir _____ eau.

26. J'aime bien _____ histoire.

27. Il y a _____ fille à la porte.

28. J'aimerais _____ vin.

29. Je déteste _____ devoirs !

30. J'ai ajouté _____ huile.

A Little of This and That: Using Demonstratives

You use demonstrative adjectives and pronouns when you want to talk about something specific, such as *this, that, these,* or *those. Demonstrative adjectives* are used with nouns; *demonstrative pronouns* are used in place of nouns. *This* section explains all about both of *these.*

Demonstrative adjectives

The demonstrative adjective goes in front of a noun to indicate that you're referring to this or that particular noun. For example, if you say *this book is more interesting than that book,* the demonstrative adjectives *this* and *that* make it clear that the book you're holding or looking at, *this book,* is more interesting than *that book,* the one over on the other table, or that someone else is holding.

Like other French adjectives, demonstrative adjectives have different forms depending on the gender and number of the noun they're used with. In addition, you use a special form with masculine nouns that begin with a vowel or mute *h* — see Table 2-4.

Table 2-4	Demonstrative Adjectives	
Gender	*Singular (This/That)*	*Plural (These/Those)*
masculine	ce	ces
masculine + vowel	cet	ces
feminine	cette	ces

Check out these examples:

Masculine: **Ce livre est intéressant.** (*This/That book is interesting.*)

Masculine + vowel: **Qui a écrit cet article ?** (*Who wrote this/that article?*)

Masculine + mute: **Cet homme est grand.** (*This/That man is tall.*)

Feminine: **Cette maison est bleue.** (*This/That house is blue.*)

Ce, cet, and **cette** can all mean *this* or *that* — French doesn't have separate words to make this distinction. You can usually tell by context, but if not, you can add the suffixes **-ci** (*here*) and **-là** (*there*) to the end of the noun:

> **Ce livre-ci est intéressant.** (*This book [here] is interesting.*)

> **Ce livre-là est stupide.** (*That book [there] is stupid.*)

The plural demonstrative adjective **ces** can mean *these* or *those;* again, you can use **-ci** and **-là** to clarify, if necessary:

> **Ces maisons sont vertes.** (*These/Those houses are green.*)

> **Ces maisons-ci sont grises.** (*These houses [here] are gray.*)

> **Ces maisons-là sont jaunes.** (*Those houses [there] are yellow.*)

French has only one plural demonstrative adjective. You use **ces** for all plurals: masculine, masculine + vowel/mute *h,* and feminine.

Demonstrative pronouns

French demonstrative pronouns are very similar to demonstrative adjectives, except that they're not used *with* nouns; rather, they're used *instead of* nouns. The English demonstrative pronouns are *this one, that one, the one(s), these,* and *those.* French has four demonstrative pronouns because it needs different forms for masculine, feminine, singular, and plural — see Table 2-5.

Table 2-5	Demonstrative Pronouns	
Gender	*Singular*	*Plural*
masculine	celui	ceux
feminine	celle	celles

A demonstrative pronoun basically replaces a demonstrative adjective + noun, and it can, like a demonstrative adjective, indicate something that's close or far. To best use it, you need to remove both the demonstrative adjective and noun and then replace them with the demonstrative pronoun. If it's a masculine singular noun, such as **cet homme** (*this man*), replace it with the masculine singular pronoun: **celui** (*this one*). For a feminine plural noun, like **ces filles** (*these girls*), use the feminine plural pronoun: **celles** (*these ones*).

Celui and **celle** can both mean *this one* or *that one,* and **ceux** and **celles** can both mean *these* or *those.* Once again, you can use the suffixes **-ci** or **-là** to specify whether you're talking about *this* or *that one* and *these* or *those.*

> **Quel livre veux-tu, celui-ci ou celui-là ?** (*Which book do you want, this one [here] or that one [there]?*)

> **J'aime cette lampe-là mieux que celles-ci.** (*I like that lamp [there] better than these [here].*)

Notice that the preceding sentence uses both a demonstrative adjective (in the phrase **cette lampe-là**) and a demonstrative pronoun (**celles-ci**).

You can also use demonstrative pronouns with the preposition **de** + a word or phrase to indicate whom something belongs to or where it's from:

> **Je voudrais acheter des vêtements qui sont aussi jolis que ceux de Pauline.**
> (*I'd like to buy some clothes that are as pretty as Pauline's. Literally: . . . as pretty as those of Pauline.*)

Demonstrate your understanding of demonstratives by filling in the blanks with the correct demonstrative adjective or demonstrative pronoun.

Q. J'aime _____ manteau.

A. J'aime **ce** manteau. (*I like this coat.*)

31. Je pense que cette maison-ci est plus jolie que _____-là.

32. Je veux _____ chien.

33. Préfères-tu le fromage de Vermont ou bien _____ de Wisconsin ?

34. Je connais _____ homme.

35. Je cherche un film — _____ que nous avons regardé ensemble.

36. J'ai acheté _____ vêtements.

37. Tes idées sont plus viables que _____ de Marc.

38. Je n'aime pas _____ idée.

39. Tu peux utiliser mon ordinateur ; — c'est _____-ci.

40. Je ne connais pas _____ femmes.

Possession: Channeling the Spirit of Ownership

No, possession has nothing to do with ghosts — at least not in this book. I'm talking about the grammatical structures you use to express who owns something. When you want to make it clear that what's mine is mine and what's yours is mine, you need to know about possession.

French has three different ways to express ownership: possessive adjectives, possessive pronouns, and the possessive **de.** These are equivalent to English possessive adjectives, possessive pronouns, and the possessive *'s.* This section explains all of these so you can make sure that everyone knows whose is whose.

Possession using "de"

In English, when you want to say that something belongs to someone or something, you use an apostrophe: either *'s* or *s'*. French is completely different. You have to reverse the order of the nouns and join them with the preposition **de.** In other words, start with the thing that's owned and then add **de** and the owner:

la maison de Michel (*Michel's house;* Literally: *the house of Michel*)

les chaussures de Sylvie (*Sylvie's shoes;* Literally: *the shoes of Sylvie*)

l'idée de l'étudiant (*the student's idea;* Literally: *the idea of the student*)

la chambre de mes sœurs (*my sisters' room;* Literally: *the room of my sisters*)

Working with possessive adjectives

Possessive adjectives go in front of nouns to tell you who or what those nouns belong to. You use them pretty much the same way in French and English, but French has a lot more of them because there are different forms for masculine, feminine, singular, and plural. In order to use the correct one, you need to consider the person who owns the noun, as well as the gender and number of the noun. To say *my house,* you need to remember that **maison** (*house*) is feminine and singular, so you want to use the feminine singular form of the adjective: **ma maison.** See Table 2-6 for the different forms of French possessive adjectives.

Table 2-6	Possessive Adjectives		
English	*Masculine*	*Feminine*	*Plural*
my	**mon**	**ma**	**mes**
your (**tu** form)	**ton**	**ta**	**tes**
his/her/its	**son**	**sa**	**ses**
our	**notre**	**notre**	**nos**
your (**vous** form)	**votre**	**votre**	**vos**
their	**leur**	**leur**	**leurs**

Singular subjects

The possessive adjectives for first-, second-, and third-person singular subjects have three forms, depending on the gender, number, and first letter of the noun they're used with — see Table 2-7.

In English, the choice of *his* or *her* depends on the gender of the person/thing that possesses the object: *Tom's sister* becomes *his sister,* and *Jane's sister* becomes *her sister.* In French, the gender of the thing possessed determines whether to say **son** or **sa:** *His sister* and *her sister* are both translated as **sa sœur** because **sœur** is feminine. Likewise, *his brother* and *her brother* are both translated as **son frère** because **frère** is masculine. But if you really need to be clear about whether you mean *his* or *her,* you can add **à lui** or **à elle: C'est son frère à lui** (*It's his brother*) and **C'est son frère à elle** (*It's her brother*).

Table 2-7	Singular-Subject Possessive Adjectives		
Masculine	*Feminine*	*Before a Vowel*	*Plural*
mon frère (*my brother*)	**ma sœur** (*my sister*)	**mon idole** (*my idol*)	**mes amis** (*my friends*)
ton frère (*your brother*)	**ta sœur** (*your sister*)	**ton idole** (*your idol*)	**tes amis** (*your friends*)
son frère (*his/her brother*)	**sa sœur** (*his/her sister*)	**son idole** (*his/her idol*)	**ses amis** (*his/her friends*)

You can use **ma, ta,** and **sa** only with a feminine noun that begins with a consonant or aspirated *h.* When a feminine noun begins with a vowel or mute *h,* you have to use the masculine adjective (**mon, ton,** or **son**).

Plural subjects

First-, second-, and third-person plural subjects have only two forms of the posses-sive adjective: singular and plural. Whether the noun being possessed is masculine or feminine — or whether it starts with a consonant or vowel — doesn't matter. See Table 2-8.

Table 2-8	Plural-Subject Possessive Adjectives
Singular	*Plural*
notre père (*our father*)	**nos amis** (*our friends*)
votre père (*your father*)	**vos amis** (*your friends*)
leur père (*their father*)	**leurs amis** (*their friends*)

Make sure you own this possessive information by translating the following into French, using the possessive **de** or a possessive adjective.

Q. Jean's pen

A. **le stylo de Jean**

41. my house _____

42. Marie-Louise's book _____

43. your computer (**tu** form) _____

44. Benoît's school _____

45. our friends _____

46. Jean-Pierre's car _____

47. their bedroom _____

48. the victim's accident _____

49. his sister's kids _____

50. her dad's apartment _____

Yours, mine, and ours: Understanding possessive pronouns

Possessive pronouns are a lot like possessive adjectives, except that they're used in place of nouns rather than with them. The English possessive pronouns are *mine, yours, his, hers, its, ours,* and *theirs.* And if you think that's a lot, just wait until you see all the different French forms!

Once again, French has different possessive pronouns for masculine, feminine, singular, and plural. This time, the singular subjects have four different forms: masculine and feminine singular and masculine and feminine plural. But the plural subjects (**we, you, and they**) forms have only three because the plural possessive pronouns are the same, regardless of gender — see Table 2-9.

Table 2-9	**Possessive Pronouns**			
English Translation	*Masculine Singular*	*Feminine Singular*	*Masculine Plural*	*Feminine Plural*
mine	**le mien**	**la mienne**	**les miens**	**les miennes**
yours (**tu** form)	**le tien**	**la tienne**	**les tiens**	**les tiennes**
his/hers/its	**le sien**	**la sienne**	**les siens**	**les siennes**
ours	**le nôtre**	**la nôtre**	**les nôtres**	**les nôtres**
yours (**vous** form)	**le vôtre**	**la vôtre**	**les vôtres**	**les vôtres**
theirs	**le leur**	**la leur**	**les leurs**	**les leurs**

Note that each possessive pronoun has to start with a definite article and that although the **nous** and **vous** forms of the possessive pronoun have a circumflex (**le nôtre, le vôtre**), the possessive adjectives don't (**notre, votre**). Here are some sentences that use possessive pronouns:

> **J'ai trouvé un stylo . . . c'est le vôtre ?** (*I found a pen . . . is it yours?*)
>
> **As-tu tes clés ? Je ne peux pas trouver les miennes.** (*Do you have your keys? I can't find mine.*)
>
> **Cette maison est jolie, mais je préfère la tienne.** (*This house is pretty, but I prefer yours.*)
>
> **Si ta voiture ne marche pas, tu peux emprunter la nôtre.** (*If your car doesn't work, you can borrow ours.*)

Just as with possessive adjectives, the third-person singular possessive pronoun's form is based on the gender of the noun being replaced, not the gender of the subject. **Le sien, la sienne, les siens,** and **les siennes** can all mean *his, hers,* or *its:* **Le sien est là-bas** (*His/Hers/Its is over there*).

Answer Key

1 **un boulanger** (*male baker*)

2 **un professeur** (*teacher* — always masculine)

3 **un employé** (*male employee*)

4 **une étudiante** (*female student*)

5 **un pharmacien** (*male pharmacist*)

6 **une infirmière** (*female nurse*)

7 **une idole** (*idol* — always feminine)

8 **un médecin** (*doctor* — always masculine)

9 **une vedette** (*movie star* — always feminine)

10 **une actrice** (*actress*)

11 **garçons** (*boys*)

12 **filles** (*girls*)

13 **feux** (*fires*)

14 **pois** (*peas*)

15 **chevaux** (*horses*)

16 **messieurs** (*sirs*)

17 **cieux** (*skies*)

18 **mesdames** (*ladies*)

19 **gaz** (*gases*)

20 **yeux** (*eyes*)

21 J'ai acheté **des** oranges. *or* J'ai acheté **les** oranges. (*I bought some oranges.* or *I bought the oranges.*)

22 Il a **une** sœur. (*He has a sister.*)

23 Avez-vous **un** stylo ? (*Do you have a pen?*)

24 **Le** chat qui habite ici est mignon. (*The cat that lives here is cute.*)

25 Je dois avoir **de l'**eau. (*I need to have some water.*)

26 J'aime bien **l'**histoire. (*I like history.*)

27 Il y a **une** fille à la porte. (*There's a girl at the door.*)

28 J'aimerais **du** vin. (*I would like some wine.*)

29 Je déteste **les** devoirs ! (*I hate homework!*)

30 J'ai ajouté **de l'**huile. (*I added some oil.*)

31 Je pense que cette maison-ci est plus jolie que **celle**-là. (*I think this house is prettier than that one.*)

32 Je veux **ce** chien. (*I want this/that dog.*)

33 Préfères-tu le fromage de Vermont ou bien **celui** de Wisconsin ? (*Do you prefer cheese from Vermont or Wisconsin?*)

34 Je connais **cet** homme. (*I know this/that man.*)

35 Je cherche un film — **celui** que nous avons regardé ensemble. (*I'm looking for a movie — the one we watched together.*)

36 J'ai acheté **ces** vêtements. (*I bought these/those clothes.*)

37 Tes idées sont plus viables que **celles** de Marc. (*Your ideas are more workable than Marc's.*)

38 Je n'aime pas **cette** idée. (*I don't like this/that idea.*)

39 Tu peux utiliser mon ordinateur — c'est **celui**-ci. (*You can use my computer — it's this one.*)

40 Je ne connais pas **ces** femmes. (*I don't know these/those women.*)

41 **ma maison** (*my house*)

42 **le livre de Marie-Louise** (*Marie-Louise's book*)

43 **ton ordinateur** (*your computer*)

44 **l'école de Benoît** (*Benoît's school*)

45 **nos amis** (*our friends*)

46 **la voiture de Jean-Pierre** (*Jean-Pierre's car*)

47 **leur chambre** (*their bedroom*)

48 **l'accident de la victime** (*the victim's accident*)

49 **les enfants de sa sœur** (*his sister's kids*)

50 **l'appartement de son père** (*her dad's apartment*)

Chapter 3

The 4-1-1 on Numbers, Dates, and Time

. . . .

In This Chapter

▶ Knowing the cardinal and ordinal numbers

▶ Talking about days, months, and years

▶ Counting the hours and minutes

. . . .

Numbers are one of the most basic and useful parts of language. In addition to simple counting, you need numbers for talking about dates, time, prices, phone numbers, addresses, and so much more. Before you can make appointments, find out how much something costs, shop in bulk, or trade phone numbers with a new friend, you have to know your numbers. But being able to say and understand numbers is only half the battle — writing them is another matter, because you need to know how to spell and abbreviate them as well. This chapter explains French cardinal and ordinal numbers and calendar words, as well as how to put everything together for talking about dates and time.

Using Numbers

Before you can do anything with numbers, you need to know what they are. French numbers have a few special characteristics that make them a little tricky for English speakers. Plus, reciting numbers and writing them are two different tasks. You may feel like you have a solid grasp of numbers, but this section highlights a few important points about cardinal and ordinal numbers so you don't make any faux pas in your writing.

Counting on cardinal numbers: 1, 2, 3

Cardinal numbers are for counting, and the low numbers are easy. You may already know them backwards and forwards, but if not, all you need to do is memorize them like any other vocab list. Check out the following list of numbers from 0 to 19:

▶ **zéro** (*0*)

▶ **un, une** (*1*)

▶ **deux** (*2*)

▶ **trois** (*3*)

▶ **quatre** (*4*)

▶ **cinq** (*5*)

- six *(6)*
- sept *(7)*
- huit *(8)*
- neuf *(9)*
- dix *(10)*

- onze *(11)*
- douze *(12)*
- treize *(13)*
- quatorze *(14)*
- quinze *(15)*

- seize *(16)*
- dix-sept *(17)*
- dix-huit *(18)*
- dix-neuf *(19)*

When you get to the 20s, you have to start doing some addition, just like in English. Take the tens number and add the ones number. For example, 23 is 20 (**vingt**) followed by 3 (**trois**) and joined by a hyphen: twenty-three — **vingt-trois.** The process is the same for all the numbers up to 69, except for 21, 31, 41, 51, and 61. For those, you replace the hyphen with the word **et** *(and).* See the following list for some examples.

- vingt *(20)*
- trente *(30)*
- quarante *(40)*
- cinquante *(50)*
- soixante *(60)*

- vingt et un *(21)*
- trente et un *(31)*
- quarante et un *(41)*
- cinquante et un *(51)*
- soixante et un *(61)*

- vingt-deux *(22)*
- trente-deux *(32)*
- quarante-deux *(42)*
- cinquante-deux *(52)*
- soixante-deux *(62)*

When you get past 69, you have to start doing some real math. To say 70 in French, you have to say **soixante-dix,** which actually means sixty-ten. *Seventy-one* is sixty and eleven (**soixante et onze**), 72 is sixty-twelve (**soixante-douze**), and so on up to *79* — sixty-nineteen (**soixante-dix-neuf**). The numbers 80 to 99 are even stranger — you have to do multiplication, too. The French term for 80 is **quatre-vingts** — four twenties. And then, 81 is **quatre-vingt-un,** 82 is **quatre-vingt-deux,** yada yada yada, 89 is **quatre-vingt-neuf,** and 90 is **quatre-vingt-dix.** The 90s then continue like the 70s, adding on the tens number: 91 — **quatre-vingt-onze,** 92 — **quatre-vingt-douze,** and so on. Notice that 80 is the only number that has an **s** on the word **vingts.** You can see these numbers in all their strange glory in in this list:

- soixante-dix *(70)*
- soixante et onze *(71)*
- soixante-douze *(72)*
- soixante-treize *(73)*
- soixante-quatorze *(74)*
- soixante-quinze *(75)*
- soixante-seize *(76)*
- soixante-dix-sept *(77)*
- soixante-dix-huit *(78)*
- soixante-dix-neuf *(79)*

- quatre-vingts *(80)*
- quatre-vingt-un *(81)*
- quatre-vingt-deux *(82)*
- quatre-vingt-trois *(83)*
- quatre-vingt-quatre *(84)*
- quatre-vingt-cinq *(85)*
- quatre-vingt-six *(86)*
- quatre-vingt-sept *(87)*
- quatre-vingt-huit *(88)*
- quatre-vingt-neuf *(89)*

- quatre-vingt-dix *(90)*
- quatre-vingt-onze *(91)*
- quatre-vingt-douze *(92)*
- quatre-vingt-treize *(93)*
- quatre-vingt-quatorze *(94)*
- quatre-vingt-quinze *(95)*
- quatre-vingt-seize *(96)*
- quatre-vingt-dix-sept *(97)*
- quatre-vingt-dix-huit *(98)*
- quatre-vingt-dix-neuf *(99)*

The French spoken in France doesn't have unique words for 70, 80, and 90, but other French-speaking countries do. In Switzerland, *seventy* is **septante,** *eighty* is **huitante** or **octante,** and *ninety* is **nonante.** In Belgium, they say **septante, quatre-vingts,** and **nonante.**

If you've waded through the calculations of the 70s through 90s, **félicitations** (*congratulations*)! The rest of the French numbers are pretty straightforward. Here are just two things to watch out for:

- **Plurals:** All the big number words — except for **mille** (*thousand*) — end in **s** when referring to more than one of that amount.

- **Billion:** The word **billion** is a *false friend* (a word that looks similar in French and English but has different meanings). In English, a billion is a thousand millions (1,000,000,000), but in French, **un billion** means *a million millions,* which equals a trillion (1,000,000,000,000).

The following list shows you the singular and plural forms of the big numbers. Note that **cent** and **mille** aren't preceded by articles: **J'ai cent dollars** means *I have a hundred dollars.*

- **cent** (*100*)
- **mille** (*1,000*)
- **un million** (*1,000,000*)
- **un milliard** (*1,000,000,000*)
- **un billion** (*1,000,000,000,000*)

- **deux cents** (*200*)
- **deux mille** (*2,000*)
- **deux millions** (*2,000,000*)
- **deux milliards** (*2,000,000,000*)
- **deux billions** (*2,000,000,000,000*)

Take a swing at the French numbers and do some counting. For each number provided, list the number that comes before and after it.

Q. un

A. **zéro, deux** (*zero, two*)

1. six _____

2. dix _____

3. treize _____

4. dix-neuf _____

5. trente _____

6. quarante et un _____

7. cinquante-neuf _____

8. soixante-dix _____

9. quatre-vingt-un _____

10. quatre-vingt-dix-neuf _____

Sorting out ordinal numbers

Suppose you want to tell people that you work on the 17th floor or that you plan to come in first in next year's Tour de France (hey, you've been training). In that case, you need *ordinal* numbers, which allow you to rank things. You form most French ordinal numbers by taking the cardinal number and adding the suffix **-ième** (see the preceding section for details on cardinal numbers). *Third,* for instance, is **troisième.** Ordinal numbers can be abbreviated with a superscript **e**, so you can write 3rd as 3e.

As you convert cardinals to ordinals, you may need to make a few spelling changes before you can add the suffix. For numbers like **quatre** and **onze**, you have to lose the **e**: **quatrième** (*fourth*), **onzième** (*eleventh*). At the end of **cinq**, you have to add a **u**: **cinquième** (*fifth*). As for **neuf**, the **f** changes to a **v**: **neuvième** (*ninth*).

The only ordinal number that doesn't end in **-ième** is *first*. It's nothing like the cardinal number **un** (*one*), and it's the only ordinal number with two forms: The masculine form is **premier,** abbreviated **1ᵉʳ,** and the feminine is **première,** or **1ᵉʳᵉ.** (See Chapter 2 for details on gender.)

Table 3-1 breaks down the numbers and shows the ordinal and corresponding cardinal numbers for one through ten.

Table 3-1		Ordinal Numbers		
Number	*Abbreviation (in English)*	*Cardinal*	*Ordinal*	*Abréviation*
first	*1st*	**un, une**	**premier, première**	**1ᵉʳ, 1ᵉʳᵉ**
second	*2nd*	**deux**	**deuxième**	**2ᵉ**
third	*3rd*	**trois**	**troisième**	**3ᵉ**
fourth	*4th*	**quatre**	**quatrième**	**4ᵉ**
fifth	*5th*	**cinq**	**cinquième**	**5ᵉ**
sixth	*6th*	**six**	**sixième**	**6ᵉ**
seventh	*7th*	**sept**	**septième**	**7ᵉ**
eighth	*8th*	**huit**	**huitième**	**8ᵉ**
ninth	*9th*	**neuf**	**neuvième**	**9ᵉ**
tenth	*10th*	**dix**	**dixième**	**10ᵉ**

The rest of the ordinal numbers follow the same pattern; the only ones to look out for are 21st, 31st, and so on, which are in the format *tens number* + **et** + **unième: vingt et unième, trente et unième,** and so on.

Make sure you have your ordinals in order. Convert each cardinal number into an ordinal and provide the abbreviation.

Q. trois

A. **troisième, 3ᵉ** (*third, 3rd*)

11. dix _____

12. sept _____

13. un _____

14. trente _____

15. quarante-quatre _____

16. cinquante et un _____

17. soixante-douze _____

18. quatre-vingt-onze _____

19. quatre-vingt-dix-neuf _____

20. cent _____

Mark Your Calendar: Expressing Days, Months, and Dates

Got plans? Knowing French calendar words and how to say what day it is makes it easier for you to make appointments, break dates, plan outings, and make sure you don't accidentally end up working all weekend. If you want to be sure everyone knows when to meet, you need to know how to talk about dates in French. This section gives you the lowdown on the days of the week, the months of the year, and all the dates on the calendar. After reading this, you can make sure your French-speaking friends never forget your birthday again.

A full sept: Knowing the days of the week

Most of the days of the week end in **-di**, except for Sunday, which begins with those two letters.

In French, the week starts on Monday, not Sunday, and you don't capitalize the days.

Here are the **jours de la semaine** (*days of the week*):

- **lundi** (*Monday*)
- **mardi** (*Tuesday*)
- **mercredi** (*Wednesday*)
- **jeudi** (*Thursday*)
- **vendredi** (*Friday*)
- **samedi** (*Saturday*)
- **dimanche** (*Sunday*)

If you want to know what day of the week it is, ask **Quel jour sommes-nous ?** or **Quel jour est-ce ?** You can answer such a question with any of the following phrases followed by the day of the week: **Nous sommes, On est,** or **C'est**. Thus, **C'est mardi** means *It's Tuesday.*

To say that something happened or is going to happen on a certain day, you just use that day with no preposition or article: **Je suis allé à la banque vendredi** means *I went to the bank on Friday.*

To say that something happens every week on a certain day, you use the definite article: **Je vais à la banque le vendredi** means *I go to the bank on Fridays.*

Here are some other useful words related to days and weeks:

- **hier** (*yesterday*)
- **aujourd'hui** (*today*)
- **demain** (*tomorrow*)
- **la semaine passée** (*last week*)

> ✔ **cette semaine** (*this week*)
>
> ✔ **la semaine prochaine** (*next week*)

An even dozen: Identifying the months

The French words for months are fairly similar to their English counterparts, but you definitely need to watch out for some spelling differences. Whenever you're writing a letter to your pen pal in Senegal or an e-mail to that business associate in Switzerland, you want to ensure that you use and spell the month correctly. This list shows you the months of the year, which, like the days of the week, aren't capitalized:

✔ **janvier** (*January*)

✔ **février** (*February*)

✔ **mars** (*March*)

✔ **avril** (*April*)

✔ **mai** (*May*)

✔ **juin** (*June*)

✔ **juillet** (*July*)

✔ **août** (*August*)

✔ **septembre** (*September*)

✔ **octobre** (*October*)

✔ **novembre** (*November*)

✔ **décembre** (*December*)

To say that something happened or will happen in a given month, use the preposition **en**: **J'ai acheté ma voiture en juin** (*I bought my car in June*).

Day, month, and year: Scoping out the "dating" scene

From meetings to parties to jetting off to the Côte d'Azur for the weekend, every event takes place on a particular date. So if you want to invite and be invited, you need to know how to talk about dates. The first thing to know (besides the days of the week and months of the year — see the earlier sections) is the question **Quelle est la date ?** (*What's the date?*).

To answer, you can say **C'est, On est,** or **Nous sommes,** followed by **le** + *cardinal number* + *month* + *year* (*optional*). Notice that the day comes before the month and has to be preceded by the definite article **le**. For example, you can say **C'est le 3 [trois] mai** (*It's May 3*) or **On est le 22 [vingt-deux] février 2008 [deux mille huit]** (*It's February 22, 2008*).

You always use the cardinal (counting) number to say the date in French except when you're talking about the first day of the month; for that, you use the ordinal: **C'est le 1ᵉʳ [premier] décembre** (*It's December 1st*). The short form of the date also goes day/month/year, so **le 25 novembre 1999** is shortened to **25/11/99**. The day always comes before the month, which isn't such a big deal when the month is spelled out, but when it's the short form, you really need to be careful — **12/10/77** is **le 12 octobre 1977,** not December 10!

Your best friend just can't keep track of the date; he's always one day behind. When he announces what day it is, tell him the correct day.

Q. C'est lundi.

A. **Non, c'est mardi.** (*No, it's Tuesday.*)

21. On est le 5 octobre. _____

22. Nous sommes vendredi. _____

23. C'est le 19 avril. _____

24. On est mardi. _____

25. Nous sommes le 30 septembre. _____

26. C'est samedi. _____

27. On est le 1ᵉʳ juin. _____

28. Nous sommes mercredi. _____

29. C'est le 31 décembre. _____

30. On est jeudi. _____

Understanding Time Differences

When writing and speaking French, knowing and telling the time is an important concept to master. Otherwise, you may show up half a day early for meetings, mix up the train schedules, or miss that lunch date you made. How do you prevent such catastrophes? Well, the first thing you need to know is how to ask what time it is: **Quelle heure est-il ?**

In French, people tell time on the 24-hour clock, like military time (but without the uniforms). So the morning hours are 1 to 12, and the afternoon and evening hours are 13 to 24. To convert back to a 12-hour clock, subtract 12 from any time greater than 12.

To give the time, you say **Il est** followed by the number, the word **heure(s),** and any modifiers that describe the minutes. For example, if it's 7 a.m., you say **Il est sept heures.** If it's 2 p.m., **Il est quatorze heures.** And if it's 1 a.m., **Il est une heure — au lit !** (*It's 1 a.m. — go to bed!*)

Now you just need the modifiers. To modify with minutes, use cardinal numbers (see the earlier section titled "Counting on cardinal numbers: 1, 2, 3"). You can add these numbers by just tacking them on after **heure(s).** For instance, 1:20 a.m. is **une heure vingt.** After you get past 30 minutes, you have a choice of either adding the minutes onto the current hour or subtracting them from the next hour with **moins** (*minus*). So 2:40 a.m. is either **deux heures quarante** or **trois heures moins vingt.**

Just as you can say *half past* or *quarter to* in English, you can use similar phrases when telling the time in French. To say that it's _____-*thirty,* add **et demie** (*and a half*). To say *quarter after* the hour, use **et quart** (*and a quarter*); and *quarter to* is **moins le quart** (*minus a quarter*):

    Il est une heure moins le quart. (*It's quarter to one [12:45 a.m.].*)

> **Il est une heure et quart** or **Il est une heure quinze** (*It's quarter after one* or *It's one-fifteen [1:15 a.m.].*)

> **Il est une heure et demie** or **Il est une heure trente.** (*It's one-thirty [1:30 a.m.].*)

Note that **moins le quart** requires the article **le,** but **et quart** doesn't.

And just like English, French has special words for the 12 o'clocks:

✔ **midi** (*noon*)

✔ **minuit** (*midnight*)

Unlike English, however, you can use **et quart** and **et demi** with these words. Note that the adjective **demi** is in the masculine because **midi** and **minuit** are **masculine,** as opposed to **heure,** which is feminine and therefore takes the feminine form **demie.** See Chapter 9 for more info about adjective agreement.

> **Il est midi et demi.** (*It's 12:30 p.m.* Literally: *It's noon thirty* or *It's half past noon.*)

The short version of French times has an **h** (short for **heures**) where English speakers use a colon:

> **14h00** (*2:00 p.m.*)

> **8h30** (*8:30 a.m.*)

Take a look at Table 3-2 to see all this timely information spelled out.

Table 3-2	French Times	
Time	*Heure*	*Abréviation*
midnight	minuit	**0h00**
1 a.m.	une heure	**1h00**
2 a.m.	deux heures	**2h00**
3 a.m.	trois heures	**3h00**
4:15 a.m.	quatre heures et quart quatre heures quinze	**4h15**
5:30 a.m.	cinq heures et demie cinq heures trente	**5h30**
6:45 a.m	sept heures moins le quart	**6h45**
noon	midi	**12h00**
1 p.m.	treize heures	**13h00**
2 p.m.	quatorze heures	**14h00**
3 p.m.	quinze heures	**15h00**

Time	Heure	Abréviation
4:05 p.m.	**seize heures cinq**	**16h05**
5:17 p.m.	**dix-sept heures dix-sept**	**17h17**
6:55 p.m	**dix-neuf heures moins cinq**	**18h55**

If you want to talk about when something (say, a conference call) is happening rather than what time it is right now, say **À quelle heure est la téléconférence ?** (*What time is the conference call?*). To answer, you just start with that event and add **est à** and the time: **La téléconférence est à midi.** (*The conference call is at noon.*)

As the department secretary, your job is to keep track of everyone's schedules and provide people with a copy of the weekly planner. But Christiane lost hers, and she remembers the day everything is happening but not the time. For each question, answer with a complete sentence, spelling out the time shown on the weekly planner.

lundi	mardi	mercredi	jeudi	vendredi
	8h30 — rendez-vous avec Martin			8h45 — conférence de presse
9h10 — téléconférence			9h50 — réunion syndicale	
11h50 — déjeuner avec Mme LeBlanc		12h00 — déjeuner avec Paul et Claire		12h40 — déjeuner avec Sophie
	16h00 — Étienne arrive			16h55 — vol à Genève
		18h30 — Le Mariage de Figaro		18h00 — Dîner à La Lune

Q. À quelle heure est le rendez-vous avec Martin ?

A. **Le rendez-vous avec Martin est à huit heures et demie.** (*The appointment with Martin is at 8:30 a.m.*)

31. À quelle heure est le dîner à La Lune ?

_____

32. À quelle heure est le déjeuner avec Paul et Claire ?

_____

33. À quelle heure est le vol à Genève ?

_____

34. À quelle heure est la réunion syndicale ?

_____

35. À quelle heure est *Le Mariage de Figaro* ?

_____

36. À quelle heure est l'arrivée d'Étienne ?

_____

37. À quelle heure est la conférence de presse ?

_____

38. À quelle heure est le déjeuner avec Mme LeBlanc ?

_____

39. À quelle heure est la téléconférence ?

_____

40. À quelle heure est le déjeuner avec Sophie ?

_____

Answer Key

1 **cinq, sept** (*five, seven*)

2 **neuf, onze** (*nine, eleven*)

3 **douze, quatorze** (*twelve, fourteen*)

4 **dix-huit, vingt** (*eighteen, twenty*)

5 **vingt-neuf, trente et un** (*twenty-nine, thirty-one*)

6 **quarante, quarante-deux** (*forty, forty-two*)

7 **cinquante-huit, soixante** (*fifty-eight, sixty*)

8 **soixante-neuf, soixante et onze** (*sixty-nine, seventy-one*)

9 **quatre-vingts, quatre-vingt-deux** (*eighty, eighty-two*)

10 **quatre-vingt-dix-huit, cent** (*ninety-eight, one hundred*)

11. **dixième, 10e** (*tenth, 10th*)

12 **septième, 7e** (*seventh, 7th*)

13 **premier, 1er** (*first, 1st*)

14 **trentième, 30e** (*thirtieth, 30th*)

15 **quarante-quatrième, 44e** (*forty-fourth, 44th*)

16 **cinquante et unième, 51e** (*fifty-first, 51st*)

17 **soixante-douzième, 72e** (*seventy-second, 72nd*)

18 **quatre-vingt-onzième, 91e** (*ninety-first, 91st*)

19 **quatre-vingt-dix-neuvième, 99e** (*ninety-ninth, 99th*)

20 **centième, 100e** (*hundredth, 100th*)

21 **Non, on est le 6 octobre.** (*No, it's October 6.*)

22 **Non, nous sommes samedi.** (*No, it's Saturday.*)

23 **Non, c'est le 20 avril.** (*No, it's April 20.*)

24 **Non, on est mercredi.** (*No, it's Wednesday.*)

25 **Non, nous sommes le 1er octobre.** (*No, it's October 1.*)

26 **Non, c'est dimanche.** (*No, it's Sunday.*)

27 **Non, on est le 2 juin.** (*No, it's June 2.*)

28 **Non, nous sommes jeudi.** (*No, it's Thursday.*)

29 **Non, c'est le 1ᵉʳ janvier.** (*No, it's January 1.*)

30 **Non, on est vendredi.** (*No, it's Friday.*)

31 **Le dîner à La Lune est à dix-huit heures.** (*Dinner at La Lune is at 6 p.m.*)

32 **Le déjeuner avec Paul et Claire est à midi.** (*Lunch with Paul and Claire is at noon.*)

33 **Le vol à Genève est à dix-sept heures moins cinq.** (*The flight to Geneva is at five to 5 p.m. [4:55 p.m.]*)

34 **La réunion syndicale est à dix heures moins dix.** (*The union meeting is at ten to 10 a.m. [9:50 a.m.]*)

35 ***Le Mariage de Figaro* est à dix-huit heures et demie.** (Le Mariage de Figaro *is at 6:30 p.m.*)

36 **L'arrivée d'Étienne est à seize heures.** (*Étienne's arrival is at 4 p.m.*)

37 **La conférence de presse est à neuf heures moins le quart.** (*The press conference is at quarter to nine a.m. [8:45 a.m.]*)

38 **Le déjeuner avec Mme LeBlanc est à midi moins dix.** (*Lunch with Mrs. LeBlanc is at ten to noon [11:50 a.m.]*)

39 **La téléconférence est à neuf heures dix.** (*The conference call is at 9:10 a.m.*)

40 **Le déjeuner avec Sophie est à midi quarante/treize heures moins vingt.** (*Lunch with Sophie is at 12:40/twenty to 1:00 p.m.*)

Part II
The Here and Now: Writing in the Present

The 5th Wave   By Rich Tennant

"Maybe next time you'll learn your negative verbs in French before having a suit made in Paris."

In this part . . .

This part puts you in the moment. The present tense is the most common verb form, and in Chapter 4, I explain how to conjugate all different kinds of verbs and how to use them so you can talk about what you're doing right now. Want to know what other people are doing? Read about asking questions in Chapter 5. When you don't want to do anything, go to Chapter 6 to tackle negation. And in Chapter 7, I introduce the infinitive (*to* + verb) and present participle (verb + *-ing*), two verb forms that exist in both French and English but act very differently in the two languages. Chapter 8 helps you express your subjectivity with the subjunctive.

Chapter 4

Right Here, Right Now: The Present Tense

In This Chapter
▶ Understanding subject pronouns
▶ Using the present tense
▶ Recognizing different types of verbs
▶ Conjugating French verbs

Here's your chance to get a handle on the present tense, your link to talking about what's going on and the way things are. This most common French verb tense — which is also one of the most complicated tenses — describes what's happening, what people's routines are, or what a current situation is like. The English simple present tense (*I sing*) and present progressive tense (*I am singing*) are both generally translated with the French present tense: **je chante.**

In order to stress that something is happening right now, the way *I'm singing* does, use the construction **être en train de: Je suis en train de chanter** — *I am (in the process of) singing (right now).*

Using the French present tense is easy; the hard part is choosing the right verb form, because the conjugations are different for regular, stem-changing, spelling-change, and irregular verbs. This chapter covers the types of verbs and present-tense verb conjugation. But first, it opens with a few ideas about the subject of the sentence.

Understanding Subject Pronouns, Your Conjugation Cues

The *subject* is the person, place, or thing that's doing something. In the sentence *My dog has fleas,* for example, *my dog* is the subject. A *subject pronoun* can replace a subject so that if you've already mentioned your dog, you can just say *he* when you refer to your dog again.

Subject pronouns exist in both French and English, but they're extra important in French because each one has its own *conjugation*, or verb form. In a verb conjugation table, each subject pronoun represents any noun that has the same number and *grammatical person* — the role the subject plays in the conversation. Subject pronouns may be singular or plural, and they may be first person (the speaker), second person (whoever's being addressed), or third person (everyone else). Table 4-1 breaks down the pronouns so you can better understand them.

Table 4-1	French Subject Pronouns and Their English Cohorts	
	Singular	*Plural*
1st person	**je** (*I*)	**nous** (*we*)
2nd person	**tu** (*you*)	**vous** (*you*)
3rd person	**il** (*he, it*) **elle** (*she, it*) **on** (*one, people, they, we*)	**ils** (*they* — masculine) **elles** (*they* — feminine)

Note: In formal situations, **vous** can be singular — see "Tu or vous: The second person" for details.

French has a different conjugation for each grammatical person, whereas English usually has only two conjugations: one for third-person singular (*he walks*) and one for everything else (*I walk, you walk, we walk, they walk*). This section takes a closer look at these pronouns to help you use them correctly.

Je or nous: The first person

Je is the first-person singular. Unlike its English equivalent *I*, **je** is capitalized only when it begins a sentence.

> **Je suis américain.** (*I am American.*)

> **Demain, je vais en France.** (*Tomorrow, I'm going to France.*)

Note that when **je** is followed by word beginning with a vowel or mute *h*, it contracts to **j'**: **Maintenant, j'habite en Californie.** (*Now I live in California.*)

Nous is the first-person plural, and it means *we.* You use it the same way in French and English.

> **Nous allons en France.** (*We're going to France.*)

> **Nous mangeons à midi.** (*We eat at noon.*)

Tu or vous: The second person

Tu and **vous** both mean *you,* but French distinguishes between different kinds of *you:*

- ✔ **Tu** is singular and informal, meaning that you use it only when you're talking to one person you know well — such as a family member, friend, classmate, or colleague — or to a child or animal.

- ✔ **Vous** is plural and formal. You have to use it

  - When talking to one person you don't know or whom you wish to show respect to, such as your teacher, doctor, or boss

  - Whenever you're talking to more than one person, whether or not you know them

If you're not sure whether to use **tu** or **vous,** be respectful and opt for **vous.** Except when you're introduced to someone by a close friend, you normally start out using **vous** with everyone you meet. At some point, if you become friends, this new person may ask you to use **tu** by saying something like **On peut se tutoyer.** (*We can use **tu** with one another.*) English has no real equivalent to this — "Call me John" is the closest, but it doesn't indicate the same shift to intimacy as switching from **vous** to **tu** does. Using **tu** without this sort of invitation can be very offensive, but the French usually make allowances for non-native speakers.

> **Tu peux commencer maintenant.** (*You can begin now.*)
>
> **Vous êtes en retard.** (*You're late.*)

Il, elle, or on: The third-person singular

Il and **elle** mean *he* and *she,* respectively. When you want to say *it,* you have to figure out the gender of the noun because you use **il** to refer to a masculine noun and **elle** to refer to a feminine noun (see Chapter 2 for details on noun gender).

> **Il a deux soeurs.** (*He has two sisters.*)
>
> **Où est mon livre ? Il est sur la table.** (*Where is my book? It's on the table.*)
>
> **Elle veut travailler ici.** (*She wants to work here.*)
>
> **Je vois la voiture. Elle est dans la rue.** (*I see the car. It's in the street.*)

On is an indefinite pronoun that literally means *one.* But **on** can also mean *you, people* in general, or *we,* informally:

> **On ne doit pas dire cela.** (*One shouldn't say that.*)
>
> **On ne sait jamais.** (*You just never know.*)
>
> **On ne fait plus attention.** (*People don't pay attention anymore.*)
>
> **On va partir à midi.** (*We're going to leave at noon.*)

Ils or elles: The third-person plural

Ils and **elles** mean *they*. **Ils** is used for

- ✔ Groups of men or masculine nouns
- ✔ Mixed groups of men and women
- ✔ Masculine and feminine nouns together

Elles is used only for groups of women or feminine nouns. Even if there's only one man in a group of a thousand women, you have to use **ils**.

> **Paul et David (ils) habitent à Bruxelles.** (*Paul and David [they] live in Brussels.*)
>
> **Où sont mes livres ? Ils sont dans ta chambre.** (*Where are my books? They're in your room.*)
>
> **Lise, Marie-Laure, Robert et Anne (ils) partent ensemble.** (*Lise, Marie-Laure, Robert, and Anne [they] are leaving together.*)
>
> **Ma mère et ma soeur (elles) aiment danser.** (*My mother and sister [they] like to dance.*)
>
> **Je vois tes clés. Elles sont sur mon bureau.** (*I see your keys. They're on my desk.*)

You work at an advertising firm, and you're writing to a colleague with an ad idea about a product called **la Sandwichière** (*the sandwich maker*). Choose the best pronoun-verb pair to fill in each blank.

Q. Marc, _____ (je suis, il est) prêt à commencer.

A. je suis (*I am*)

1. Michel, _____ (j'ai, il a) une idée pour une nouvelle publicité. _____ (Peux-tu, Pouvez-vous) m'aider ? _____ (Nous pouvons, Vous pouvez) travailler ensemble.

2. Voici mon idée. Il y a un père, une mère et un enfant dans la cuisine. Le père dit à sa femme, _____ (veux-tu, voulez-vous) quelque chose à manger ?

3. _____ (Il répond, Elle répond, On répond) : Oui, et _____ (je pense, tu penses, il pense, nous pensons) que David a faim aussi.

4. David dit à ses parents : Oui, moi aussi — _____ (peux-tu, pouvez-vous) me faire un sandwich ?

5. _____ (Ils répondent, Elles répondent) : Non, _____ (tu peux, vous pouvez) le faire. _____ (J'ai, Nous avons) acheté une Sandwichière — _____ (il est, elle est, on est) tellement simple qu'un enfant peut faire son propre sandwich.

The Mainstream: Conjugating Regular Verbs

Regular verbs are groups of verbs that are all conjugated the same way, so when you know how to conjugate one, you can conjugate them all — kind of a package deal. Verbs that aren't yet conjugated appear in their *infinitive* form (the one you find in the dictionary), and the three groups of regular verbs are classified by their infinitive endings: **-er**, **-ir**, and **-re**. This section shows you how to get them in shape.

The most common regular verbs: -er

The verbs that end in **-er** are by far the largest category of French verbs. To conjugate **-er** verbs, remove **-er** from the infinitive to find the *stem* and then add the appropriate ending: **-e, -es, -e, -ons, -ez,** or **-ent.** The following table conjugates **parler** (*to speak*).

parler (*to speak*)	
je parl**e**	nous parl**ons**
tu parl**es**	vous parl**ez**
il/elle/on parl**e**	ils/elles parl**ent**
Je **parle** français. (*I speak French.*)	

Thousands of French verbs end in **-er**. Here are several of the more common ones:

- **aimer** (*to like, to love*)
- **chercher** (*to look for*)
- **danser** (*to dance*)
- **détester** (*to hate*)
- **donner** (*to give*)
- **jouer** (*to play*)
- **penser** (*to think*)
- **regarder** (*to watch, to look at*)
- **travailler** (*to work*)
- **trouver** (*to find*)

Another common regular verb ending: -ir

The **-ir** verbs fill the No. 2 slot on the charts of the most common verb types. To conjugate **-ir** verbs, remove **-ir** from the infinitive and add the endings: **-is, -is, -it, -issons, -issez,** and **-issent.** Here's how you conjugate **finir** (*to finish*).

finir (*to finish*)	
je fin**is**	nous fin**issons**
tu fin**is**	vous fin**issez**
il/elle/on fin**it**	ils/elles fin**issent**
Il **finit** le dessin. (*He's finishing the drawing.*)	

You can find hundreds of regular **-ir** French verbs. Check out some of the more common ones:

- ✔ **avertir** (*to warn*)
- ✔ **bâtir** (*to build*)
- ✔ **choisir** (*to choose*)
- ✔ **établir** (*to establish*)
- ✔ **grandir** (*to grow*)

- ✔ **réagir** (*to react*)
- ✔ **remplir** (*to fill*)
- ✔ **réunir** (*to meet*)
- ✔ **réussir** (*to succeed*)
- ✔ **vieillir** (*to grow old*)

The third type of regular verbs: -re

The **-re** verbs round out the list of regular French verbs. To conjugate **-re** verbs, remove **-re** from the infinitive and add the endings: **-s, -s,** nothing, **-ons, -ez,** and **-ent.** Here's how you conjugate **perdre** (*to lose*).

perdre (*to lose*)	
je perd**s**	nous perd**ons**
tu perd**s**	vous perd**ez**
il/elle/on perd	ils/elles perd**ent**
Nous **perdons** du poids. (*We're losing weight.*)	

French has dozens of regular **-re** verbs, including the following:

- ✔ **attendre** (*to wait [for]*)
- ✔ **défendre** (*to defend*)
- ✔ **descendre** (*to descend*)
- ✔ **entendre** (*to hear*)
- ✔ **étendre** (*to stretch*)

- ✔ **fondre** (*to melt*)
- ✔ **prétendre** (*to claim*)
- ✔ **rendre** (*to give back, return something*)
- ✔ **répondre** (*to answer*)
- ✔ **vendre** (*to sell*)

See how well you understand regular French verbs by conjugating the verb in parentheses for the grammatical person provided.

0. je _____ (jouer)

A. je **joue** (*I play*)

6. j'_____ (aimer)

7. tu _____ (chercher)

8. il _____ (donner)

9. nous _____ (penser)

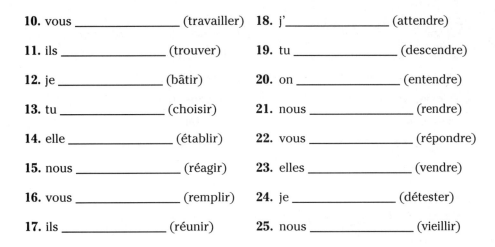

10. vous _____ (travailler)

11. ils _____ (trouver)

12. je _____ (bâtir)

13. tu _____ (choisir)

14. elle _____ (établir)

15. nous _____ (réagir)

16. vous _____ (remplir)

17. ils _____ (réunir)

18. j'_____ (attendre)

19. tu _____ (descendre)

20. on _____ (entendre)

21. nous _____ (rendre)

22. vous _____ (répondre)

23. elles _____ (vendre)

24. je _____ (détester)

25. nous _____ (vieillir)

Preserving Pronunciation with Spelling-Change Verbs

Spelling-change verbs have the same endings as regular **-er** verbs (see the earlier section), but for pronunciation reasons, they have a slight spelling change in certain conjugations. French has two types of spelling-change verbs: those that end in **-cer** and those that end in **-ger.** This section helps you conjugate them.

Working with -cer verbs

In French, the letter *c* has two sounds: hard, like the *c* in *coal,* and soft, like the *c* in *celery.* The French *c* is

- ✔ Hard when it precedes the vowels *a, o,* or *u*
- ✔ Soft when it precedes *e, i,* or *y*

The *c* at the end of **-cer** verbs is soft because it precedes *e,* which means it needs to be soft in all conjugations. For example, take the verb **prononcer** (*to pronounce*), which is conjugated like a regular **-er** verb with one exception. In the **nous** form, **prononcer** would have an *o* after the *c,* which would become hard. To avoid that, the **c** changes to **ç.** Now you have **nous prononçons,** and the *c* is soft, just like in the infinitive and all the other conjugations. Take a look at the verb table.

prononcer *(to pronounce)*	
je prononc**e**	nous pronon**ç**ons
tu prononc**es**	vous prononc**ez**
il/elle/on prononc**e**	ils/elles prononc**ent**
Tu **prononces** bien. (*Your pronunciation is good.* Literally: *You pronounce well.*)	

French has dozens of **-cer** verbs, including the following:

- **annoncer** (*to announce*)
- **avancer** (*to advance*)
- **balancer** (*to sway*)
- **commencer** (*to begin*)
- **dénoncer** (*to denounce*)

- **divorcer** (*to divorce*)
- **effacer** (*to erase*)
- **influencer** (*to influence*)
- **lancer** (*to throw*)
- **remplacer** (*to replace*)

Managing -ger verbs

Like *c,* the letter *g* also has two sounds in French: hard, like the *g* in *glass,* and soft, like the *g* in *massage.* The French *g* is

- Hard when it precedes *a, o,* or *u*
- Soft when it precedes *e, i,* or *y*

The *g* at the end of **-ger** verbs is soft, so it has to be soft in all its conjugations. For example, take the verb **bouger** (*to move*). You conjugate it like a regular **-er** verb, except for the **nous** form, where, to avoid the hard *g,* you add en *e:* **bougeons.** This change makes the *g* soft, like in the infinitive and all the other conjugations.

bouger (*to move*)	
je boug**e**	nous boug**eons**
tu boug**es**	vous boug**ez**
il/elle/on boug**e**	ils/elles boug**ent**
Ils **bougent** beaucoup. (*They're moving a lot.*)	

French has dozens of **-ger** verbs, including these:

- **arranger** (*to arrange*)
- **changer** (*to change*)
- **corriger** (*to correct*)
- **déménager** (*to move house*)
- **déranger** (*to disturb*)

- **diriger** (*to direct*)
- **exiger** (*to demand, insist*)
- **loger** (*to lodge*)
- **manger** (*to eat*)
- **voyager** (*to travel*)

Dissecting Stem-Changing Verbs

Stem-changing verbs take the same endings as regular **-er** verbs, but they have two different stems. There are five types of stem-changing verbs, but the rules for their conjugation are the same: The **nous** and **vous** forms of the verb take the regular *stem* (the infinitive minus **-er**), and the singular forms and third-person plural have a stem change. This section takes a closer look at the five types.

To help you remember which four forms have stem changes, draw a line encircling them — it makes the shape of a boot.

Tackling -yer verbs

Verbs that end in **-yer** have two stems:

- ✔ A regular stem with **y** for the **nous** and **vous** conjugations
- ✔ An irregular stem with **i** in place of **y** for the other conjugations

Here I conjugate **employer** (*to employ*).

employer (*to employ, make use of*)	
j'emplo**ie**	nous emplo**yons**
tu emplo**ies**	vous emplo**yez**
il/elle/on emplo**ie**	ils/elles emplo**ient**
Tu **emploies** bien ton temps. (*You make good use of your time.*)	

There are dozens of **-yer** verbs, such as

- ✔ **balayer** (*to sweep*)
- ✔ **effrayer** (*to frighten*)
- ✔ **ennuyer** (*to bore, annoy*)
- ✔ **envoyer** (*to send*)
- ✔ **essayer** (*to try*)
- ✔ **essuyer** (*to wipe*)
- ✔ **nettoyer** (*to clean*)
- ✔ **payer** (*to pay*)
- ✔ **tutoyer** (*to use **tu***)
- ✔ **vouvoyer** (*to use **vous***)

This stem change, although required for verbs that end in **-oyer** and **-uyer,** is optional for verbs that end in **-ayer.** Verbs like **payer** can be conjugated with or without the stem-change: **Je paie** and **je paye** are both acceptable.

Figuring out -eler verbs

Verbs that end in **-eler** have a regular stem with a single **l** in the **nous** and **vous** conjugations and an irregular **ll** for the other conjugations. This example conjugates **épeler** (*to spell*).

épeler (*to spell*)	
j'épe**lle**	nous épe**lons**
tu épe**lles**	vous épe**lez**
il/elle/on épe**lle**	ils/elles épe**llent**
Vous **épelez** trop lentement. (*You spell too slowly.*)	

There are only a few **-eler** verbs:

- ✔ **appeler** (*to call*)
- ✔ **rappeler** (*to call back, recall*)
- ✔ **renouveler** (*to renew*)

The verbs **geler** (*to freeze*) and **peler** (*to peel*) don't follow this pattern of doubling the **l**. You conjugate them like **-e*er** verbs (see the "Looking at -e*er verbs" section later in this chapter for more info).

Focusing on -eter verbs

Verbs that end in **-eter** have a regular stem with a single **t** in the **nous** and **vous** conjugations and an irregular **tt** for the other conjugations. See how you conjugate **jeter** (*to throw*).

jeter (*to throw*)	
je je**tte**	nous je**tons**
tu je**ttes**	vous je**tez**
il/elle/on je**tte**	ils/elles je**ttent**
Elle **jette** Marc à l'eau. (*She's throwing Marc in the water.*)	

The most common **-eter** verbs are

- ✔ **feuilleter** (*to leaf through*)
- ✔ **hoqueter** (*to hiccup*)
- ✔ **projeter** (*to project*)
- ✔ **rejeter** (*to reject*)

The verb **acheter** (*to buy*) is an exception; it's conjugated like **-e*er** verbs. See the next section.

Looking at -e*er verbs

Verbs that end in **-e*er** have an unstressed **e** in the infinitive followed by a consonant such as **n** or **v**. Conjugated, these verbs have a regular stem with an unaccented **e** and an irregular stem with a grave accent **è**. Consider the following example of **mener** (*to lead*).

mener (*to lead*)	
je mè**ne**	nous men**ons**
tu mè**nes**	vous men**ez**
il/elle/on mè**ne**	ils/elles mè**nent**
Ils **mènent** le chien. (*They're leading/walking the dog.*)	

The French language has many common **-e*er** verbs (including the exceptions to the **-eler** and **-eter** verbs I mention previously in this chapter). Some of these verbs include the following:

- ✔ **acheter** (*to buy*)
- ✔ **amener** (*to take*)
- ✔ **élever** (*to bring up, raise*)
- ✔ **emmener** (*to take*)
- ✔ **enlever** (*to remove*)

- ✔ **geler** (*to freeze*)
- ✔ **lever** (*to lift, raise*)
- ✔ **peler** (*to peel*)
- ✔ **peser** (*to weigh*)
- ✔ **promener** (*to walk*)

Dealing with -é*er verbs

Verbs that end in **-é*er** have a regular stem that keeps the acute accent **é** for **nous** and **vous** and an irregular stem that changes to the grave accent **è.** The following example conjugates **gérer** (*to manage*).

gérer (*to manage*)	
je gè**re**	nous g**érons**
tu gè**res**	vous g**érez**
il/elle/on gè**re**	ils/elles gè**rent**
Nous **gérons** le projet. (*We're managing the project.*)	

Some **-é*er** verbs include

- ✔ **célébrer** (*to celebrate*)
- ✔ **compléter** (*to complete*)
- ✔ **considérer** (*to consider*)
- ✔ **espérer** (*to hope*)
- ✔ **modérer** (*to moderate*)

- ✔ **posséder** (*to possess*)
- ✔ **préférer** (*to prefer*)
- ✔ **répéter** (*to repeat*)
- ✔ **suggérer** (*to suggest*)
- ✔ **tolérer** (*to tolerate*)

While writing cautionary memos to several employees, your computer crashed and all the conjugated verbs turned into infinitives! Fill in the blanks with the correct conjugation for the spelling-change and stem-changing verbs provided.

Q. vous _____ (tolérer)

A. **tolérez**

Attention
Memo à David et Philippe :

Je m' **(26)**_____ (appeler) Anne et je **(27)**_____ (gérer) la section B7. Les autres gérants et moi **(28)**_____ (changer) notre politique de courriel. Vous **(29)**_____ (envoyer) souvent des messages personnels, et nous **(30)**_____ (considérer) que c'est une infraction de vos contrats. Nous **(31)**_____ (commencer) à surveiller vos ordinateurs ; si vous **(32)**_____ (répéter) cette activité, nous ne **(33)**_____ (renouveler) pas vos contrats. J' **(34)**_____ (espérer) que vous **(35)**_____ (essayer) de ne plus écrire à vos amis quand vous travaillez.

Attention
Memo à Sylvie :

Nous **(36)**_____ (rejeter) ta note de frais. Quand tu **(37)**_____ (voyager), tu **(38)**_____ (payer) trop pour des hôtels trois étoiles. Nous **(39)**_____ (exiger) que nos employés se **(40)**_____ (loger) dans des hôtels deux étoiles. Même si tu **(41)**_____ (préférer) les hôtels de luxe, nous **(42)**_____ (suggérer) que tu **(43)**_____ (considérer) les frais et que tu te **(44)**_____ (modérer).

```
Attention
Memo à Georges :


Il y a deux problèmes. D'abord, tu ne (45) _____
(compléter) pas ton travail — tu n' (46) _____ (épeler) pas
bien et tu ne (47) _____ (corriger) pas tes erreurs. Nous
te (48) _____ (diriger) de relire ce que tu (49) _____
(projeter) dans les meetings. De surcroît, te (50) _____
(rappeler) — tu que nous n' (51) _____ (employer) pas de
femmes de service ? Nous (52) _____ (enlever) les tableaux
blancs parce que tu les (53) _____ (effacer) mais tu ne les
(54) _____ (nettoyer) pas.
```

The Rebels: Conjugating Irregular Verbs

As if all the different regular verb patterns weren't enough to remember, French also has numerous irregular verbs, which have either unique conjugations or patterns limited to just a few verbs. Unfortunately, I don't know of any shortcut for memorizing them, but irregular verbs don't have to be the bane of your existence. You just have to practice conjugations until they feel natural.

To get better at conjugating verbs, try this quick exercise. Choose a verb and practice writing and reciting the conjugations for each subject pronoun. Take 10 minutes to do this every day, and the conjugations should become second nature in no time.

This section looks at several types of irregular French verbs and helps you keep track of them all.

Coming right up: Verbs like venir

Venir (*to come*), **tenir** (*to hold*), and all their derivatives are conjugated with a stem-change as well as irregular endings. In the singular conjugations and the third-person plural, the **e** in the stem changes to **ie**; there's no stem change in the **nous** and **vous** forms. (As for stem-changing verbs, you can remember which persons get stem changes by drawing a line around the singular forms and the third-person plural of **venir** and **tenir** to make a boot shape.) Then add the endings **-s, -s, -t, -ons, -ez,** and **-nent.** The best way to understand these verbs is to take a look at the following table, memorize the pattern, and apply it to related verbs.

venir (*to come*)	
je v**iens**	nous ven**ons**
tu v**iens**	vous ven**ez**
il/elle/on v**ient**	ils v**iennent**
Il **vient** dans deux heures. (*He's coming in two hours.*)	

Other verbs that follow this conjugation include **contenir** (*to contain*), **maintenir** (*to maintain*), and **revenir** (*to come back*).

Going out . . . and out like a light: Verbs like sortir and dormir

Dormir (*to sleep*) and most verbs that end in **-tir**, like **sortir** (*to go out*), are conjugated with the endings of regular **-re** verbs, except in the third-person singular. In the singular conjugations, the consonant plus **-ir** ending is dropped before adding the endings **-s**, **-s**, and **-t.** In the plurals, just **-ir** is dropped and the endings are **-ons, -ez,** and **-ent.**

sortir (*to go out*)	
je sor**s**	nous sort**ons**
tu sor**s**	vous sort**ez**
il/elle/on sor**t**	ils/elles sort**ent**
Nous **sortons** ce soir. (*We're going out tonight.*)	

Other verbs that follow this same conjugation include **mentir** (*to lie*), **sentir** (*to smell, to feel*), and **partir** (*to leave*).

Offering and opening: Verbs like offrir and ouvrir

Verbs that end in **-frir** and **-vrir,** like **offrir** (*to offer*) and **ouvrir** (*to open*), are irregular **-ir** verbs that are conjugated with the same endings as regular **-er** verbs. So you basically drop the **-ir** ending to find the stem and add the following endings: **-e, -es, -e, -ons, -ez,** and **-ent.**

Check out the following example.

ouvrir (*to open*)	
j'ouvr**e**	nous ouvr**ons**
tu ouvr**es**	vous ouvr**ez**
il/elle/on ouvr**e**	ils/elles ouvr**ent**
Elles **ouvrent** la porte. (*They're opening the door.*)	

Other similarly conjugated verbs include **découvrir** (*to discover*), **couvrir** (*to cover*), and **souffrir** (*to suffer*).

Taking: Verbs like prendre

Prendre (*to take*) and all its derivatives are conjugated with regular **-re** endings in the singular conjugations (**-s, -s**, nothing). The plural forms, however, drop the **d**, and the third-person plural also takes on an extra **n**; these forms then take the regular **-re** verb endings **-ons, -ez,** and **-ent**.

prendre (*to take*)	
je prend**s**	nous pre**nons**
tu prend**s**	vous pre**nez**
il/elle/on prend	ils/elles pre**nnent**
Tu **prends** beaucoup de photos. (*You take a lot of pictures.*)	

Similarly conjugated verbs include **apprendre** (*to learn*), **comprendre** (*to understand*), and **surprendre** (*to surprise*).

Beating and putting: Verbs like battre and mettre

Verbs that end in **-ttre**, like **battre** (*to beat*) and **mettre** (*to put*), as well as all their derivatives, drop a **t** in the singular conjugations. Then all the conjugations use the regular **-re** verb endings **-s, -s,** nothing, **-ons, -ez,** and **-ent**.

battre (*to beat*)	
je ba**ts**	nous batt**ons**
tu ba**ts**	vous batt**ez**
il/elle/on ba**t**	ils/elles batt**ent**
Ils **battent** toujours l'autre équipe. (*They always beat the other team.*)	

Examples of similarly conjugated verbs include **admettre** (*to admit*), **promettre** (*to promise*), and **transmettre** (*to transmit, to convey*).

Abilities and wants: Pouvoir and vouloir

The conjugations for **pouvoir** (*to be able to*) and **vouloir** (*to want*) are very similar. They have both stem changes and irregular endings. Check out the tables that follow.

pouvoir (*can, to be able to*)	
je p**eux**	nous p**ouvons**
tu p**eux**	vous p**ouvez**
il/elle/on p**eut**	ils/elles p**euvent**
Tu **peux** partir. (*You may leave.*)	

vouloir (*to want*)	
je v**eux**	nous v**oulons**
tu v**eux**	vous v**oulez**
il/elle/on v**eut**	ils/elles v**eulent**
Elles **veulent** danser. (*They want to dance.*)	

Seeing is believing: Voir, c'est croire

Voir (*to see*) and **croire** (*to believe*) are conjugated the same way. Take a look.

voir (*to see*)	
je v**ois**	nous v**oyons**
tu v**ois**	vous v**oyez**
il/elle/on v**oit**	ils/elles v**oient**
Nous **voyons** le volcan. (*We see the volcano.*)	

croire (*to believe*)	
je cr**ois**	nous cr**oyons**
tu cr**ois**	vous cr**oyez**
il/elle/on cr**oit**	ils/elles cr**oient**
Il **croit** à Père Noël. (*He believes in Santa Claus.*)	

Provide the correct conjugation for the verb in parentheses.

Q. Je _____ (partir) à midi.

A. Je **pars** à midi. (*I'm leaving at noon.*)

55. Je ne _____ (comprendre) pas.

56. Il _____ (vouloir) manger.

57. Vous _____ (pouvoir) venir.

58. Je _____ (dormir) en classe.

59. _____-tu (sortir) chaque soir ?

60. Ils _____ (ouvrir) la fenêtre même quand il fait froid.

61. Nous _____ (prendre) beaucoup de notes.

62. Elle _____ (mettre) trop d'argent sur les vêtements.

63. Si tu _____ (croire) que c'est juste, d'accord.

64. _____-vous (voir) l'hôtel ?

Tackling unique irregular verbs

Some of the most important French verbs have completely unique conjugations. They have nothing in common, other than the fact that they're some of the most commonly used French verbs. Write out the conjugations and practice saying them. (As you expand your vocab, use these verbs to discuss the cool things you have, talk about where your neighbor is going, or tell other people what they absolutely have to do.) Do this regularly, and the conjugations will be rolling off your tongue and out of your pen in no time.

avoir (*to have*)	
j'**ai**	nous **avons**
tu **as**	vous **avez**
il/elle/on **a**	ils/elles **ont**
J'**ai** une idée. (*I have an idea.*)	

être (*to be*)	
je **suis**	nous **sommes**
tu **es**	vous **êtes**
il/elle/on **est**	ils/elles **sont**
Tu **es** très intelligent. (*You are very smart.*)	

aller (*to go*)	
je **vais**	nous **allons**
tu **vas**	vous **allez**
il/elle/on **va**	ils/elles **vont**
Nous **allons** en France. (*We're going to France.*)	

faire (*to do, make*)	
je **fais**	nous **faisons**
tu **fais**	vous **faites**
il/elle/on **fait**	ils/elles **font**
Il **fait** le lit. (*He's making the bed.*)	

devoir (*should, to have to*)	
je **dois**	nous **devons**
tu **dois**	vous **devez**
il/elle/on **doit**	ils/elles **doivent**
Vous **devez** essayer. (*You have to try.*)	

savoir (*to know*)	
je **sais**	nous **savons**
tu **sais**	vous **savez**
il/elle/on **sait**	ils/elles **savent**
Elles **savent** nager. (*They know how to swim.*)	

dire *(to say, tell)*	
je **dis**	nous **disons**
tu **dis**	vous **dites**
il/elle/on **dit**	ils/elles **disent**
Tu **dis** des mensonges. (*You're telling lies.*)	

boire *(to drink)*	
je **bois**	nous **buvons**
tu **bois**	vous **buvez**
il/elle/on **boit**	ils/elles **boivent**
Elle **boit** trop. (*She drinks too much.*)	

vivre *(to live)*	
je **vis**	nous **vivons**
tu **vis**	vous **vivez**
il/elle/on **vit**	ils/elles **vivent**
Nous **vivons** ensemble. (*We live together.*)	

Translate these sentences with unique verbs into French.

Q. We are here.

A. **Nous sommes ici.**

65. You (plural) have a lot of questions. _____

66. We drink a lot of wine. _____

67. I have to open the door. _____

68. We're going to Belgium. _____

69. They know the answer. _____

70. She has a problem. _____

Answer Key

1 Michel, **j'ai** une idée pour une nouvelle publicité. **Peux-tu** m'aider ? **Nous pouvons** travailler ensemble. (*Michel, I have an idea for a new ad. Can you help me? We can work together.*)

2 Voici mon idée. Il y a un père, une mère et un enfant dans la cuisine. Le père dit à sa femme, **veux-tu** quelque chose à manger ? (*Here's my idea. A father, mother, and child are in the kitchen. The father says to his wife, do you want something to eat?*)

3 **Elle répond :** Oui, et **je pense** que David a faim aussi. (*She responds: Yes, and I think David is hungry, too.*)

4 David dit à ses parents : Oui, moi aussi — **pouvez-vous** me faire un sandwich ? (*David says to his parents: Yes, me too, can you make me a sandwich?*)

5 **Ils répondent :** Non, **tu peux** le faire. **Nous avons** acheté une Sandwichière — **elle est** tellement simple qu'un enfant peut faire son propre sandwich. (*They respond: No, you can do it. We bought a sandwich maker — it's so simple that a child can make his own sandwich.*)

6 j'**aime** (*I like*)

7 tu **cherches** (*you are looking for*)

8 il **donne** (*he gives*)

9 nous **pensons** (*we think*)

10 vous **travaillez** (*you work*)

11 ils **trouvent** (*they find*)

12 je **bâtis** (*I build*)

13 tu **choisis** (*you choose*)

14 elle **établit** (*she is establishing*)

15 nous **réagissons** (*we are reacting*)

16 vous **remplissez** (*you are filling*)

17 ils **réunissent** (*they are meeting*)

18 j'**attends** (*I'm waiting for*)

19 tu **descends** (*you are going down*)

20 on **entend** (*one hears*)

21 nous **rendons** (*we're returning*)

22 vous **répondez** (*you answer*)

23 elles **vendent** (*they sell*)

24 je **déteste** (*I hate*)

25 nous **vieillissons** (*we're getting old*)

Attention

Memo à David et Philippe :

Je m'(26) **appelle** Anne et je (27) **gère** la section B7. Les autres gérants et moi (28) **changeons** notre politique de courriel. Vous (29) **envoyez** souvent des messages personnels, et nous (30) **considérons** que c'est une infraction de vos contrats. Nous (31) **commençons** à surveiller vos ordinateurs ; si vous (32) **répétez** cette activité, nous ne (33) **renouvelons** pas vos contrats. J'(34) **espère** que vous (35) **essayez** maintenant de ne plus écrire à vos amis quand vous travaillez.

(My name is Anne, and I manage section B7. The other managers and I are changing our e-mail policy. You often send personal messages, and we consider that a breach of your contracts. We are starting to watch your computers; if you repeat this activity, we are not renewing your contracts. I hope that you now try not to write to your friends anymore when you work.)

Attention

Memo à Sylvie :

Nous (36) **rejetons** ta note de frais. Quand tu (37) **voyages**, tu (38) **paies** (or **payes**) trop pour des hôtels trois étoiles. Nous (39) **exigeons** que nos employés se (40) **logent** dans des hôtels deux étoiles. Même si tu (41) **préfères** les hôtels de luxe, nous (42) **suggérons** que tu (43) **considères** les frais et que tu te (44) **modères**.

(We are rejecting your expense report. When you travel, you pay too much for three-star hotels. We insist that our employees stay in two-star hotels. Even if you prefer luxury hotels, we suggest that you consider the costs and moderate yourself.)

Attention
Memo à Georges :

Il y a deux problèmes. D'abord, tu ne (45) **complètes** pas ton travail — tu n'(46) **épelles** pas bien et tu ne (47) **corriges** pas tes erreurs. Nous te (48) **dirigeons** de relire ce que tu (49) **projettes** dans les meetings. De surcroît, te (50) **rappelles**-tu que nous n'(51) **employons** pas de femmes de service ? Nous (52) **enlevons** les tableaux blancs parce que tu les (53) **effaces** mais tu ne les (54) **nettoies** pas.

(There are two problems. First of all, you do not complete your work — you donît spell well, and you don't correct your mistakes. We direct you to reread what you project in meetings. In addition, do you remember that we don't employ cleaners? We are removing the whiteboards because you erase them but you don't clean them.)

55 Je ne **comprends** pas. (*I don't understand.*)

56 Il **veut** manger. (*He wants to eat.*)

57 Vous **pouvez** venir. (*You can come.*)

58 Je **dors** en classe. (*I sleep in class.*)

59 **Sors**-tu chaque soir ? (*Do you go out every night?*)

60 Ils **ouvrent** la fenêtre même quand il fait froid. (*They open the window even when it's cold.*)

61 Nous **prenons** beaucoup de notes. (*We take a lot of notes.*)

62 Elle **met** trop d'argent sur les vêtements. (*She spends too much money on clothes.*)

63 Si tu **crois** que c'est juste, d'accord. (*If you believe it's fair, okay.*)

64 **Voyez**-vous l'hôtel ? (*Do you see the hotel?*)

65 **Vous avez beaucoup de questions.**

66 **Nous buvons beaucoup de vin.**

67 **Je dois ouvrir la porte.**

68 **Nous allons en Belgique.**

69 **Ils savent la réponse.**

70 **Elle a un problème.**

Chapter 5

Asking and Answering Questions

- -

In This Chapter

▶ Asking yes/no questions

▶ Requesting information

▶ Answering questions

- -

*E*veryone knows that being a good listener is important, but if you want to have a real discussion, you can't just stand there and let others jabber on — you have to contribute, too. Questions are one of the foundations of a good conversation or letter, and knowing how to ask and answer questions will greatly improve both your spoken and written French. When you exchange letters with your friend in Brussels and your colleague in Montreal, don't let them do all the talking — ask some questions of your own.

 In French texts, the question mark and all other two-part punctuation marks — exclamation points, **guillemets** (*French quotation marks*), colons, and semicolons — must be preceded by a space. When typing, be sure to use a non-breaking space in front of the punctuation mark to avoid its wrapping to the next line. Or if you set the language of your word-processing software to French, it should add the spaces for you.

This chapter explains how to ask and answer the different types of questions, and it provides all the interrogative vocabulary that goes along with them.

Oui ou Non: Asking Yes/No Questions

If all you need is a simple *yes* or *no,* then asking questions in French couldn't be easier. You can ask questions in various ways, and which one you use depends on what kind of a conversation you're having or the type of letter you're writing. In most cases, you want to choose between the less formal **est-ce que** and the more formal inversion. This section helps you make the right decision and shows you how to use each form.

Posing informal questions

Using **est-ce que** (Literally: *is it that?*) is the easiest way to ask questions. All you have to do is tack **est-ce que** to the beginning of any statement and stick a question mark at the end of it. When followed by a word that begins with a vowel, like **il**, **elle** and **on**, **est-ce que** contracts to **est-ce qu'**. Check out some examples:

Est-ce que tu es prêt ? (*Are you ready?*)

Est-ce que vous avez mangé ? (*Have you eaten?*)

Est-ce que David sait nager ? (*Does David know how to swim?*)

Est-ce qu'elle parle français ? (*Does she speak French?*)

Est-ce qu'on a de l'argent ? (*Do we have any money?*)

Est-ce que is somewhat informal, and it's rarely written — it's used mainly when speaking. Another very common way to ask questions informally when writing or speaking is just to tack a question mark at the end of a statement, such as **Tu veux venir avec nous ?** (*You want to come with us?*). However, this structure is very informal, and it should never be used in anything official or business-related. Inversion (see the next section) is the best way to ask questions in any kind of formal situation.

If you're pretty sure the answer to your question is yes, you can tack **n'est-ce pas** (Literally: *isn't it that?*) on the end of a statement: **Tu viens avec nous, n'est-ce pas ?** (*You're coming with us, right/aren't you?*) This is also informal.

Turn each of the following statements into a question with **est-ce que**.

Q. Elle est intéressante.

A. **Est-ce qu'elle est intéressante ?** (*Is she interesting?*)

1. Vous voulez étudier. _____

2. Tu vas commencer maintenant. _____

3. Vous avez faim. _____

4. Il travaille ici. _____

5. Elle veut voyager. _____

6. Tu es heureux. _____

7. Nous allons marcher. _____

8. Elle habite au Sénégal. _____

Asking formal questions with inversion

Inversion is a little bit more complicated than the informal methods. Whereas you can ask any question with **est-ce que,** inversion works only with a subject pronoun, not a noun or a name. Inversion is also more formal, so in a business setting, such as a job interview or conversation with your boss, it's the better option.

To ask a question with inversion, you switch the order of the subject pronoun and verb and join them with a hyphen:

Es-tu prêt ? (*Are you ready?*)

Sait-il nager ? (*Does he know how to swim?*)

You can invert only subject pronouns, not actual subjects. So when you ask a question with a subject, such as **Pierre** or **le chat** (*the cat*), you have to either replace the subject with a pronoun or start the question with the subject, followed by the inverted verb and subject pronoun.

> **Pierre est-il prêt ?** (*Is Pierre ready?*)
>
> **Le chat sait-il nager ?** (*Does the cat know how to swim?*)

When the verb ends in a vowel and is followed by a third-person singular pronoun, you have to add **t** between the verb and pronoun:

> **Parle-t-elle français ?** (*Does she speak French?*)
>
> **A-t-on de l'argent ?** (*Do we have any money?*)

Turn each of the following statements into a question with inversion.

Q. Il est beau.

A. **Est-il beau ?** (*Is he handsome?*)

9. Tu as un chien. _____

10. Vous êtes prêts. _____

11. Vous devez partir. _____

12. Elle travaille ici. _____

13. Elles aiment danser. _____

14. Tu es triste. _____

15. Nous sommes en retard. _____

16. Ils habitent en France. _____

Asking Who, What, Which, When, Where, Why, and How Questions

Questions that ask for information, such as *who, when, why,* and *how,* are sometimes called *wh* questions in English because all these question words begin with *w* or *h*. French has three types of question words, and you need to understand the difference between them in order to ask *wh* questions:

> ✔ **Interrogative adverbs:** These adverbs ask for more information about something that happens. French has five important interrogative adverbs:
>
> - **comment** (*how*)
> - **combien (de)** (*how much/many*)
> - **quand** (*when*)

- **où** (*where*)
- **pourquoi** (*why*)

Comment means *how*, as in **Comment as-tu fait ça ?** (*How did you do that?*). However, used alone, **Comment ?** means *What?* — for example, when you need someone to repeat what he or she just said.

Quand means *when*, and the answer can be a time or date: **Quand vas-tu en France ? Dans deux semaines.** (*When are you going to France? In two weeks.*) If you want to know what time something happens, use **à quelle heure** (*at what time*). **Quelle** is an interrogative adjective, which I mention later in this list.

✔ **Interrogative pronouns:** Interrogative pronouns ask *who* or *what*, and because they're pronouns, you can't use them in front of a noun. *Who* in French is pretty easy — it's usually translated as **qui.** *What* is a lot more complicated. If it's at the beginning of a question, the French translation is **que,** but if it's after a preposition, it's **quoi** (see Chapter 12 for details on prepositions). In addition, if you're asking *what* but you really mean *which,* you want an interrogative adjective, which I discuss in the next bullet point.

Don't get too attached to the idea that **que** means *what* and **qui** means *who*. They usually do, but not always. When asking questions, **qui** and **que** also indicate whether you're using *who* or *what* as the subject or object of the question — see the next section for details.

✔ **Interrogative adjectives:** These adjectives are perhaps the most difficult question words. In English, when you ask a question about two or more similar objects, you can just use *what* plus the noun, even though *which* may be the grammatically correct option, as in *What (Which) shirt do you like better?* But in French, you simply can't use the interrogative pronoun **que** in front of a noun — you have to use **quel** whenever you're asking someone to make a distinction between two or more nouns: **Quelle chemise préfères-tu ?**

Quel is an adjective, which means that it has to agree in gender and number with the noun it modifies:

- Masculine singular: **quel homme** (*what/which man*)
- Feminine singular: **quelle femme** (*what/which woman*)
- Masculine plural: **quels hommes** (*what/which men*)
- Feminine plural: **quelles femmes** (*what/which women*)

This section shows you the *wh* question words and explains how to use them with both the **est-ce que** and the inversion methods.

Asking wh questions with "est-ce que"

You can ask *wh* questions with interrogative adverbs and adjectives plus **est-ce que** by putting the question word at the beginning of the question, followed by **est-ce que,** the subject, and the verb. Don't forget that **quel** has to be followed by a noun and that it has to agree with that noun in gender and number.

Où est-ce que tu vas ? (*Where are you going?*)

Combien d'argent est-ce que vous avez ? (*How much money do you have?*)

Pourquoi est-ce qu'il aime le jazz ? (*Why does he like jazz?*)

Quand est-ce que Laure va arriver ? (*When is Laure going to arrive?*)

Quel livre est-ce que tu veux ? (*Which book do you want?*)

When you're asking a question with *who* or *what,* **est-ce que** gets more complicated. **Que** + **est-ce que** has to contract to **qu'est-ce que.** And if the question has *who* or *what* as the *object* of the question, the basic rules still apply, such as with **Qu'est-ce que tu veux faire ?** (*What do you want to do?*). However, if *who* or *what* is the subject of the question, you have to change **est-ce que** to **est-ce qui,** as in **Qu'est-ce qui se passe ?** (*What's happening?*) or **Qui est-ce qui veut m'aider ?** (*Who wants to help me?*). Note that **qui** doesn't contract with **est-ce que** or any other word.

In the prior examples, the first word — the word that comes before **est-ce que** or **est-ce-qui** — determines the meaning. If the first word is **qui,** you're asking *who?* If the first word is **que,** you're asking *what?* The word that comes after **est-ce** indicates whether the word that becomes before **est-ce** is the subject or object. If the word at the end is **qui,** the first word is the subject, and if the word is **que,** it's the object.

If you're not sure how to tell whether something is a subject or object, try rewording it. When you rearrange *What do you want to do?* you get *You want to do what?* which makes it easier to see that *you* is the subject and *what* is the object. Table 5-1 lays out this information for you.

Table 5-1	Interrogative Pronouns with Est-ce Que	
Pronoun	*Subject of Question*	*Object of Question*
Who	**Qui est-ce qui (or Qui)**	**Qui est-ce que**
What	**Qu'est-ce qui**	**Qu'est-ce que**

You can also ask questions with a preposition plus *who* or *what.* Remember that after a preposition, **que** changes to **quoi.**

À qui est-ce que tu écris ? (*Whom are you writing to?* or *To whom are you writing?*)

De quoi est-ce que vous parlez ? (*What are you talking about?*)

À quelle heure est-ce que tu pars ? (*What time are you leaving?*)

Your boss sent out an important memo, but you spilled coffee on it and some of the words are illegible. For each of the partial sentences provided here, ask a question with **est-ce que** that'll get the information you need to fill the blanks.

Q. _____ va commencer un nouveau projet.

A. **Qui est-ce qui** va commencer un nouveau projet ? (*Who is going to start a new project?*)

NOTE DE SERVICE

| À tous les employés : | | | |
| De la part du chef : | | | |

Il s'agit de ▬▬▬▬▬
(17)

Il y aura ▬▬▬▬▬ employés sur l'équipe.
(18)

L'équipe sera basée à ▬▬▬▬▬
(19)

Elle travaillera avec ▬▬▬▬▬
(20)

Elle va faire ▬▬▬▬▬
(21)

Il faut commencer demain parce que ▬▬▬▬▬
(22)

L'équipe doit se rassembler à ▬▬▬▬▬
heures . . .
(23)

. . . dans le bureau ▬▬▬▬▬
(24)

Le ▬▬▬▬▬ est très important.
(25)

Le projet durera ▬▬▬▬▬ mois.
(26)

Asking wh questions with inversion

To ask a *wh* question using inversion, just put the interrogative word at the beginning and follow it with the inverted verb and subject.

Though most yes/no and *wh* questions can be asked with either **est-ce que** or inversion, certain common questions are virtually always asked with inversion. Table 5-2 lists these fixed questions.

Table 5-2	Common Questions with Inversion
English	*French*
Do you speak French/English?	**Parles-tu français/anglais ?** or **Parlez-vous français/anglais ?**
How are you?	**Comment vas-tu ?** or **Comment allez-vous ?**
How old are you?	**Quel âge as-tu ?** or **Quel âge avez-vous ?**
How's the weather?	**Quel temps fait-il ?**
What day is it?	**Quel jour sommes-nous ?**

English	French
What is your name?	**Comment t'appelles-tu ?** or **Comment vous appelez-vous ?**
What time is it?	**Quelle heure est-il ?**
Where are you going?	**Où vas-tu ?** or **Où allez-vous ?**
Who is it?	**Qui est-ce ?**

Answering Questions

Knowing how to ask questions is only half the battle. What kind of world would it be if questions got asked but never answered? Would that make them rhetorical? What good would that do? Am I annoying you yet? So you see, you also have to know how to answer questions — and understand other people's answers, too. This section gives you an overview of responding to different types of questions.

Answering yes/no questions

Yes/no questions aren't just easy to ask — they're also easy to answer. You can take the easy road and just answer **oui** (*yes*) or **non** (*no*):

> **Est-ce que tu es prêt ? Oui.** (*Are you ready? Yes.*)

> **Avez-vous mangé ? Non.** (*Have you eaten? No.*)

You can also repeat the question as a statement after you say yes or no:

> **Oui, je suis prêt.** (*Yes, I'm ready.*)

> **Oui, elle parle français.** (*Yes, she speaks French.*)

French has another word for yes, **si,** which you use when someone asks a question in the negative but you want to respond in the affirmative. For example, if someone says "Don't you like to swim?" and you do in fact like to swim, in English, you have to say, "Yes, I do like to swim." But in French, someone can ask **N'aimes-tu pas nager ?** and you can just answer **Si.** (Check out Chapter 6 for more information about responding to negative questions and giving negative answers.)

Of course, not all questions merit a simple *yes* or *no.* The following are some useful ways to answer questions:

- **oui** (*yes*)
- **si** (*yes* — in response to a negative)
- **bien sûr** (*of course*)
- **non** (*no*)
- **pas du tout** (*not at all*)

- **pas encore** (*not yet*)
- **peut-être** (*maybe*)
- **je ne sais pas** (*I don't know*)
- **ça m'est égal** (*I don't care*)

Answering wh questions

The answers to *wh* questions are a lot more complicated than responses to yes/no questions. Because they're asking for information, you have to respond with that information in place of the question words:

> **Quelle heure est-il ? Il est midi.** (*What time is it? It's noon.*)

> **Comment t'appelles-tu ? Je m'appelle Jean.** (*What's your name? My name is Jean.*)

You can use the following words to help you answer *wh* questions (see Chapter 3 for details on dates and times):

✔ **à** (*at, in, to*)

✔ **c'est, on est** (*it is* — with dates)

✔ **il est** (*it is* — with time)

✔ **parce que** (*because*)

✔ **pendant** (*for* — with time)

Try answering the following questions in French. Because they're personal, there are no right or wrong answers, but you can read some possible answers in the Answer Key to make sure yours are in the correct format. (For info on negative sentences, please see Chapter 6.)

Q. Comment vous appelez-vous ?

A. **Je m'appelle Laura.** (*My name is Laura.*)

27. Est-ce que vous habitez en France ? _____

28. Est-ce que vous aimez voyager ? _____

29. Où est-ce que vous travaillez ? _____

30. Qu'est-ce que vous aimez faire le samedi ? _____

31. Savez-vous nager ? _____

32. Quelle musique aimez-vous ? _____

33. Qui est votre meilleur ami ? _____

34. Quelle est la date de votre anniversaire ? _____

35. Combien de frères et de sœurs avez-vous ? _____

Answer Key

1 **Est-ce que vous voulez étudier ?** (*Do you want to study?*)

2 **Est-ce que tu vas commencer maintenant ?** (*Are you going to start now?*)

3 **Est-ce que vous avez faim ?** (*Are you hungry?*)

4 **Est-ce qu'il travaille ici ?** (*Does he work here?*)

5 **Est-ce qu'elle veut voyager ?** (*Does she want to travel?*)

6 **Est-ce que tu es heureux ?** (*Are you happy?*)

7 **Est-ce que nous allons marcher ?** (*Are we going to walk?*)

8 **Est-ce qu'elle habite au Sénégal ?** (*Does she live in Sénégal?*)

9 **As-tu un chien ?** (*Do you have a dog?*)

10 **Êtes-vous prêts ?** (*Are you ready?*)

11 **Devez-vous partir ?** (*Do you have to leave?*)

12 **Travaille-t-elle ici ?** (*Does she work here?*)

13 **Aiment-elles danser ?** (*Do they like to dance?*)

14 **Es-tu triste ?** (*Are you sad?*)

15 **Sommes-nous en retard ?** (*Are we late?*)

16 **Habitent-ils en France ?** (*Do they live in France?*)

NOTE DE SERVICE

À tous les employés :				
De la part du chef :				

(17) **De quoi est-ce qu'**il s'agit? (*What is it about?*) (18) **Combien d'**employés **est-ce qu'**il y aura sur l'équipe? (*How many employees will be on the team?*) (19) **Où est-ce que** l'équipe sera basée? (*Where will the team be based?*) (20) **Avec quoi** OR **qui est-ce qu'**elle travaillera? (*What* OR *Who will it work with?*) (21) **Qu'est-ce qu'**elle va faire? (*What will it do?*) (22) **Pourquoi est-ce qu'**il faut commencer demain? (*Why do we need to start tomorrow?*) (23) **À quelle heure** OR **Quand est-ce que** l'équipe doit se rassembler? (*At what time* OR *When does the team have to meet?*) (24) **Dans quel** bureau est-ce qu'elle doit se rassembler? (*In which office does it have to meet?*) (25) **Qu'est-ce qui** est très important? (*What is very important?*) (26) **Combien de** mois **est-ce que** le projet durera? (*How many months will the project last?*)

27 **Oui, j'habite en France** or **Non, je n'habite pas en France.** (*Yes, I live in France* or *No, I don't live in France.*)

28 **Oui, j'aime voyager.** (*Yes, I like to travel.*)

29 **Je travaille à IBM/dans une banque.** (*I work at IBM/in a bank.*)

30 **Le samedi j'aime aller à la plage.** (*I like to go to the beach on Saturdays.*)

31 **Oui, je sais nager.** (*Yes, I know how to swim.*)

32 **J'aime la musique classique/le rap.** (*I like classical music/rap.*)

33 **Henri est mon meilleur ami.** (*Henri is my best friend.*)

34 **Mon anniversaire est le 10 septembre.** (*My birthday is September 10.*)

35 **J'ai deux frères et une sœur** or **Je n'ai pas de frères.** (*I have two brothers and one sister* or *I don't have any brothers or sisters.*)

Chapter 6

Just Say No: The Negative

In This Chapter
▶ Understanding French negation
▶ Using negative words
▶ Responding to negative questions and statements

*E*ven if you'd rather be a yes-man (or yes-woman), sometimes you've just got to say no. Otherwise, you may discover that you've agreed to visit your pen pal in the Malian desert or accepted a weekend work assignment with no extra pay. In French, being negative is twice as hard as it is in English because French requires at least two words, whereas English only needs one. This chapter explains all the different ways to be negative in French, as well as how to respond — whether you agree or disagree — when someone says something negative to you.

Using Negative Adverbs

Other than the short and sweet *no,* negative adverbs are the most common construction used to negate statements and questions. In English, the negative adverb is usually a single word, such as *not* or *never.* In French, it's at least two words, and one of them is always **ne.** This section takes a closer look at the most common negative adverb as well as some other options you have.

The most common negative adverb: Ne . . . pas

The French equivalent of *not,* as in *I do not sing,* is **ne . . . pas.** These two words have to surround the verb — you put **ne** in front of it and **pas** after. When you have **ne** + a vowel or mute *h,* it contracts to **n':**

> **Je ne suis pas prêt.** (*I'm not ready.*)
>
> **Elle n'est pas là.** (*She's not there.*)

When you have two verbs in a sentence, as with the near future construction (see Chapter 18), **ne . . . pas** surrounds just the conjugated verb:

> **Il ne va pas travailler.** (*He isn't going to work.*)
>
> **Tu ne dois pas venir.** (*You don't have to come.*)

In compound tenses like the **passé composé** (see Chapter 15), the negative adverb surrounds the auxiliary verb, and the past participle comes after **pas:**

> **Elles ne sont pas arrivées.** (*They didn't arrive.*)

> **Je n'ai pas mangé.** (*I didn't eat.*)

For questions with inversion (check out Chapter 5), the **ne . . . pas** surrounds the inverted verb-plus-subject:

> **Ne viennent-ils pas ?** (*Aren't they coming?*)

> **N'as-tu pas faim ?** (*Aren't you hungry?*)

Ne . . . pas can't be used with **est-ce que** questions. If you're pretty sure that the answer to your question is *yes,* you can say something and then end the sentence with **n'est-ce pas ?** which means *right?* or *isn't that so?* For instance, **Tu as faim, n'est-ce pas ?** means *You're hungry, right?*

When your negative statement or question has reflexive, object, or adverbial pronouns (see Chapter 13), those have to stay directly in front of the verb. So **ne** precedes the whole group of them, and **pas** follows the conjugated verb as usual:

> **Je ne te crois pas.** (*I don't believe you.*)

> **Tu ne me l'as pas donné.** (*You didn't give it to me.*)

In informal spoken French, **ne** is often dropped, so **pas** has to be negative all on its own:

> **Je ne sais pas.** → **Je sais pas.** (*I don't know.*)

> **Il ne veut pas étudier.** → **Il veut pas étudier.** (*He doesn't want to study.*)

Remember that partitive articles (**du, de la, des**) and indefinite articles (**un, une, des**) change to **de** after a negation. (See Chapter 2 for more info on articles.)

> **J'ai un frère.** → **Je n'ai pas de frère.** (*I have a brother.* → *I don't have any brothers.*)

Other negative adverbs

Although **ne . . . pas** is the most common negative adverb, several others are also very useful. Take a look at the following:

- ✔ **ne . . . jamais** (*never*)
- ✔ **ne . . . nulle part** (*nowhere*)
- ✔ **ne . . . pas du tout** (*not at all*)
- ✔ **ne . . . pas encore** (*not yet*)
- ✔ **ne . . . pas que** (*not only*)
- ✔ **ne . . . pas toujours** (*not always*)
- ✔ **ne . . . plus** (*not anymore, no more, no longer*)
- ✔ **ne . . . que** (*only*)

All negative adverbs follow the same placement rules as **ne . . . pas,** with **ne** preceding the conjugated verb and with **plus, jamais,** or whatever else following it:

> **Elle ne ment jamais.** (*She never lies.*)

> **Je ne suis pas encore prêt.** (*I'm not ready yet.*)

> **Nous n'avons que 5 euros.** (*We have only 5 euros.*)

As with **ne . . . pas,** in informal spoken French, you can drop the **ne** with other negative adverbs:

> **Je ne fume plus.** → **Je fume plus.** (*I don't smoke any more.*)

> **Je n'y suis jamais allé.** → **J'y suis jamais allé.** (*I've never gone there.*)

You do have to be careful when dropping **ne,** because the second part of the adverb can have a different meaning when used affirmatively. **Plus,** for example, can mean *more* when it's not used with **ne,** so make sure that you add any other info necessary to get your point across.

In questions, **jamais** without **ne** means *ever,* such as with **As-tu jamais vu ce film ?** (*Have you ever seen this movie?*).

Rewrite each of these in the negative using the negative adverb provided.

0. J'ai faim. (ne . . . pas)

A. Je **n'ai pas** faim. (*I'm not hungry.*)

1. Elle parle français. (ne . . . pas) _____

2. Il est allé en France. (ne . . . jamais) _____

3. Je peux travailler. (ne . . . plus) _____

4. Veux-tu partir ? (ne . . . pas) _____

5. Ils ont fait. (ne . . . rien) _____

6. Elle le veut. (ne . . . pas du tout) _____

7. J'ai un frère. (ne . . . que) _____

8. Il est en retard. (ne . . . pas toujours) _____

Using Negative Adjectives, Pronouns, and Conjunctions

Negative adverbs are the most common type of negative structure, but you can use them only to negate verbs. If you want to negate other parts of speech, such as nouns, you need negative adjectives, pronouns, and conjunctions — words that can add a little spice to your negativity. This section points out what you need to know when using these other negative parts of speech.

Negative adjectives

Like negative adverbs, French negative adjectives also have two parts. Rather than negating verbs, they negate nouns by limiting or refusing them. But their placement is pretty much the same as for negative adverbs: **ne** goes in front of the conjugated verb and the second part goes after the verb.

  ✔ **ne . . . aucun/aucune** (*no, not any, not one*)

  ✔ **ne . . . nul/nulle** (*no, not any*)

  ✔ **ne . . . pas un/une** (*no, not one*)

  ✔ **ne . . . pas un seul/une seule** (*not a single*)

Like other kinds of French adjectives, negative adjectives have to agree in gender with the nouns they're negating. However, negative adjectives are never plural, because you're saying there's not even one of the noun.

Even though there are four different negative adjectives, they all mean pretty much the same thing — *no* or *not any,* with the exception of **ne . . . pas un seul,** which is a bit stronger than the others — *not a single one.* But there is a difference in how you use them.

You can use **ne . . . pas un** and **ne . . . pas un seul** only for *countable* nouns (such as books, employees, and houses), and you can use **ne . . . nul** only for *uncountable* nouns (such as intelligence, money, and furniture). The last negative adjective, **ne . . . aucun,** is less picky — you can use it with countable and uncountable nouns.

> **Je n'ai pas une idée.** (*I don't have one idea, I have no idea.*)
>
> **Il ne connaît pas un seul bon resto.** (*He doesn't know one single good restaurant.*)
>
> **Ils n'ont nulle foi.** (*They have no faith.*)
>
> **Je n'ai aucune solution.** (*I have no solution, I have not one solution.*)
>
> **Il ne connaît aucun bon café.** (*He doesn't know a single good café.*)
>
> **Ils n'ont aucune intégrité.** (*They have no integrity.*)

In English, when you say *there aren't any* of something, the verb is in the third-person plural and the noun is plural: *There are no books.* The equivalent expression in French is **il y a,** which has the third-person singular subject and takes a third-person singular verb. So when you use a negative adjective in French, the verb has to be in the third-person singular and the noun following the negative adjective is always singular: **Il n'y a aucun livre; Il n'y a pas un livre.**

Normally, when you have a sentence with an indefinite article (**un** or **une**) that you want to make negative, the article changes to **de,** meaning *(not) any.* When you use the negative adverb **ne . . . pas un,** you're keeping the indefinite article in order to stress the negative aspect of the statement — that there is not a single one. Compare these two statements:

> **Il n'a pas d'amis.** (*He doesn't have any friends.*)
>
> **Il n'a pas un ami.** (*He doesn't have one friend, a single friend.*)

You can start a sentence with a negative adjective by putting the second part of the adjective at the beginning, followed by the noun, **ne,** and the verb:

> **Nul argent ne sera remboursé.** (*No money will be reimbursed.*)
>
> **Aucun bruit ne parvenait à mes oreilles.** (*Not a sound reached my ears.*)

You're taking inventory of the office, and it turns out that you're out of everything. For each of the items listed, say that there are none. Note that more than one negative adjective is possible for each answer.

Q. des crayons

A. **Il n'y a pas un crayon/Il n'y a aucun crayon.** (*There isn't a single pencil.*)

9. des stylos _____

10. du papier _____

11. des chemises _____

12. des agrafes _____

13. de la mine de crayon _____

14. des timbres _____

15. du café _____

Negative pronouns

Negative adjectives and negative pronouns are a lot alike; in fact, all the adjectives can also be used as pronouns. The difference between these two negative structures is that negative adjectives are used *with* the nouns they negate, and negative pronouns *replace* the nouns.

The French negative pronouns are

- ✔ **ne . . . aucun/aucune (de)** (*none [of], not any [of]*)
- ✔ **ne . . . nul/nulle** (*no one*)
- ✔ **ne . . . pas un/une (de)** (*not one [of]*)
- ✔ **ne . . . pas un seul/une seule (de)** (*not a single one [of]*)
- ✔ **ne . . . personne** (*no one*)
- ✔ **ne . . . rien** (*nothing, not anything*)

Like many other pronouns, negative pronouns have to agree in gender with the nouns they replace. You can use **ne . . . pas un** and **ne . . . pas un seul** only for countable nouns, and you can use **ne . . . aucun** for countable or uncountable nouns. These three negative pronouns can be used in one of two ways:

- ✔ Followed by **de** + some additional information about what you're negating
- ✔ With an *antecedent* (a noun that you're referring back to) and the pronoun **en** (**en,** which replaces **de** + noun, is explained in Chapter 13.)

Je n'aime aucune de ces idées. (*I don't like any of these ideas.*)

Pas un des employés n'est arrivé. (*Not one of the employees has arrived.*)

Il a trois voitures et je n'en ai pas une seule. (*He has three cars and I don't have a single one.*)

Ne . . . nul and **ne . . . personne** mean *no one, not anyone,* and **ne . . . rien** means *nothing, not anything:*

> **Personne n'est venu à la fête.** (*No one came to the party.*)
>
> **Rien ne m'inspire.** (*Nothing inspires me.*)

Note that the negative pronoun **personne** (*no one*) is always masculine, unlike **une personne** (*person*), which is always feminine.

Note: **Ne . . . nul** means *no, not one* as a negative adjective and *no one* as a negative pronoun.

> **Je n'ai nulle idée.** (*I don't have any ideas.*)
>
> **Nul n'est prophète en son pays.** (*No man is a prophet in his own country.*)

Negative pronouns can be subjects, direct objects, or objects of a preposition:

- ✔ Subject: **Personne n'est venu.** (*No one came.*)
- ✔ Direct object: **Je ne connais personne.** (*I don't know anyone.*)
- ✔ Object of a preposition: **Je ne parle à personne.** (*I'm not talking to anyone.*)

You can modify negative pronouns with **d'entre** + **nous/vous/eux/elles** to mean *of us/you/them.*

> **Aucun d'entre nous ne peut y aller.** (*None of us can go.*)
>
> **Nul d'entre eux n'est innocent.** (*None of them is innocent.*)

You can answer questions with just the negative pronoun:

> **Combien d'enfants avez-vous ? Aucun.** (*How many kids do you have? None.*)
>
> **Qui as-tu vu à la fête ? Personne.** (*Whom did you see at the party? No one.*)

Table 6-1 shows that the opposite of negative pronouns are indefinite pronouns.

Table 6-1	Negative and Indefinite Pronouns		
Negative Pronouns	**English**	**Indefinite Pronouns**	**English**
ne . . . aucun(e), ne . . . pas un(e)	none	quelques	some
ne . . . personne	no one	quelqu'un	someone
ne . . . rien	nothing	quelque chose	something

Your colleague is just too nosy! Respond to all of his questions using negative pronouns.

Q. Qu'est-ce que tu as fait hier ?

A. **Je n'ai rien fait hier.** (*I didn't do anything yesterday.*)

16. Qui était au téléphone ? _____

17. Combien de frères as-tu ? _____

18. Qu'est-ce que tu aimes faire ? _____

19. Connais-tu des vedettes ? _____

20. Que vas-tu faire demain ? _____

21. Qui habite à côté de toi ? _____

22. Combien de tes amis parlent français ? _____

23. As-tu une voiture ? _____

Negative conjunctions

French has one negative conjunction: **ne . . . ni . . . ni,** which means *neither . . . nor.* You use it just like the other negative expressions, placing **ne** in front of the verb and **ni** in front of each noun, pronoun, adjective, or verb you're negating.

> **Hier, mon appartement n'avait ni eau ni électricité.** (*Yesterday my apartment had neither water nor electricity.*)

> **Ni toi ni moi ne pouvons savoir.** (*Neither you nor I can know.*)

You can use **ni** more than twice for a longer list:

> **Ni Paul ni Timothée ni Jean-Marc n'aiment voyager.** (*Paul, Timothée, and Jean-Marc don't like to travel/Neither Paul nor Timothée nor Jean-Marc likes to travel.*)

Ni is also found in a few expressions with no verb:

- ✔ **ni l'un ni l'autre** (*neither one*)
- ✔ **ni moi non plus** (*me neither*)
- ✔ **ni plus ni moins** (*no more, no less*)

The opposite of **ne . . . ni . . . ni** is either **ou . . . ou** or **soit . . . soit.**

> **Ou toi ou moi devons commencer.** (*Either you or I have to start.*)

Responding to Negative Questions and Statements

Negative questions and statements aren't necessarily correct — sometimes you agree, and sometimes you don't. Because these sentences are in the negative, responding to them accurately can be a little bit confusing. This section explains the correct ways to answer these types of questions and statements.

Replying with no

When someone asks you a negative question or makes a negative statement that you agree with, you can respond with just **non,** or you can repeat the question as a negative statement.

Tu n'as pas soif ? Non, (je n'ai pas soif). (*Aren't you thirsty? No, [I'm not thirsty].*)

Pierre n'est pas prêt. Non, (il n'est pas prêt). (*Pierre isn't ready. No, [he's not ready].*)

You can also respond with a negative adverb, adjective, pronoun, or conjunction or with an expression like **c'est vrai** (*that's true*) or **exact** (*right, exactly*).

Le nouveau chef n'est pas sympa. Non, pas du tout. (*The new boss isn't very nice. No, not at all.*)

Nicolas et François ne sont jamais à l'heure. C'est vrai./Non, ni l'un ni l'autre. (*Nicolas and François are never on time. That's true./No, neither one [of them].*)

Of course, you can also use the various negative constructions to answer affirmative questions (see Chapter 5) negatively.

Answering with yes

In English, if someone says, "Aren't you hungry?" but in fact you are hungry, you can't just say *yes,* because the asker won't know whether you mean *yes, that's right* or *yes, I am.* You have to spell it out: "Yes, [actually] I am hungry," or "Yes, that's right. I'm not hungry." Not so in French. When someone asks or says something negative that you don't agree with, French has a unique word, **si,** which all by its lonesome means *yes, I am* or *yes, I do* or *yes, the opposite of whatever you just said.* Of course, you can still repeat the statement as part of your answer if you want, but in French you don't have to.

N'est-il pas prêt ? Si (il est prêt). (*Isn't he ready? Yes, [he is ready].*)

Tu ne veux pas savoir. Si (je veux savoir). (*You don't want to know. Yes, [I do want to know].*)

Ton frère n'est pas beau. (*Your brother isn't good-looking.*)
— Non ! (*No [he's not]!*)
— Si ! (*Yes [he is]!*)

English only has one word for *yes,* but French has two: **oui** and **si.** You use **oui** to say *yes* to a regular question and **si** to say *yes* to a negative question. Note that **si** (*yes*) never contracts, unlike **si** (*if*), which contracts with **il: s'il** (*if he*).

Respond to these questions and statements with complete sentences, using the answer in parentheses. If the question has **tu** or **vous,** you need to respond with **je** or **nous.**

Q. Sais-tu la réponse ? (no)

A. **Non, je ne sais pas la réponse.** (*No, I don't know the answer.*)

24. Veux-tu nager ? (yes) _____

25. Vont-ils voyager ensemble ? (no) _____

26. N'a-t-elle pas une suggestion ? (yes) _____

27. Ne lis-tu pas ? (never) _____

28. Ne peut-il pas travailler ? (yes) _____

29. N'aimes-tu pas danser ? (not at all) _____

30. Il ne va jamais arriver ! (yes) _____

Answer Key

1 Elle **ne parle pas** français. (*She doesn't speak French.*)

2 Il **n'est jamais** allé en France. (*He has never gone to France.*)

3 Je **ne peux plus** travailler. (*I can't work anymore.*)

4 **Ne veux-tu pas** partir ? (*Don't you want to leave?*)

5 Ils **n'ont rien** fait. (*They didn't do anything.*)

6 Elle **ne le veut pas du tout.** (*She doesn't want it at all.*)

7 Je **n'ai qu'un** frère. (*I have only one brother.*)

8 Il **n'est pas toujours** en retard. (*He isn't always late.*)

9 **Il n'y a pas un stylo. / Il n'y a aucun stylo.** (*There is no pen.*)

10 **Il n'y a nul papier. / Il n'y a aucun papier.** (*There is no paper.*)

11 **Il n'y a pas une chemise. / Il n'y a aucune chemise.** (*There is no folder.*)

12 **Il n'y a pas une agrafe. / Il n'y a aucune agrafe.** (*There is no staple, not a single staple.*)

13 **Il n'y a nulle mine de crayon. / Il n'y a aucune mine de crayon.** (*There is no pencil lead.*)

14 **Il n'y a pas un timbre. / Il n'y a aucun timbre.** (*There is no stamp, not a single stamp.*)

15 **Il n'y a nul café. / Il n'y a aucun café.** (*There is no coffee.*)

16 **Personne n'était au téléphone.** (*No one was on the phone.*)

17 **Je n'en ai aucun. / Je n'en ai pas un.** (*I don't have one.*)

18 **Je n'aime rien faire.** (*I don't like to do anything.*)

19 **Je n'en connais aucune. / Je n'en connais pas une.** (*I don't know any.*)

20 **Je ne vais rien faire demain.** (*I'm not doing anything tomorrow.*)

21 **Personne n'habite à côté de moi.** (*No one lives next to me.*)

22 **Aucun de mes amis ne parle français.** (*None of my friends speak French.*)

23 **Je n'en ai aucune. / Je n'en ai pas une.** (*I don't have one.*)

24 **Oui, je veux nager.** (*Yes, I do want to swim.*)

25 **Non, ils ne vont pas voyager ensemble.** (*No, they're not going to travel together.*)

26 **Si, elle a une suggestion.** (*Yes, she has a suggestion.*)

27 **Non, je ne lis jamais.** (*No, I never read.*)

28 **Si, il peut travailler.** (*Yes, he can work.*)

29 **Non, je n'aime pas du tout danser.** (*No, I don't like to dance at all.*)

30 **Si, il va arriver.** (*Yes, he's going to arrive.*)

Chapter 7

"To Be" or "Being" Is the Question: Infinitives and Present Participles

In This Chapter
▶ Recognizing infinitives
▶ Conjugating present participles

*I*nfinitives and present participles are *impersonal* verb forms, but that doesn't mean they don't have any friends. It just means that they each have only one form — you don't conjugate them for the different grammatical persons like you do with other verb tenses and moods. In English, the infinitive is the word *to* + a verb, and the present participle ends in *-ing*. In French, the infinitive is a single word, and the present participle ends in **-ant.**

Although infinitives and present participles exist in both French and English, you use them very differently in the two languages. However, both verb forms can act as other parts of speech, such as nouns. The French present participle is much less common than its English counterpart; in fact, the English present participle is often equivalent to the French infinitive.

This chapter explains how to recognize infinitives, how to form present participles, and how to use them both.

How to Use Infinitives

The *infinitive* is the default form of a verb, its basic, unconjugated state. When you don't know what a verb means, you look up the infinitive in the dictionary, and when you need to conjugate a verb, you often start with the infinitive.

In English, the infinitive has two parts — *to* + a verb — as in *to go, to choose,* and *to hear.* In French, the infinitive is a single word that ends in **-er, -ir,** or **-re: aller, choisir, entendre.** You use these *infinitive endings* to classify French verbs because many verbs in each group follow the same conjugation rules (see Chapter 4).

According to some dusty old grammar books, the English infinitive isn't supposed to be split; that is, no word is supposed to come between the *to* and its verb. For example, *to gladly go* has an adverb (*gladly*) splitting the infinitive *to go.* Because the French infinitive is a single word, it truly can't be split: In French, *to go gladly* is **aller volontiers.**

In addition to using the infinitive as a base to conjugate many verb tenses, you can also use the infinitive as a verb or noun. This section shows you how.

With the verb: Expressing action

You use the French infinitive most often as a verb. To do this, you conjugate a verb for the subject of the sentence (as in **je veux** or **il faut**) and follow that with an infinitive (such as **aller** or **réserver**):

>**Je veux aller en France.** (*I want to go to France.*)

>**Il faut réserver à l'avance.** (*You need to book in advance.*)

Even though the French infinitive already includes the idea of *to,* many French verbs require a preposition between the conjugated verb and the infinitive. When you translate this into English, the extra preposition has no English equivalent:

>**J'ai décidé de partir.** (*I decided to leave.*)

>**J'hésite à parler.** (*I hesitate to speak.*)

 The preposition you have to use in French — if any — depends on the conjugated verb, not on the infinitive. In other words, you don't have to precede **partir** with **de,** but rather, you have to follow **décider** with **de.** Likewise, **hésiter** has to be followed by **à.** On the other hand, **vouloir** (*to want*) doesn't need a preposition. See Chapter 12 for an explanation of prepositions and verbs that require them.

The English modal verbs *can* and *must* are followed by the verb, without *to.* The French equivalents of these verbs, **pouvoir** and **devoir,** are followed by the infinitive:

>**Peux-tu nager ?** (*Can you swim?*)

>**Je dois travailler.** (*I must work.*)

When the infinitive is a pronominal verb (that is, a verb that needs a reflexive pronoun — see Chapter 11), the reflexive pronoun has to agree with the subject, as with **Je dois me lever** (*I have to get up*) or **Vas-tu t'habiller ?** (*Are you going to get dressed?*).

You can often translate the French infinitive as either the English present participle or the English infinitive:

>**J'aime chanter.** (*I like singing/to sing.*)

>**Il préfère marcher.** (*He prefers walking/to walk.*)

In French, you can also use the infinitive to give *impersonal* commands, such as on signs and in instructions (Chapter 10 explains more about the different ways to give orders in French):

>**Marcher lentement.** (*Walk slowly.*)

>**Agiter avant l'emploi.** (*Shake well before use.*)

Nouns: Standing as subjects

When the French infinitive is the subject of the sentence, it always takes the third-person singular conjugation. So you just put the infinitive in your sentence where you'd put any other noun and follow it with a verb conjugated in the third-person singular. Note that the French infinitive in this construction is equivalent to the present participle in English:

>**Avoir des amis est important.** (*Having friends is important.*)

>**Pleurer ne sert à rien.** (*Crying doesn't do any good.*)

>**Voir, c'est croire.** (*Seeing is believing.*)

The infinitive is the only French verb form that can be used in this way, as a subject. All other verb forms need a separate subject; for example, **J'ai des amis** (*I have some friends*) has **je** as the subject and **avoir** conjugated as the verb.

Even though you're using these French infinitives as nouns in these sentences, they still have to "act" like verbs. The infinitives refer to the action of a verb, so you can't use them with articles or adjectives or make them plural. However, some French infinitives are also legitimate nouns with non-verb-like meanings. These infinitive nouns act just like regular nouns, meaning that you can modify them with articles, adjectives, and plurals. See Table 7-1 for some common examples.

Table 7-1		French Infinitive Nouns	
French Verb	*English Verb*	*French Noun*	*English Noun*
déjeuner	*to have lunch*	**le déjeuner**	*lunch*
devoir	*should, must*	**le devoir**	*duty*
dîner	*to have dinner*	**le dîner**	*dinner*
être	*to be*	**l'être**	*(human) being*
goûter	*to taste*	**le goûter**	*snack*
pouvoir	*can, to be able*	**le pouvoir**	*power*
rire	*to laugh*	**le rire**	*laughter*
savoir	*to know*	**le savoir**	*knowledge*
sourire	*to smile*	**le sourire**	*smile*

You also use the French infinitive after prepositions, where you'd use the present participle in English, such as with **sans attendre** (*without waiting*) and **avant de manger** (*before eating*).The French preposition **à** + an infinitive often means *for,* as with **à vendre** (*for sale*) and **à louer** (*for rent*).

Understanding word order with infinitives

When your sentence has a conjugated verb followed by an infinitive, you have to pay attention to where you put some of the smaller sentence elements. For instance, object and adverbial pronouns such as **le** (*it*) and **y** (*there*) (see Chapter 13) always come right before the infinitive, not the conjugated verb:

> **Je peux le faire.** (*I can do it.*)

> **Il va nous téléphoner.** (*He's going to call us.*)

In a negative sentence (see Chapter 6) with an infinitive, you have to consider the meaning of your sentence: Are you negating the main, conjugated verb or the infinitive? If it's the main verb, the negative structure surrounds that. Think about where you'd put the negative word in English. If *not* or another negative word goes with the conjugated verb, including a form of *be* or *do,* you're negating the conjugated verb in French:

> **Il n'aime pas lire.** (*He doesn't like to read.*)

> **Je ne peux pas trouver mon portefeuille.** (*I can't find my wallet.*)

If you're saying anything with *not to* in English, you're negating the French infinitive. In that case, both parts of the negative structure stay together in front of the infinitive:

> **Je t'ai dit de ne pas commencer sans moi.** (*I told you not to start without me.*)

> **Il préfère ne pas parler.** (*He prefers not to talk.*)

> **Être ou ne pas être . . .** (*To be or not to be . . .*)

Your boss has written up a strict new set of guidelines for the office, and your job is to translate them into French. See whether you understand how to use the infinitive.

Q. Everyone needs to follow these guidelines.

A. **Tout le monde doit suivre ces directives.**

1. Being on time (à l'heure) is essential.

_____

2. If you are going to be late (en retard) . . .

_____

3. . . . it's necessary to call the receptionist.

_____

4. He can inform your department about this fact.

_____

5. Eating lunch at noon is required.

_____

6. Employees cannot make personal calls.

_____

7. If you like working here . . .

_____

8. . . . you have to pay attention.

_____

9. If you want to leave early (tôt) . . .

_____

10. . . . you can ask the manager.

_____

Presenting Present Participles

In English, the present participle ends in -*ing,* and in French, it ends in **-ant.** The present participle is all over the place, grammatically speaking. It can be a verb, gerund, adjective, or noun. It's also something of a misnomer because the present participle doesn't actually have a tense; you can use it in the present, past, and future.

In French, the present participle is *variable* (it has different forms for masculine, feminine, singular, and plural) when it's an adjective or noun and is *invariable* when it's a verb or gerund. In this section, I discuss how to create the present participle and how to correctly use it.

Forming present participles

For nearly all verbs — regular, stem-changing, spelling-change, and irregular — you form the French present participle by taking the present-tense **nous** form of the verb, dropping **-ons,** and adding **-ant.** See Table 7-2.

Table 7-2	Creating Present Participles	
Infinitive	*Nous Form*	*Present Participle*
parler (*to talk, speak*)	parl**ons**	parl**ant** (*talking, speaking*)
choisir (*to choose*)	choisiss**ons**	choisiss**ant** (*choosing*)
entendre (*to hear*)	entend**ons**	entend**ant** (*hearing*)
aller (*to go*)	all**ons**	all**ant** (*going*)
commencer (*to begin*)	commenç**ons**	commenç**ant** (*beginning*)
voir (*to see*)	voy**ons**	voy**ant** (*seeing*)

This rule has only three exceptions. These three present participles still end in **-ant,** but they're not conjugated from the **nous** form of the verb:

- ✔ **avoir** (*to have*): **ayant**
- ✔ **être** (*to be*): **étant**
- ✔ **savoir** (*to know*): **sachant**

The present participle of pronominal verbs (see Chapter 11) is preceded by the reflexive pronoun:

- ✔ **se lever** (*to get up*): **se levant**
- ✔ **se coucher** (*to go to bed*): **se couchant**
- ✔ **s'habiller** (*to get dressed*): **s'habillant**

Note that the reflexive pronoun always changes to agree with the subject:

> **En me levant**, **j'ai vu les fleurs.** (*Upon getting up, I saw the flowers.*)

> **Nous parlions en nous habillant.** (*We talked while getting dressed.*)

Using present participles

In both French and English, you can use the present participle as an adjective, noun, verb, or gerund, but the two languages are very different. The following sections show how to use present participles in different situations.

Present participles as adjectives

When you use the French present participle as an adjective, it acts just like any other adjective, meaning that it usually follows the noun it modifies and that it has to agree in gender and number. Remember that you add **-e** for feminine adjectives, **-s** for plural adjectives, and **-es** for feminine plural adjectives. (See Chapter 9 for more information about adjectives.)

> **un livre intéressant** (*an interesting book*)

> **une soucoupe volante** (*a flying saucer*)

> **des appartements charmants** (*some charming apartments*)

> **des tables pliantes** (*some folding tables*)

You can't turn just any French verb into a present-participle adjective. This form is far less common in French than in English — always check your adjectives in a French dictionary.

Nouns that are present participles

You can use some French present participles as nouns that refer to people. Therefore, like the present participle as an adjective, the present participle as a noun has different forms for masculine, feminine, singular, and plural. You follow the same rules for making these feminine and plural as for other nouns: **assistant** is masculine, **assistante** is feminine, **assistants** is masculine plural, and **assistantes** is feminine plural. (See Chapter 2 for more information about nouns.)

un assistant, une assistante (*an assistant*)

un dirigeant, une dirigeante (*a leader*)

un étudiant, une étudiante (*a student*)

un participant, une participante (*a participant*)

un survivant, une survivante (*a survivor*)

In English, you can use an *-ing* word as a noun that refers to the action of a verb, as in *Running is good exercise* or *Smoking is bad for you.* An *-ing* word used as a noun is called a *gerund* in English, and it's identical to the present participle. However, you can't use the French present participle this way. You can translate this use of the English gerund only with the French infinitive or an equivalent French noun. See Table 7-3 for some examples of words you'd use to replace an English gerund.

Table 7-3	English -ing Nouns and Their French Counterparts	
English Noun	*French Noun*	*Infinitive*
dancing	**la danse**	**danser**
fishing	**la pêche**	**pêcher**
hunting	**la chasse**	**chasser**
reading	**la lecture**	**lire**
running	**la course**	**courir**
smoking	**le tabagisme**	**fumer**
swimming	**la natation**	**nager**
writing	**l'écriture**	**écrire**

J'aime la pêche. or **J'aime pêcher.** (*I like fishing.*)

L'écriture est difficile. or **Écrire est difficile.** (*Writing is difficult.*)

The French present participle is much rarer than the English one, and its use as a noun is extremely limited. If you have any doubts at all about whether to use the French present participle as a noun in a particular sentence, don't — it would likely be wrong.

Verbs: Describing action with present participles

French uses present participles to indicate an action that's happening at the same time as another action. To do this, use the present participle followed by an adjective or other descriptive information:

Étant fatigué, il voulait rentrer. (*Being tired, he wanted to go home.*)

J'ai vu un homme marchant très vite. (*I saw a man walking very quickly.*)

When you have two nouns in a sentence, as in the second example, the meaning of the present participle can be ambiguous. Was I walking very quickly, or was the man? To avoid confusion, think about whether you're modifying the subject of the sentence or the object. If it's the subject, use the **gérondif** (explained in the next section), as with **En marchant très vite, j'ai vu un homme** (*While [I was] walking very quickly, I saw a man*). If it's the object, use **qui** (*who*) + verb, as with **J'ai vu un homme qui marchait très vite** (*I saw a man who was walking very quickly*). Note that the verb **marchait** (*was walking*) is in the imperfect because it explains what was happening when something else happened. You can read about the imperfect in Chapter 16.

Determine whether the present participles in these sentences are adjectives, nouns, or verbs and therefore whether they should agree. Circle the correct form of the present participle and write its function in the blank.

Q. C'est une idée (choquant/choquante). _____

A. C'est une idée **choquante. adjective** (*It's a shocking idea.*)

11. Mes (assistant/assistants) ne travaillent pas le lundi. _____

12. Tous les invités (assistant/assistants) à la réception sont tombés malades. _____

13. La fille (habitant/habitante) à côté est très sympa. _____

14. Les (habitant/habitants) de cette ville n'aiment pas les étrangers. _____

15. Il a une voix (chantant/chantante). _____

16. J'ai entendu une dame (chantant/chantante) dans la douche. _____

17. Il m'a raconté une histoire (amusant/amusante). _____

18. Il a raconté des histoires, (amusant/amusantes) tous les enfants. _____

19. J'espère que les (gagnant/gagnants) seront contents. _____

20. Quels étaient les numéros (gagnant/gagnants) ? _____

While, as, and by: Expressing simultaneous action with the gérondif

A **gérondif** (*gerund*) in French is the present participle preceded by **en,** which means *while, as,* or *by* in English. Because the **gérondif** modifies another verb, it's essentially acting as an adverb. (See Chapter 9 for information on French adverbs.) To use the present participle as a **gérondif,** just put **en** in front of it and any descriptive information after.

> **En quittant le bâtiment, j'ai vu mon frère.** (*While leaving [As I left] the building, I saw my brother.*)
>
> **Je l'ai fait en rêvant de mes vacances.** (*I did it while dreaming of my vacation.*)
>
> **En me brossant les dents, j'ai avalé du dentifrice.** (*While brushing my teeth, I swallowed some toothpaste.*)

The English *gerund* is simply the *-ing* form of a verb that you use as a noun. The French **gérondif** is the **en** + verb + **-ant** construction that you use to express something that was happening at the same time as something else.

You can add **tout** in front of the **gérondif** to obtain one of two effects:

✔ Emphasize the simultaneity of the **gérondif** and main verb

✔ Contrast the meanings of the **gérondif** and main verb

Consider these examples:

> **Je me suis habillé tout en mangeant.** (*I got dressed while eating [at the same time].*)

> **Tout en acceptant ton invitation, je ne te pardonne pas.** (*While/Whereas I accept your invitation, I don't forgive you.*)

Present participles as verbs (see the preceding section) and as **gérondifs** are both *invariable* — they never change in gender or number to agree with anything else. The differences between them are that the **gérondif** includes **en** and can modify only a verb, whereas the participle can modify a noun.

> **J'ai vu une fille lisant le journal.** (*I saw a girl [who was] reading the paper.*) The participle, **lisant,** modifies the noun **fille.**

> **J'ai vu une fille en lisant le journal.** (*I saw a girl [while I was] reading the paper.*) The **gérondif, en lisant,** modifies the verb **ai vu** — it tells you that something happened while something else was happening.

Using other verb forms in lieu of the French present participle

In English, you often use a conjugated verb followed by the present participle. You can't do this in French — that grammatical structure simply doesn't exist. Here are some considerations to remember when translating the English present participle into French.

✔ If the verb is *is/am/are + -ing,* the French equivalent is the simple present (see Chapter 4), as with **J'écris une lettre** (*I am writing a letter*).

✔ If it's *was/were + -ing,* the French equivalent is the imperfect (see Chapter 16), such as **Dormais-tu ?** (*Were you sleeping?*).

✔ If the conjugated verb is something other than *to be* and is introducing the verb in the present participle, the French equivalent is the infinitive, as in **J'aime voyager** (*I like traveling*) or **Nous détestons faire la cuisine** (*We hate cooking*).

Translate each of these sentences into French, paying careful attention to whether you need to use the present participle or infinitive (or neither). See Chapters 15 and 16 to read about the **passé composé** and **imparfait** conjugations you need to translate some of these.

Q. I like dancing.

A. **J'aime danser.**

21. As I ate lunch, I watched TV. _____

22. He hates fishing. _____

23. Traveling is expensive. _____

24. We are leaving at noon. _____

25. Do you like running? _____

26. They were working all day. _____

27. Wanting to leave, he excused himself. _____

28. By using the computer . . . _____

29. . . . you can save a lot of time. _____

30. Were you (plural) driving? _____

31. Hunting is dangerous. _____

32. I am trying to understand. _____

33. I saw you reading the newspaper. _____

34. Can you help us? _____

35. As I worked, I thought about my decision. _____

Answer Key

1 Être à l'heure est essentiel.

2 Si vous allez être en retard . . .

3 . . . il faut téléphoner au réceptionniste.

4 Il peut informer votre département de ce fait.

5 Manger à midi est requis.

6 Les employés ne peuvent pas faire d'appels personnels.

7 Si vous aimez travailler ici . . .

8 . . . vous devez faire attention.

9 Si vous voulez partir tôt . . .

10 . . . vous pouvez demander au directeur.

11 Mes **assistants** ne travaillent pas le lundi. **noun** (*My assistants don't work on Monday.*)

12 Tous les invités **assistant** à la réception sont tombés malades. **verb** (*All the guests attending the reception got sick.*)

13 La fille **habitant** à côté est très sympa. **verb** (*The girl living next door is very nice.*)

14 Les **habitants** de cette ville n'aiment pas les étrangers. **noun** (*The inhabitants of this town don't like strangers.*)

15 Il a une voix **chantante. adjective** (*He has a lilting voice.*)

16 J'ai entendu une dame **chantant** dans la douche. **verb** (*I heard a woman singing in the shower.*)

17 Il m'a raconté une histoire **amusante. adjective** (*He told me an amusing story.*)

18 Il a raconté des histoires, **amusant** tous les enfants. **verb** (*He told stories, amusing all the kids.*)

19 J'espère que les **gagnants** seront contents. **noun** (*I hope the winners will be happy.*)

20 Quels étaient les numéros **gagnants** ? **adjective** (*What were the winning numbers?*)

21 **En déjeunant, j'ai regardé la télé.** The word *as* lets you know that the **gérondif** is required in French.

22 **Il déteste pêcher/la pêche.** English gerunds referring to actions are equivalent to the French infinitive or a noun.

23 **Voyager/Le voyage est cher.** English gerunds referring to actions are equivalent to the French infinitive or a noun.

24 **Nous partons à midi.** *Be* + *-ing* is equivalent to the French present tense.

25 **Aimes-tu/Aimez-vous courir/la course ?** English gerunds referring to actions are equivalent to the French infinitive or a noun.

26 **Ils travaillaient pendant toute la journée.** *Be* in the past + *-ing* is equivalent to the French imperfect.

27 **Voulant partir, il s'est excusé.** *Wanting* describes the subject *he,* so you use the French present participle.

28 **En utilisant l'ordinateur . . .** The word *by* lets you know that the **gérondif** is required in French.

29 **. . . on peut/tu peux/vous pouvez gagner du temps.** Pouvoir must be followed by the infinitive.

30 **Conduisiez-vous ?** *Be* in the past + *-ing* is equivalent to the French imperfect.

31 **Chasser est dangereux** or **La chasse est dangereuse.** English gerunds referring to actions are equivalent to the French infinitive or a noun.

32 **J'essaie de comprendre.** *Be* + *-ing* is equivalent to the French present tense.

33 **Je t'ai vu lisant le journal.** *Reading* is describing the object **te,** so you need a present participle in French.

34 **Pouvez-vous nous aider ? Pouvoir** must be followed by the infinitive.

35 **En travaillant, j'ai pensé à ma décision.** The word *as* lets you know that the **gérondif** is required in French.

Chapter 8

Deciphering the Subjunctive Mood

. . . .

In This Chapter

▶ Conjugating the subjunctive

▶ Using the subjunctive

▶ Avoiding the subjunctive

. . . .

The **subjonctif** (*subjunctive*) may make you tense, but it's not a verb tense — it's a mood, with an attitude. The difference between a tense and a mood is that a *tense* tells you when something is happening, and a *mood* tells you the speaker's attitude toward the action of the verb. The subjunctive mood indicates subjectivity — the speaker may want something to happen or think it's important for something to happen, but the subjunctive tells you that something may or may not actually happen. The *indicative*, in contrast, is the "normal" verb mood that indicates the way something actually is. This chapter tells you all about the subjunctive: how to conjugate it, when to use it, and how and when to avoid it.

Conjugating the Subjunctive

The subjunctive is one of the easier verb conjugations. All regular verbs, no matter what endings they have, are conjugated the same way. Stem-changing verbs and all but seven irregular verbs are conjugated in a second way. So that leaves just a handful of verbs that are irregular in the subjunctive, making the subjunctive conjugations (if not the uses) relatively easy to master. This section covers both the regular conjugations as well as the conjugations of irregular verbs.

Regular verbs

All regular **-er, -ir,** and **-re** verbs use the third-person plural (**ils**) present indicative as the root for subjunctive conjugations. To conjugate any regular verb, just take the **ils** form of the present tense, drop **-ent,** and add the subjunctive ending **-e, -es, -e, -ions, -iez,** or **-ent.** (See Chapter 4 for more info on present-tense conjugations.) These subjunctive endings are the same for all regular verbs, all stem-changing verbs, all spelling-change verbs, and nearly all irregular verbs.

The present indicative **ils** form of the regular **-er** verb **parler** (*to speak*), for instance, is **parlent,** so the subjunctive stem is **parl-.** The following table shows what **parler** looks like in the subjunctive.

parler (*to speak*) — stem: **parl-**	
je parl**e**	nous parl**ions**
tu parl**es**	vous parl**iez**
il/elle/on parl**e**	ils/elles parl**ent**
Il veut que nous **parlions** en français. (*He wants us to speak in French.*)	

Spelling-change verbs have no spelling change in the subjunctive because all the subjunctive endings begin with soft vowels (**e** or **i**). The present-tense **ils** form of **manger** (*to eat*) is **mangent,** so the stem is **mang-.**

manger (*to eat*) — stem: **mang-**	
je mang**e**	nous mang**ions**
tu mang**es**	vous mang**iez**
il/elle/on mang**e**	ils/elles mang**ent**
Il faut que tu **manges** immédiatement. (*You have to eat immediately.*)	

You'd say **ils finissent** in the present indicative, so the subjunctive stem of **finir** (*to finish*) is **finiss-.**

finir (*to finish*) — stem: **finiss-**	
je finiss**e**	nous finiss**ions**
tu finiss**es**	vous finiss**iez**
il/elle/on finiss**e**	ils/elles finiss**ent**
Il faut que tu **finisses** avant midi. (*You have to finish before noon.*)	

The subjunctive stem of **vendre** (*to sell*) is **vend-.**

vendre (to sell) — stem: **vend-**	
je vend**e**	nous vend**ions**
tu vend**es**	vous vend**iez**
il/elle/on vend**e**	ils/elles vend**ent**
Penses-tu qu'il **vende** des fraises ? (*Do you think he sells strawberries?*)	

Stem-changing and most irregular verbs

Stem-changing verbs and all but seven irregular verbs enjoy a little variety — they have two subjunctive stems. Like regular verbs, stem-changing and irregular verbs use the **ils** conjugation minus -**ent** as the stem — but only for the **je, tu, il/elle/on,** and

ils/elles subjunctive conjugations. For **nous** and **vous,** the verbs use the present-tense **nous** conjugation minus **-ons.** Regardless of the stem, they all take the same subjunctive endings as regular verbs (**-e, -es, -e, -ions, -iez,** and **-ent**).

With **envoyer** (*to send*), for instance, you write **ils envoient** or **nous envoyons** in the normal present tense. So in the subjunctive, the two stems are **envoi-** and **envoy-.** Take a look at the table.

envoyer (*to send*) — stems: **envoi-, envoy-**	
j'envoi**e**	nous envoy**ions**
tu envoi**es**	vous envoy**iez**
il/elle/on envoi**e**	ils/elles envoi**ent**
Il est bon que vous **envoyiez** le chèque. (*It's good that you're sending the check.*)	

For the subjunctive stems of **lever** (*to lift*), write **ils lèvent** minus **-ent** to get **lèv-** and **nous levons** minus **-ons** to get **lev-.**

lever (*to lift*) — stems: **lèv-, lev-**	
je lèv**e**	nous lev**ions**
tu lèv**es**	vous lev**iez**
il/elle/on lèv**e**	ils/elles lèv**ent**
Il ne faut pas que vous **leviez** la main. (*You don't have to raise your hand.*)	

For the irregular verb **devoir** (*to have to*), **ils doivent** minus -ent is **doiv-,** and **nous devons** minus -ons is **dev-.**

devoir (*to have to*) — stems: **doiv-, dev-**	
je doiv**e**	nous dev**ions**
tu doiv**es**	vous dev**iez**
il/elle/on doiv**e**	ils/elles doiv**ent**
Penses-tu que je **doive** partir ? (*Do you think I have to leave?*)	

Really irregular verbs

The preceding conjugation rules apply to all but seven irregular verbs. The seven irregular verbs that are also irregular in the subjunctive are as follows:

- ✔ **aller** (*to go*)
- ✔ **avoir** (*to have*)
- ✔ **être** (*to be*)

✔ **faire** (*to do, make*)

✔ **pouvoir** (*can, to be able*)

✔ **savoir** (*to know*)

✔ **vouloir** (*to want*)

Faire, pouvoir, and **savoir** have a single irregular stem for all conjugations: **fass-**, **puiss-**, and **sach-**, respectively. **Aller** and **vouloir** have two irregular stems: **aill-** and **veuill-** for the third-person plural and all the singular conjugations, and **all-** and **voul-** for the **nous** and **vous** forms. These five verbs take the same subjunctive endings as the rest (**-e, -es, -e, -ions, -iez,** and **-ent**) — see the following tables.

faire (*to do, make*) — stem: **fass-**	
je fass**e**	nous fass**ions**
tu fass**es**	vous fass**iez**
il/elle/on fass**e**	ils/elles fass**ent**
Il est bon que tu le **fasses.** (*It's good [that] you're doing it.*)	

pouvoir (*can, to be able*) — stem: **puiss-**	
je puiss**e**	nous puiss**ions**
tu puiss**es**	vous puiss**iez**
il/elle/on puiss**e**	ils/elles puiss**ent**
Elle ne croit pas que je **puisse** nager. (*She doesn't believe that I can swim.*)	

savoir (*to know*) — stem: **sach-**	
je sach**e**	nous sach**ions**
tu sach**es**	vous sach**iez**
il/elle/on sach**e**	ils/elles sach**ent**
Il est important que vous **sachiez** lire. (*It's important for you to know how to read.*)	

aller (*to go*) — stems: **aill-, all-**	
j'aill**e**	nous all**ions**
tu aill**es**	vous all**iez**
il/elle/on aill**e**	ils/elles aill**ent**
Veux-tu que j'**aille** avec toi ? (*Do you want me to go with you?*)	

vouloir (*to want*) — stems: **veuill-, voul-**	
je veuill**e**	nous voul**ions**
tu veuill**es**	vous voul**iez**
il/elle/on veuill**e**	ils/elles veuill**ent**
Il est possible qu'elles **veuillent** partir tôt. (*It's possible that they want to leave early.*)	

Finally, **avoir** and **être** have completely irregular subjunctive conjugations.

avoir (*to have*)	
j'**aie**	nous **ayons**
tu **aies**	vous **ayez**
il/elle/on **ait**	ils/elles **aient**
Je suis heureux que tu **aies** une nouvelle voiture. (*I'm happy [that] you have a new car.*)	

être (*to be*)	
je **sois**	nous **soyons**
tu **sois**	vous **soyez**
il/elle/on **soit**	ils/elles **soient**
Nous avons peur qu'elle **soit** malade. (*We're afraid she's sick.*)	

Provide the subjunctive conjugation for the grammatical person and verb listed.

Q. je (marcher)

A. je **marche** (*I walk*)

1. tu (choisir) _____

2. il (rendre) _____

3. nous (chanter) _____

4. vous (réussir) _____

5. elles (perdre) _____

6. je (partir) _____

7. tu (jeter) _____

8. elle (envoyer) _____

9. nous (avoir) _____

10. vous (être) _____

11. ils (aller) _____

12. je (savoir) _____

13. tu (pouvoir) _____

14. on (faire) _____

15. nous (vouloir) _____

16. vous (aller) _____

17. ils (être) _____

18. je (vouloir) _____

19. tu (être) _____

20. il (avoir) _____

Getting Unreal: Using the Subjunctive

The most important thing to understand about the subjunctive mood is that, as its name suggests, it expresses subjectivity. When any desire, doubt, emotion, judgment, or necessity is expressed in a sentence, you have to use the subjunctive to show that the action of the verb is not a fact but rather is based on the subjective notion in the phrase that precedes it. The verb in the subjunctive tells you about what someone wants, needs, or feels but not whether that is actually going to happen. It may be good, bad, important, necessary, or doubtful, but is it real? Will it actually happen? The subjunctive indicates the unreality of the situation.

The subjunctive is nearly always found in a dependent clause preceded by **que.** This **que** is required, unlike its English equivalent *that,* which is often optional:

> **Il est bon que tu partes.** (*It's good [that] you're leaving.*)
>
> **Je suggère que nous mangions à midi.** (*I suggest [that] we eat at noon.*)

The subjunctive exists in English, but it's so rare and so easily avoided that many native speakers aren't even aware of it. For example, in the sentence *It's important that you be good,* the verb *be* is in the subjunctive. But English speakers are far more likely to say *It's important for you to be good.* The only real holdouts are a few verbs like *suggest, recommend,* and *demand,* as well as the expressions *If I were you* and *I wish I were. I were* is the subjunctive; the indicative is *I was.*

The French subjunctive is required after many expressions, verbs, and conjunctions, and it's optional after others. This section explains when you need to use the subjunctive and how to use it correctly.

With impersonal expressions

Impersonal expressions require the subjunctive when they indicate some kind of subjectivity, will, possibility, or judgment, whether on the part of the speaker or of society as a whole. Impersonal expressions include the following:

- **il est bon que** (*it's good that*)
- **il est dommage que** (*it's too bad that*)
- **il est douteux que** (*it's doubtful that*)
- **il est étonnant que** (*it's amazing that*)
- **il est important que** (*it's important that*)
- **il est impossible que** (*it's impossible that*)
- **il est improbable que** (*it's improbable that*)
- **il est naturel que** (*it's natural that*)
- **il est nécessaire que** (*it's necessary that*)
- **il est normal que** (*it's normal that*)
- **il est possible que** (*it's possible that*)
- **il est rare que** (*it's rare that*)

> ✔ **il est regrettable que** (*it's regrettable that*)
>
> ✔ **il est surprenant que** (*it's surprising that*)
>
> ✔ **il est urgent que** (*it's urgent that*)

Check out some examples, noting the subjunctive verb in the clause after the **que:**

Il est bon que tu travailles pour ton père. (*It's good that you work for your father.*)

Il est important que tout le monde fasse de l'exercice. (*It's important that everyone exercises.*)

Il n'est pas possible qu'il ait autant de temps libre. (*It's not possible that he has so much free time.*)

In English, you can often more naturally translate a French impersonal expression + subjunctive as *for* + a subject and infinitive:

Il est normal que tu aies peur. (*It's normal for you to be afraid.*)

Il est rare qu'il mente. (*It's rare for him to lie.*)

You can also begin impersonal expressions with **c'est: c'est dommage** (*it's too bad*), **c'est bon** (*it's good*), and so on. The meaning is the same, but **c'est** is slightly informal.

Translate the following sentences into French.

Q. It's urgent that you call your brother.

A. **Il est urgent que tu téléphones/vous téléphoniez à ton/votre frère.**

21. It's too bad we don't have a car.

_____

22. It's amazing that I can't swim.

_____

23. It's natural for him to want to travel.

_____

24. It's regrettable that we are poor.

_____

25. It's impossible for me to help you.

_____

26. It's doubtful that she knows the answer.

_____

27. It's improbable that we'll finish today.

_____

28. It's good that you have a lot of friends.

_____

29. Is it necessary for you to do that?

_____

30. It's not surprising that they're tired.

_____

Once more, with feelings (and orders and opinions)

Because feelings, such as fear, doubt, regret, surprise, and happiness, are subjective, they require the subjunctive. Some common phrases that express feelings and opinions include the following:

- **avoir peur que** (_to be afraid that_)
- **craindre que** (_to fear that_)
- **détester que** (_to hate_)
- **douter que** (_to doubt that_)
- **être content que** (_to be happy that_)
- **être désolé que** (_to be sorry that_)

- **être étonné que** (_to be amazed that_)
- **être heureux que** (_to be happy that_)
- **être surpris que** (_to be surprised that_)
- **être triste que** (_to be sad that_)
- **regretter que** (_to regret that_)

Consider these examples:

J'ai peur qu'il soit blessé. (_I'm afraid that he's wounded._)

Nous sommes contents que tu veuilles voyager. (_We're happy you want to travel._)

In the preceding expressions, the words following **être** (**contents, désolé,** and so on), are adjectives. Like all adjectives, they have to agree with the nouns or pronouns they modify, which in this case is the subject of the verb **être**. See Chapter 9 for info on adjectives.

When you use **douter** (_to doubt_) in the negative, it doesn't take the subjunctive because saying that you don't doubt something means that you believe it to be true, and when you believe something, you can't use the subjunctive. Compare the following sentences — only the first requires the subjunctive:

Je doute qu'il ait raison. (_I doubt he's right._)

Je ne doute pas qu'il a raison. (_I don't doubt he's right._)

Verbs that indicate the speaker's will, wants, or opinions express something that may or may not happen and therefore require the subjunctive. Some common phrases include

- **demander que** (_to ask that [someone do something]_)
- **désirer que** (_to desire that_)
- **exiger que** (_to demand that_)
- **ordonner que** (_to order that_)

> ✔ **préférer que** (*to prefer that*)
>
> ✔ **proposer que** (*to propose that*)
>
> ✔ **souhaiter que** (*to wish that*)
>
> ✔ **suggérer que** (*to suggest that*)
>
> ✔ **vouloir que** (*to want that*)

Here are some examples:

> **J'exige que vous partiez.** (*I demand that you leave.*)
>
> **Il veut que je fasse moins.** (*He wants me to do less.*)

You and some friends are planning a trip to France. You're in charge and want to make sure that everyone has a good time, so you're writing a letter with some suggestions and ideas. I provide some ideas in the Answer Key that you can compare with your own.

Q. Je suis content(e) que . . .

A. **nous allions en France ensemble.** (*I'm happy that we're going to France together.*)

	14-3-2008
Salut Juliette,	
31. Je veux que _____	
32. Je préfère que _____	
33. Je propose que _____	
34. Je demande que _____	
35. Je doute que _____	
36. Je regrette que _____	
37. Jíexige que _____	
38. J'ai peur que _____	
39. Je suis surpris(e) que _____	
40. Je souhaite que _____	

Why not? With certain verbs in the negative or interrogative

Verbs and expressions that indicate what a person believes, a general statement of fact, or something that's probable don't take the subjunctive when you use them in a statement because they indicate something that's reality, at least in the mind of the speaker. However, these same terms do require the subjunctive when you use them in a question or negation because that question or negation indicates doubt, which requires the subjunctive. Some examples include the following:

- ✔ **croire que** (*to believe that*)
- ✔ **dire que** (*to say that*)
- ✔ **espérer que** (*to hope that*)
- ✔ **être certain que** (*to be certain that*)
- ✔ **être clair que** (*to be clear/obvious that*)
- ✔ **être sûr que** (*to be sure that*)
- ✔ **il est évident que** (*it's obvious that*)

- ✔ **il est probable que** (*it's probable that*)
- ✔ **il est vrai que** (*it's true that*)
- ✔ **il paraît que** (*it appears that*)
- ✔ **penser que** (*to think that*)
- ✔ **savoir que** (*to know that*)
- ✔ **trouver que** (*to find/think that*)

Check out the following sentences. Notice that the last two use the subjunctive:

> **Je pense que tu as raison.** (*I think you're right.*)
>
> **Je ne pense pas que tu aies raison.** (*I don't think you're right.*)
>
> **Penses-tu que j'aie raison ?** (*Do you think I'm right?*)

And with conjunctions

Conjunctions that express some sort of condition, concession, or feeling require the subjunctive. Some common conjunctions include

- ✔ **à moins que** (*unless*)
- ✔ **afin que** (*so that*)
- ✔ **avant que** (*before*)
- ✔ **bien que** (*although*)
- ✔ **de crainte/peur que** (*for fear that*)
- ✔ **en attendant que** (*while, until*)

- ✔ **jusqu'à ce que** (*until*)
- ✔ **pour que** (*so that*)
- ✔ **pourvu que** (*provided that*)
- ✔ **quoique** (*even though*)
- ✔ **quoi que** (*whatever, no matter what*)
- ✔ **sans que** (*without*)

Here are some examples:

> **Je suis parti pour qu'il puisse se concentrer.** (*I left so that he could concentrate.*)
>
> **Il travaille bien que sa famille soit riche.** (*He works even though his family is rich.*)

Note: There's a present subjunctive and a past subjunctive but no future subjunctive. If the action is supposed to happen in the future, you use the present subjunctive: **Je te téléphonerai bien que tu sois en France la semaine prochaine.** (*I'll call you even though you'll be in France next week.*)

Conjunctions that express anything considered real aren't followed by the subjunctive:

- ✔ **ainsi que** (*just as, so as*)
- ✔ **alors que** (*while, whereas*)
- ✔ **après que** (*after, when*)
- ✔ **aussitôt que** (*as soon as*)
- ✔ **en même temps que** (*at the same time that*)
- ✔ **depuis que** (*since*)
- ✔ **dès que** (*as soon as, immediately*)

- ✔ **parce que** (*because*)
- ✔ **pendant que** (*while*)
- ✔ **plutôt que** (*instead of, rather than*)
- ✔ **puisque** (*since, as*)
- ✔ **quand** (*when*)
- ✔ **tandis que** (*while, whereas*)

Note: When you use **après que, aussitôt que, depuis que,** or **dès que** after a verb in the future tense, the verb in the clause following the conjunction must also be in the future (for more on the **futur** [*future tense*], see Chapter 18).

The following sentences use the normal, indicative mood after the conjuctions. The first example has the **passé composé** (*past tense;* see Chapter 15) in the first clause and the **imparfait** (*imperfect*) in the second (see Chapter 16), and the second sentence has the **futur** in both clauses (see Chapter 18):

> **Il est tombé parce que le trottoir était glissant.** (*He fell because the sidewalk was slippery.*)

> **Nous en parlerons quand tu seras prêt.** (*We'll talk about it when you're ready.*)

With superlatives: Simply the best

When you use superlatives, such as *best, worst, nicest,* and so on, you need to use the subjunctive. Superlatives (see Chapter 9 for more info) are subjective notions and therefore require the subjunctive:

> **C'est le meilleur médecin que je connaisse.** (*He's the best doctor I know.*)

> **Voici le plus bel appartement que je puisse trouver.** (*Here's the prettiest apartment I can find.*)

Words referring to something unique, such as *only, first,* and *last,* are optional subjunctives. You use the subjunctive when you're talking about something that you're claiming is unique: the first ever, the only one in the world. However, you don't use the subjunctive when talking about something that's factual.

> **C'est le premier livre que je comprenne.** (*That's the first book I understand.*) This is a unique book in that it is the first — and so far only — one that I'm able to understand. But I may be able to understand other books out there, too, and I express this possibility with the subjunctive.

> **C'est le premier livre que j'ai lu.** (*That's the first book I read.*) This is a fact — I know it's the first book that I read, and there's no possibility that some other book will show up, claiming that I read it first. Because the statement's factual, I use the indicative.

> **Ma voiture est la seule qui soit verte à pois jaunes.** (*My car is the only one that's green with yellow polka dots.*) It's the only car like this in the world — at least I think so. I can't know for sure because I haven't seen every car in the world, so I use the subjunctive.

> **C'est la seule voiture que j'ai.** (*That's the only car I have.*) I have just one car — this one. It's a fact, so I use the indicative.

Something else: Words with indefinite and negative pronouns

The indefinite pronouns **quelqu'un** (*someone*) and **quelque chose** (*something*) and the negative pronouns **ne . . . personne** (*no one*) and **ne . . . rien** (*nothing*) plus **qui** are optional subjunctives. You use the subjunctive when you're not sure whether something exists or when you're sure that it doesn't, but you don't use the subjunctive when you're sure that it does exist. Once again:

- **Positive it doesn't exist:** Subjunctive
- **Not sure it exists:** Subjunctive
- **Sure it exists:** No subjunctive

Look at these two sentences:

> **Je ne connais personne qui sache pourquoi.** (*I don't know anyone who knows why.*) I don't believe that there's anyone in the world who knows why, so I use the subjunctive.

> **Je ne connais personne qui sait conduire.** (*I don't know anyone who knows how to drive.*) Many people know how to drive — I know they exist, but I just don't happen to know any of them. Therefore, I don't use the subjunctive.

Your company is considering a merger, and you're writing a letter to explain a few things to employees. Fill in the blanks with the correct form of the verb in parentheses, paying careful attention to whether you need to use the subjunctive.

Q. Savez-vous que notre entreprise _____ (considérer) une fusion avec Abc, Cie. ?

A. **considère** (*Do you know that our company is considering a merger with Abc, Inc.?*)

XYZ, Cie.
11, rue de Dai
Paris

Il est probable que vous (41) _____ (entendre) des rumeurs, et je sais que vous (42) _____ (avoir) peur. J'espère que tout le monde (43) _____ (lire) bien cette lettre. Avant que vous (44) _____ (prendre) une décision, il faut que vous (45) _____ (comprendre) les faits. Il est vrai que cette fusion (46) _____ (pouvoir) avoir des conséquences négatives, mais il n'est pas vrai que tout le monde (47) _____ (perdre) son emploi. Je suis sûr qu'Abc (48) _____ (vouloir) continuer notre mission. Nous sommes la seule entreprise qui (49) _____ (faire) ce type de travail, alors qu'Abc (50) _____ ne (être) qu'une source de financement.

All by itself

The subjunctive usually goes in a subordinate clause after a verb, expression, or conjunction, but it also has a few solo tricks up its sleeve. On its own, the subjunctive can express certain kinds of commands. When you take **que** and add the subjunctive, you get a third-person command:

Qu'il se taise ! (*Make him shut up! If only he'd shut up!*)

Que tout le monde me laisse en paix ! (*I wish everyone would leave me alone!*)

Qu'ils mangent de la brioche ! (*Let them eat brioche!* — Marie Antoinette's legendary exclamation, which is commonly translated as *Let them eat cake!*)

A few verbs can make third-person commands without **que** (Chapter 10 explains more about giving orders):

✔ **Être** (*to be*): **Soit !** (*So be it!*)

✔ **Pouvoir** (*can, may*): **Puisse Dieu vous aider !** (*May God help you!*)

✔ **Vivre** (*to live*): **Vive la France !** (*Long live France!*)

Savoir (*to know*) and **vouloir** (*to want*) have special meanings as main-clause subjunctives, both of which are formal:

✔ **Je ne sache pas que . . .** (*I'm not aware that . . ., As far as I know . . .*)

✔ **Pas que je sache.** (*Not as far as I know, Not to my knowledge.*)

✔ **Veuillez m'excuser.** (*Won't you please excuse me?*)

Avoiding the Subjunctive

The subjunctive is an essential verb mood that expresses subjectivity, but you can avoid it in some instances, with the potential for a certain amount of variation in meaning. Of course, this doesn't mean that you can ignore the subjunctive entirely, but knowing how to express something in different ways is always good. Plus, you can express different nuances by using different constructions. In the following sections, I run through some of these bypasses.

Shared and implied subjects: Using de + infinitive

When you use the subjunctive verbs and expressions in this chapter in English, you may use them with the same subject in both clauses, as in *I'm sad that I don't have time to meet you.* In French, however, when the main clause and the subordinate clause have the same subject, you can't use the subjunctive. Instead, you must use **de** in place of **que** and follow it with the infinitive:

Je suis content que j'habite à la plage. → **Je suis content d'habiter à la plage.** (*I'm happy that I live at the beach.* → *I'm happy to live at the beach.*)

Es-tu surpris que tu aies raison ? → **Es-tu surpris d'avoir raison ?** (*Are you surprised that you're right?* → *Are you surprised to be right?*)

Tu dois manger avant que tu partes. → **Tu dois manger avant de partir.** (*You have to eat before you leave.* → *You have to eat before leaving.*)

When you have an impersonal expression with an implied subject, you can again replace **que** with **de** and follow it with the infinitive. Note that doing so in the second example turns something specific (it's good for *you* to be happy) into a general statement of fact (it's good to be happy):

> **Il est important que tout le monde travaille. → Il est important de travailler.**
> (*It's important for everyone to work. → It's important to work.*)

> **Il est bon que vous soyez content. → Il est bon d'être content.** (*It's good that you're happy. → It's good to be happy.*)

Slipping in some indirect objects

You can avoid the subjunctive with orders and requests by changing the subject of the subjunctive clause to an indirect object, replacing **que** with **de,** and turning the subjunctive into an infinitive:

> **J'ordonne que tu le fasses. → Je t'ordonne de le faire.** (*I order that you do it. → I order you to do it.*)

> **Il propose que je voyage avec lui. → Il me propose de voyager avec lui.** (*He proposes that I travel with him.*)

You can rewrite subjunctive sentences that have impersonal verbs, such as **falloir** (*to be necessary*), with no change in meaning. Just replace the subject after **que** with an indirect object and replace the subjunctive with an infinitive.

> **Il faut que tu le fasses. → Il te faut le faire.** (*You have to do it.*)

> **Il arrive que j'aie tort. → Il m'arrive d'avoir tort.** (*It sometimes happens that I am wrong.*)

Swapping the subjunctive for a noun

With time-related conjunctions like **avant que** (*before*), you can sometimes replace the subjunctive clause with a noun, with little or no change in meaning. Note that you have to drop **que:**

> **Nous allons manger avant que tu arrives. → Nous allons manger avant ton arrivée.** (*We're going to eat before you arrive/before your arrival.*)

> **Je travaille en attendant que le film commence. → Je travaille en attendant le début du film.** (*I'm working until the film starts/until the start of the film.*)

Doubting: Saying if only . . .

With verbs like **douter** (*to doubt*), you can replace **que** with **si** (*if*), which can't be followed by the subjunctive. This change makes the meaning a bit more doubtful:

> **Je doute qu'il soit là. → Je doute s'il est là.** (*I doubt he's there.*)

Rewrite these sentences to avoid the subjunctive.

Q. Elle veut qu'elle soit riche.

A. **Elle veut être riche.** (*She wants to be rich.*)

51. Il faut que je travaille demain.

_____

52. Il est possible que vous tombiez.

_____

53. Tu dois ranger ta chambre avant que nous voyagions.

_____

54. Nous doutons qu'il mente.

_____

55. Nous ne pensons pas que nous lisions assez.

_____

56. Il est bon que tout le monde lise les journaux.

_____

57. Il arrive que nous dormions trop.

_____

58. Tu peux regarder la télé en attendant que le dîner soit prêt.

_____

59. Il doute que j'aie assez de temps.

_____

60. J'ai peur que j'agisse mal.

_____

Answer Key

1 tu **choisisses** (*you choose*)

2 il **rende** (*he returns*)

3 nous **chantions** (*we sing*)

4 vous **réussissiez** (*you succeed*)

5 elles **perdent** (*they lose*)

6 je **parte** (*I leave*)

7 tu **jettes** (*you throw*)

8 elle **envoie** (*she sends*)

9 nous **ayons** (*we have*)

10 vous **soyez** (*you are*)

11 ils **aillent** (*they go*)

12 je **sache** (*I know*)

13 tu **puisses** (*you can*)

14 on **fasse** (*one does*)

15 nous **voulions** (*we want*)

16 vous **alliez** (*you go*)

17 ils **soient** (*they are*)

18 je **veuille** (*I want*)

19 tu **sois** (*you are*)

20 il **ait** (*he has*)

21 **Il est dommage que nous n'ayons pas de voiture.**

22 **Il est étonnant que je ne puisse pas nager.**

23 **Il est naturel qu'il veuille voyager.**

24 **Il est regrettable que nous soyons pauvres.**

25 **Il est impossible que je t'aide/que je vous aide.**

26 **Il est douteux qu'elle sache la réponse.**

27 **Il est improbable que nous finissions aujourd'hui.**

28 **Il est bon que tu aies/vous ayez beaucoup d'amis.**

29 **Est-il nécessaire que tu fasses/vous fassiez cela ?**

30 **Il n'est pas étonnant qu'ils soient fatigués.**

31 Je veux que **tout le monde s'amuse bien.** (*I want everyone to have a good time.*)

32 Je préfère que **nous restions groupés.** (*I prefer that we stay in a group.*)

33 Je propose que **nous visitions le Louvre ensemble.** (*I propose that we visit the Louvre together.*)

34 Je demande que **tout le monde porte une montre.** (*I ask that everyone wear a watch.*)

35 Je doute que **nous puissions prendre des photos dans les musées.** (*I doubt we can take pictures in the museums.*)

36 Je regrette que **notre hôtel soit cher.** (*I regret that our hotel is expensive.*)

37 J'exige que **vous payiez en avance.** (*I demand that you pay in advance.*)

38 J'ai peur que **nos cartes de crédit ne marchent plus en fin de voyage.** (*I'm afraid that our credit cards won't work at the end of the trip.*)

39 Je suis surpris que **personne ne veuille visiter la tour Eiffel.** (*I'm surprised no one wants to visit the Eiffel Tower.*)

40 Je souhaite que **vous aimiez bien la France.** (*I hope you really like France.*)

XYZ, Cie.
11, rue de Dai
Paris

Il est probable que vous (41) **entendez** des rumeurs, et je sais que vous (42) **avez** peur. J'espère que tout le monde (43) **lira** bien cette lettre. Avant que vous (44) **preniez** une décision, il faut que vous (45) **compreniez** les faits. Il est vrai que cette fusion (46) **peut** avoir des conséquences négatives, mais il n'est pas vrai que tout le monde (47) **perde** son emploi. Je suis sûr qu'Abc (48) **veut** continuer notre mission. Nous sommes la seule entreprise qui (49) **fasse** ce type de travail, alors qu'Abc ne (50) **soit** qu'une source de financement.

(You've probably heard some rumors, and I know you're afraid. I hope everyone will read this letter carefully. Before you make a decision, you have to understand the facts. It's true that this merger could have some negative effects, but it's not true that everyone will lose his or her job. I'm sure that Abc wants to continue our mission. We are the only company that does this type of work, whereas Abc is only a source of financing.)

---

51 **Il me faut travailler demain.** (*I have to work tomorrow.*) You can't use the subjunctive with the same subject in both clauses, so you rewrite with the infinitive.

52 **Il est possible de tomber.** (*It's possible to fall.*) Using the infinitive instead of the subjunctive changes this to a general statement.

53 **Tu dois ranger ta chambre avant notre voyage.** (*You have to clean your room before our trip.*) You can avoid the subjunctive by changing the conjunction to a preposition and the verb to a noun.

54 **Nous doutons s'il ment.** (*We doubt he's lying.*) **Douter** can be followed by **si** + indicative to make the statement a little more doubtful.

55 **Nous ne pensons pas lire assez.** (*We don't think we read enough.*) You can't use the subjunctive with the same subject in both clauses, so you rewrite with the infinitive.

56 **Il est bon de lire les journaux.** (*It's good to read the newspapers.*) Using the infinitive instead of the subjunctive changes this to a general statement.

57 **Il nous arrive de dormir trop.** (*We sometimes sleep too much.*) I avoid the subjunctive by turning the subject of the subordinate clause into the object of the main clause.

58 **Tu peux regarder la télé en attendant le dîner.** (*You can watch TV while waiting for dinner.*) You can avoid the subjunctive by changing the conjunction to a preposition and the verb to a noun.

59 **Il doute si j'ai assez de temps.** (*He doubts I have enough time.*) **Douter** can be followed by **si** + indicative to make the statement a little more doubtful.

60 **J'ai peur de mal agir.** (*I'm afraid of doing [something] wrong.*) You can't use the subjunctive with the same subject in both clauses, so you rewrite with the infinitive.

Part III

Writing with Panache: Dressing Up Your Sentences

In this part . . .

Writing well in French requires not only excellent grammar but also a certain flair for description. The adjectives and adverbs I explain in this part can help you paint a mental picture and clarify details. This part also tells you about giving commands with and without the imperative, reflects on pronominal verbs, and discusses prepositions. Finally, you can examine object and adverbial pronouns and connect with an explanation of conjunctions and relative pronouns.

Chapter 9

Describing with Flair: Adjectives and Adverbs

. . . .

In This Chapter

▶ Understanding adjectives

▶ Using adverbs properly

▶ Making comparisons

. . . .

Adjectives are descriptive words, and adverbs sometimes help them out. Although nouns and verbs are the building blocks and actions of language, adjectives and adverbs are the colors, shapes, sizes, speeds, frequencies, and styles that bring those blocks and actions to life. For example, in the first sentence, *descriptive* is an adjective and *sometimes* is an adverb. You can see that without them, the sentence would've been missing some important information: Adjectives are words, and adverbs help them out. So adjectives and adverbs provide detail and clarification to the nouns, verbs, and other words they modify. This chapter explains all about adjectives and adverbs, including how to use them, where to put them in the sentence, the different types, and how to make comparisons.

Describing the Role of Adjectives

Adjectives describe nouns and pronouns. They can tell you what something looks, tastes, feels, sounds, and smells like, as well as how smart it is, where it's from, what it's for, and sometimes even why you should or shouldn't care about it. This section focuses on what you need to know about adjectives to use them correctly in your French writing and speaking.

Adjectives that refer to nationalities, languages, and religions aren't capitalized in French: **américain** (*American*), **français** (*French*), **chrétien** (*Christian*), and so on.

Making your adjectives agree

In French, most adjectives come after the noun they modify, rather than before, and they have to agree with the nouns in gender and number. In order to make adjectives *agree,* you need to add and/or change certain letters. Most of the rules for making adjectives feminine and plural are the same as for making nouns feminine and plural.

(Chapter 2 explains noun gender and number in detail.)

When ensuring that adjectives agree, you need to know that most French adjectives have four forms:

- ✔ Masculine singular
- ✔ Feminine singular
- ✔ Masculine plural
- ✔ Feminine plural

 The masculine singular is the default form of the adjective — that's what you'd look up in the dictionary. For example, **vert** (*green*) and **beau** (*beautiful*) are masculine; your dictionary likely doesn't have entries for the feminine equivalents, **verte** and **belle,** or the masculine plural, **verts** and **beaux.**

Making adjectives feminine

In order to make a masculine adjective feminine, all you have to do for many adjectives is add an **-e** to the end:

> **petit** (*small*) becomes **petite**
>
> **joli** (*pretty*) becomes **jolie**
>
> **préféré** (*favorite*) becomes **préférée**
>
> **bleu** (*blue*) becomes **bleue**

If the masculine adjective already ends in **-e,** you don't make any changes to get the feminine form:

> **grave** (*serious*) remains **grave**
>
> **rouge** (*red*) remains **rouge**

Like nouns, certain adjective endings have irregular feminine forms. Many of these words involve a doubling of the final consonant before adding the **-e:**

- ✔ For adjectives that end in **-el, -il,** or **-ul,** add **-le** for the feminine:

  > **formel** (*formal*) becomes **formelle**
  >
  > **pareil** (*similar*) becomes **pareille**
  >
  > **nul** (*none*) becomes **nulle**

- ✔ For masculine adjectives that end in **-en** or **-on,** add **-ne** for the feminine form:

  > **tunisien** (*Tunisian*) becomes **tunisienne**
  >
  > **bon** (*good*) becomes **bonne**

- ✔ For most adjectives that end in **-s,** add **-se** for the feminine:

  > **bas** (*low*) becomes **basse**

  However, for adjectives that refer to nationalities, just add **-e** without doubling the **s:**

  > **chinois** (*Chinese*) becomes **chinoise**

French also has several other irregular feminine forms, which follow these patterns:

- ✔ -c to -che: **blanc** (*white*) becomes **blanche**
- ✔ -eau to -elle: **nouveau** (*new*) becomes **nouvelle**
- ✔ -er to -ère: **cher** (*expensive*) becomes **chère**
- ✔ -et to -ète: **secret** (*secret*) becomes **secrète**
- ✔ -eux to -euse: **heureux** (*happy*) becomes **heureuse**
- ✔ -f to -ve: **vif** (*lively*) becomes **vive**
- ✔ -is to -îche: **frais** (*fresh*) becomes **fraîche**
- ✔ -x to -ce: **doux** (*sweet*) becomes **douce**

Making adjectives plural

In order to make most French adjectives plural, all you do is add an **-s.** For instance, **joli** (*pretty*) becomes **jolis, blanc** (*white*) changes to **blancs,** and **triste** (*sad*) becomes **tristes.**

If the masculine adjective ends in **-s** or **-x,** the plural form is the same as the singular. For example, **français** (*French*) and **vieux** (*old*) can modify both singular and plural nouns. Here are a couple of other situations to remember:

- ✔ Adjectives that end in **-al** become plural with **-aux: social** (*social*) becomes **sociaux,** and **idéal** (*ideal*) changes to **idéaux.**
- ✔ Adjectives that end in **-eau** add an **-x** for the plural: **nouveau** (*new*) becomes **nouveaux,** and **beau** (*beautiful*) switches to **beaux.**

To make an adjective feminine and plural, make it feminine first, according to the rules in the preceding section; then make it plural according to the rules in this section. Table 9-1 shows some French adjectives in all four forms.

Table 9-1	French Adjectives, Ready to Agree			
English	**Masc. Singular**	**Fem. Singular**	**Masc. Plural**	**Fem. Plural**
green	**vert**	**verte**	**verts**	**vertes**
gray	**gris**	**grise**	**gris**	**grises**
red	**rouge**	**rouge**	**rouges**	**rouges**
white	**blanc**	**blanche**	**blancs**	**blanches**

Adjectives that end in **-s,** like **gris,** have only three forms because the masculine singular and plural are the same. Adjectives that end in **-e,** like **rouge,** have only two forms because the masculine and feminine forms are the same.

For each of these singular masculine adjectives, provide the feminine singular, masculine plural, and feminine plural forms.

Q. noir

A. **noire, noirs, noires** (*black*)

1. difficile _____

2. gras _____

3. gentil _____

4. premier _____

5. heureux _____

6. neuf _____

7. anglais _____

8. intéressant _____

9. nouveau _____

10. bon _____

Correctly positioning adjectives with nouns

Using adjectives with nouns is a great way to add description to a sentence. But in order to put adjectives in their correct places, you need to think about the type of adjective and what it means. Most *descriptive* French adjectives — that is, adjectives that describe the nature or appearance of a noun, such as color, shape, or origin — follow the nouns they modify:

une voiture verte (*a green car*)

un garçon mince (*a slender boy*)

des vêtements européens (*European clothing*)

une fille heureuse (*a happy girl*)

In addition, present and past participles used as adjectives always follow nouns (see Chapters 7 and 15 for more on participles):

des yeux étincelants (*sparkling eyes*)

une histoire compliquée (*a complicated story*)

However, a few descriptive adjectives and all other types of French adjectives come before nouns. Descriptive adjectives that refer to the following qualities have to come in front of the nouns they modify (you can remember them with the acronym *BAGS*):

✔ Beauty and ugliness

✔ Age

✔ Goodness and badness

✔ Size

Here are some examples:

une jolie femme (*a pretty woman*)

un jeune homme (*a young man*)

une nouvelle voiture (*a new car*)

une bonne idée (*a good idea*)

un mauvais rhume (*a bad cold*)

un petit appartement (*a small apartment*)

Grand is an exception to this rule. When it precedes the noun, it means *big* (for an object) or *great* (for a person): **une grande maison** (*a big house*), **un grand homme** (*a great man*). But to say that a person is *tall,* **grand** has to follow the noun it modifies: **un homme grand** (*a tall man*). See "Identifying adjectives with meaning changes" for details.

All non-descriptive adjectives (possessive, demonstrative, interrogative, indefinite, negative, and numerical adjectives) come before the noun. (You can read more about possessive and demonstratives in Chapter 2, interrogatives in Chapter 5, negatives in Chapter 6, and numbers in Chapter 2.)

> **ma fille** (*my daughter*)
>
> **cette voiture** (*this car*)
>
> **Quelle maison ?** (*Which house?*)
>
> **certains livres** (*certain books*)
>
> **aucune idée** (*no idea*)

Using special forms for six adjectives that precede nouns

Most adjectives have four different forms: masculine singular, feminine singular, masculine plural, and feminine plural. But six French adjectives have a fifth: a special vowel form that you use only in very specific constructions. This masculine singular form exists for six of the adjectives that go in front of nouns, and you use it in front of a vowel or mute *h.* Its goal is to make pronunciation easier so you don't have to say back-to-back vowel sounds. See Table 9-2.

Table 9-2		Adjectives with Special Masculine Singular Forms			
English	*Masc. Singular*	*Masc. Singular before a Vowel or Mute h*	*Fem. Singular*	*Masc. Plural*	*Fem. Plural*
beautiful	**beau**	**bel**	**belle**	**beaux**	**belles**
this	**ce**	**cet**	**cette**	**ces**	**ces**
new	**nouveau**	**nouvel**	**nouvelle**	**nouveaux**	**nouvelles**
crazy	**fou**	**fol**	**folle**	**fous**	**folles**
soft	**mou**	**mol**	**molle**	**mous**	**molles**
old	**vieux**	**vieil**	**vieille**	**vieux**	**vieilles**

You use this special form only with masculine nouns and only when the adjective directly precedes a vowel or mute *h:*

> **un bel homme** (*a handsome man*)
>
> **mon nouvel avocat** (*my new lawyer*)
>
> **cet ingénieur** (*this engineer*)

If a second adjective that doesn't begin with a vowel or mute *h* is used between the two words, you can't use the special form, as with **ce grand ingénieur** (*this great engineer*). On the other hand, if you precede a masculine noun that doesn't begin with a vowel or mute *h* with another adjective that does, you do use the special form, as with **cet ancien maire** (*this former mayor*).

The letter the noun actually starts with doesn't necessarily tell you whether you have to use the special form. If the adjective directly precedes **homme** (*man*) or **éclair** (*flash of lightning*), for example, you use the special form. If the adjective precedes another adjective, such as **intéressant** (*interesting*) or **ancien** (*old*), you use the special form as long as the noun is masculine (even if the noun itself begins with a consonant). And if another adjective like **jeune** (*young*) or **grand** (*big*) comes before the noun, you can't use the special form — even if the noun begins with a vowel or mute *h*. You use the special form only if all three of these conditions are met:

✔ The noun is masculine.

✔ The noun is singular.

✔ The word that actually follows the adjective — whether it's the noun itself or another adjective — begins with a vowel or mute *h*.

Identifying adjectives with meaning changes

Some French adjectives have different meanings depending on whether they precede or follow the noun. When these adjectives have a literal meaning, you place them after the noun. When they have a figurative meaning, you place them before the noun:

un ancien médecin (*former doctor*)

un médecin ancien (*old doctor*)

la pauvre femme (*poor, wretched woman*)

la femme pauvre (*poor, penniless woman*)

See Table 9-3 for some common French adjectives with meaning changes.

Table 9-3	**Adjectives with Meaning Changes**	
Adjective	*Meaning before Noun*	*Meaning after Noun*
brave	*good, decent*	*brave*
cher	*dear*	*expensive*
curieux	*odd, strange*	*inquisitive*
dernier	*final*	*previous*
franc	*real, genuine*	*frank*
grand	*great*	*tall*
premier	*first*	*basic, primary*
prochain	*following*	*next*

Adjective	Meaning before Noun	Meaning after Noun
propre	*(my, his, our) own*	*clean*
triste	*sorry, pathetic*	*sad*

Translate the following phrases into French, paying careful attention to the placement of the French adjectives.

Q. an orange book

A. **un livre orange**

11. a yellow house _____

12. a beautiful country _____

13. a funny movie _____

14. a young girl _____

15. an interesting story _____

16. a new apartment _____

17. a great doctor _____

18. a small car _____

19. a tall woman _____

20. an old friend _____

Identifying an Adverb's Role

Like adjectives, adverbs are descriptive words. But instead of describing nouns, *adverbs* describe verbs, adjectives, or other adverbs. Adverbs tell you when, where, why, how, how often, and how much. Unlike adjectives, which have to agree with the nouns they modify, adverbs are invariable: They have only one form. This section covers what you need to know, including recognizing types of adverbs, forming adverbs, and positioning them, so you can correctly use adverbs in your writing and speech.

Identifying types of adverbs

Different types of adverbs have different purposes, and the type you want to use depends on what you want to say — are you talking about how often something happens, where it happens, when, . . .? Adverb position depends in part on the type of adverb you're using.

Adverbs of frequency
Adverbs of frequency express how often or how consistently something happens:

- **encore** (*again*)
- **jamais** (*ever*)
- **parfois** (*sometimes*)
- **rarement** (*rarely*)
- **souvent** (*often*)
- **toujours** (*always, still*)
- **quelquefois** (*sometimes*)

Check out some examples:

> **Je vais souvent aux musées.** (*I often go to museums.*)
>
> **Habites-tu toujours au Québec ?** (*Do you still live in Quebec?*)

Adverbs of place

Adverbs of place tell you where something happens:

- **autour** (*around*)
- **dedans** (*inside*)
- **dehors** (*outside*)
- **derrière** (*behind, in back*)
- **dessous** (*below*)
- **dessus** (*above*)
- **devant** (*in front*)
- **en bas** (*below, down[stairs]*)

- **en haut** (*up[stairs]*)
- **ici** (*here*)
- **là** (*there*)
- **loin** (*far away*)
- **partout** (*everywhere*)
- **près** (*near*)
- **quelque part** (*somewhere*)

Take a look at some example sentences:

> **Je préfère m'asseoir derrière.** (*I prefer sitting in back.*)
>
> **Qui habite en haut ?** (*Who lives upstairs?*)

Many adverbs of place are also prepositions. The difference is that an adverb acts by itself to modify a verb — **J'habite en bas** (*I live below*) — and a preposition joins its object (the noun that follows it) with another word — **J'habite en bas de Michel** (*I live below Michel*). See Chapter 12 for more information about French prepositions.

Adverbs of time

Adverbs of time explain when something happens:

- **actuellement** (*currently*)
- **après** (*after*)
- **aujourd'hui** (*today*)
- **aussitôt** (*immediately*)
- **autrefois** (*formerly, in the past*)
- **avant** (*before*)
- **bientôt** (*soon*)
- **d'abord** (first, at first)
- **déjà** (*already*)
- **demain** (*tomorrow*)

- **depuis** (*since*)
- **enfin** (*at last, finally*)
- **ensuite** (*next*)
- **hier** (*yesterday*)
- **immédiatement** (*immediately*)
- **longtemps** (*for a long time*)
- **maintenant** (*now*)
- **récemment** (*recently*)
- **tard** (*late*)
- **tôt** (*early*)

Note: **Actuellement** means *currently,* not *actually.* **En fait** means *actually.*

Here are some sentences that use adverbs of time:

>   **Nous allons partir demain.** (*We're going to leave tomorrow.*)

>   **J'ai enfin visité Paris.** (*I finally visited Paris.*)

Adverbs of quantity

Adverbs of quantity tell you how many or how much of something:

- **assez (de)** (*quite, fairly, enough*)
- **autant (de)** (*as much, as many*)
- **beaucoup (de)** (*a lot, many*)
- **bien de** (*quite a few*)
- **combien (de)** (*how many, how much*)
- **encore de** (*more*)
- **moins (de)** (*less, fewer*)

- **pas mal de** (*quite a few*)
- **(un) peu (de)** (*few, little, not very*)
- **la plupart de** (*most*)
- **plus (de)** (*more*)
- **tant (de)** (*so much, so many*)
- **très** (*very*)
- **trop (de)** (*too much, too many*)

Note: The parentheses around **de** in many of these phrases indicate that the **de** is required only if followed by a noun. **J'ai assez mangé** (*I ate enough*) doesn't need **de** because **assez** is followed by a verb, but **j'ai assez de temps** (*I have enough time*) does because *time* is a noun. The adverbs of quantity **bien de, encore de, pas mal de,** and **la plupart de** are always followed by a noun.

>   **C'est combien ?** (*How much is it?*)

>   **Je parle très vite.** (*I speak very quickly.*)

You can use also these adverbs of quantity as adjectives, to modify nouns.

>   **Il y a trop de circulation.** (*There's too much traffic.*)

>   **Il a beaucoup d'amis.** (*He has a lot of friends.*)

When most adverbs of quantity are followed by a noun, as in the preceding two examples, you need to include the preposition **de** between them, and you usually don't use an article in front of the noun. However, there are a couple of exceptions:

- When the noun after **de** refers to specific people or things, you need an article. In general, if the English translation includes *of the* rather than just *of,* you need the article. Compare these two sentences:

    > **Cette ville a beaucoup de circulation.** (*This town has a lot of traffic.*)

    > **Beaucoup de la circulation à Marseille est à destination de l'aéroport.** (*A lot of the traffic in Marseilles is going toward the airport.*)

- **Bien de, encore de,** and **la plupart de** always need an article, as in **La plupart de la plage est rocheuse** (*Most of the beach is rocky*).

French also has three other types of adverbs that you need to know about. They include the following:

- Adverbs of manner (see the next section)
- Interrogative adverbs (see Chapter 5)
- Negative adverbs (see Chapter 6)

Forming adverbs of manner

Many adverbs are formed from adjectives, in both French and English. These *adverbs of manner* express how something happens, and they usually end in *-ly* in English (*clearly, quickly, frankly*), whereas their French equivalents end in **-ment** (**clairement, rapidement, franchement**).

The rules for turning adjectives into adverbs are fairly straightforward. For masculine adjectives that end in a single vowel, just add **-ment:**

> **poli** (*polite*) becomes **poliment** (*politely*)
>
> **carré** (*square*) becomes **carrément** (*squarely*)
>
> **triste** (*sad*) becomes **tristement** (*sadly*)

Other words need a little more tweaking. Keep the following rules in mind when forming adverbs:

- When the masculine adjective ends in a consonant (except for **-ant** or **-ent**) or multiple vowels, take the feminine form of the adjective and add **-ment**. Most French adjectives of manner are formed like this:

  > **certain** (*certain,* masc.)/**certaine** (fem.) becomes **certainement** (*certainly*)
  >
  > **heureux** (*happy,* masc.)/**heureuse** (fem.) becomes **heureusement** (*happily, fortunately*)
  >
  > **dernier** (*last,* masc.)/**dernière** (fem.) becomes **dernièrement** (*lastly*)
  >
  > **nouveau** (*new,* masc.)/**nouvelle** (fem.) becomes **nouvellement** (*newly*)

- For adjectives that end in **-ant** or **-ent,** replace that ending with **-amment** or **-emment:**

  > **constant** (*constant*) becomes **constamment** (*constantly*)
  >
  > **intelligent** (*intelligent*) becomes **intelligemment** (*intelligently*)

However, remember a few specific exceptions to the preceding rules:

- **continu** (*continuous*) becomes **continûment** (*continuously*)
- **énorme** (*enormous*) becomes **énormément** (*enormously*)
- **gentil** (*nice, kind*) becomes **gentiment** (*nicely, kindly*)
- **lent** (*slow*) becomes **lentement** (*slowly*)
- **vrai** (*true*) becomes **vraiment** (*truly*)

Some French adverbs of manner don't end in **-ment:**

- **bien** (*well*)
- **debout** (*standing up*)
- **exprès** (*on purpose*)
- **mal** (*poorly, badly*)
- **mieux** (*better*)
- **pire** (*worse*)
- **vite** (*quickly*)
- **volontiers** (*gladly*)

Here are some sentences that use adverbs of manner:

Elle parle très poliment. (*She speaks very politely.*)

Tu l'as fait exprès ! (*You did it on purpose!*)

Turn these adjectives into adverbs.

Q. joli

A. **joliment** (prettily)

21. naturel _____

22. clair _____

23. lent _____

24. malheureux _____

25. vrai _____

26. premier _____

27. abondant _____

28. gentil _____

29. affreux _____

30. prudent _____

Positioning adverbs

The position of French adverbs depends on what they're modifying and the type of adverb. Read on.

After the verb

When French adverbs modify a verb, they usually follow it:

Je le ferai volontiers ! (*I'll gladly do it, I'll be glad to do it!*)

Nous voyageons souvent en été. (*We often travel in the summer.*)

If there are two verbs, the adverb goes after the conjugated verb, not after the infinitive or past participle:

J'aime beaucoup nager. (*I like swimming a lot.*)

Il a déjà mangé. (*He already ate.*)

When you negate a sentence with an adverb following a verb, the second part of the negative structure (explained in Chapter 6) comes before the adverb.

Je ne me sens pas bien. (*I don't feel well.*)

Il ne travaille jamais vite. (*He never works quickly.*)

Other places

You can usually put adverbs that refer to a point in time like **aujourd'hui** and **hier** at the beginning or end of the sentence, as in **Je dois travailler aujourd'hui** (*I have to work today*). The same is true for long adverbs, as in **Normalement, je me lève à 7h00** (*Usually, I get up at 7 a.m.*). However, when you want to stress the meaning of the adverb, you put it after the conjugated verb, as in **Il a violemment critiqué la nouvelle loi.** (*He strongly criticized the new law.*)

The best place for adverbs of place is after the direct object or, if there isn't one, after the verb:

> **Tu trouveras tes valises en haut.** (*You'll find your suitcases upstairs.*)

> **J'aimerais vivre ici.** (*I'd like to live here.*)

Adverbs that modify adjectives or other adverbs go in front of those words:

> **Elle est très belle.** (*She is very beautiful.*)

> **J'habite ici depuis assez longtemps.** (*I've lived here for a fairly long time.*)

Your colleague Marianne asked you to look over a memo she wrote, and you think it's a bit dull and imprecise because she didn't use any adverbs. Help her out by adding the adverb in parentheses to each of these sentences.

Q. Nous allons parler de la fête annuelle. (aujourd'hui)

A. **Aujourd'hui,** nous allons parler de la fête annuelle. (*Today, we're going to talk about the annual party.*)

NOTE DE SERVICE

À:	Tous les employés			
De:	Marianne			
Sujet:	Fête annuelle			

31. Elle se tient dans le bureau. (normalement)

_____

32. Mais cette fois, nous pouvons trouver un endroit intéressant. (plus)

_____

33. À mon avis, un restaurant est un bon choix. (très)

_____

34. Comme ça, nous mangeons ce que nous voulons. (exactement)

_____

35. J'ai téléphoné à plusieurs restaurants . . . (hier)

_____

36. . . . et j'en ai trouvé trois qui semblent idéaux. (presque)

_____

37. Le premier a du charme. (beaucoup)

_____

38. Le deuxième est ici. (près de)

_____

39. Et le troisième est fréquenté par des célébrités. (souvent)

_____

40. Répondez pour me dire lequel vous préférez. (immédiatement)

_____

Comparing with Comparatives and Superlatives

The two kinds of comparisons you can make in French are comparatives and superlatives. *Comparatives* say that something is *more _____ than, less _____ than,* or *as _____ as* something else; *superlatives* proclaim that something is the *most _____* or *least _____* of all.

More or less, equal: Relating two things with comparatives

Comparatives can indicate one of three things:

✔ Superiority

✔ Inferiority

✔ Equality

You use the comparative **plus _____ que** in French to indicate superiority — that something is *more _____ than* or *_____-er than* something else. The construction works for both adjectives and adverbs:

> **Elle est plus belle que moi.** (*She is more beautiful than I am.*)

> **Jacques parle plus rapidement que toi.** (*Jacques speaks more quickly than you.*)

In French comparatives and superlatives, you use stressed pronouns, rather than subject pronouns, after **que,** as in the preceding examples. *Stressed pronouns* are special forms that you use after prepositions and in comparatives or superlatives. See Table 9-4.

Table 9-4	Pronouns that Follow Que in Comparatives and Superlatives	
Person	**Singular**	**Plural**
First	moi	nous
Second	toi	vous
Third	lui/elle	leur

If the object you're comparing to is implied or has already been mentioned, you can leave out the **que: J'ai lu ton livre, mais le mien est plus intéressant [que le tien].** (*I read your book, but mine is more interesting [than yours].*)

The adjective in a comparative has to agree with the noun it follows. In order to do so, follow the agreement rules in "Making your adjectives agree" (as always, adverbs don't agree):

> **Paul est plus grand que Camille.** (*Paul is taller than Camille.*)

> **Camille est plus grande que Paul.** (*Camille is taller than Paul.*)

To say that something is inferior — *less _____ than* — use the comparative **moins _____ que:**

> **Yvette est moins aventureuse que son frère.** (*Yvette is less adventurous than her brother.*)

> **Ce livre est moins intéressant [que l'autre].** (*This book is less interesting [than the other one].*)

> **Il chante moins distinctement que son frère.** (*He sings less distinctly than his brother.*)

You express equality with **aussi _____ que** in French, which is equivalent to *as _____ as* in English:

> **L'exercice est aussi important que la nutrition.** (*Exercise is as important as nutrition.*)

> **Ma mère est aussi grande que mon père.** (*My mother is as tall as my father.*)

> **Vous vivez aussi bien qu'un roi.** (*You live as well as a king.*)

All these comparatives are between two people or things, but you can also make comparisons with two adjectives:

> **Je suis plus agacé que fâché.** (*I'm more annoyed than [I am] angry* — I'm annoyed, rather than angry.)

> **Il est aussi audacieux que courageux.** (*He's as audacious as [he is] courageous.*)

Supersizing with superlatives

Superlatives talk about the two extremes: *the most, the least, the _____-est.* In order to form the superlative, you need to know the three parts involved:

- The definite article
- **Plus** (*most*) or **moins** (*least*)
- The adjective or adverb

Adjectives

The definite article and the adjective both have to be masculine or feminine, and singular or plural to agree with the noun they're modifying. Then to form the superlative, use the definite article + **plus** or **moins** + the adjective.

Before you can use superlatives, you have to know whether the adjective you're using goes before or after the verb (see the section "Correctly positioning adjectives with nouns," earlier in this chapter) because adjectives that follow the noun have to be in that same position in superlatives. When the superlative follows the noun, you have to use the definite article twice — it precedes both the noun and the superlative:

> **C'est la solution la plus équitable.** (*That's the fairest solution.*)

> **Mon frère est l'homme le moins sportif du monde.** (*My brother is the least athletic man in the world.*)

Adjectives that precede the noun can either precede or follow the noun in superlatives. When they precede it, you use only one definite article:

> **Il est l'homme le plus beau.** or **Il est le plus bel homme.** (*He is the most handsome man.*)

> **les accidents les moins mauvais** or **les moins mauvais accidents** (*the least bad accidents*)

Adverbs

Superlatives with adverbs are a little different from superlatives with adjectives. Because adverbs don't agree with the words they modify, the definite article in superlatives doesn't either, so it's always **le,** the masculine singular. Also, because most adverbs follow verbs, comparative and superlatives adverbs always follow verbs as well, and superlatives with adverbs never have two definite articles the way superlatives with adjectives sometimes do. Instead, superlatives with adverbs simply take the form **le** + **plus** or **moins** + adverb:

> **Elle danse le plus parfaitement.** (*She dances the most perfectly.*)

> **Ils conduisent le moins lentement.** (*They drive the least slowly.*)

For better or worse: Special comparative and superlative forms

Two French adjectives have special forms in the superior comparative and superlative: **bon** (*good*) and **mauvais** (*bad*). The comparative of **bon** is **meilleur** (*better*) and the superlative is **le meilleur** (*the best*). Like all adjectives, they have to agree with the nouns they modify:

> **Ton vélo est meilleur que le mien.** (*Your bike is better than mine.*)

> **Ma question est la meilleure.** (*My question is the best.*)

> **Leurs idées sont moins bonnes.** (*Their ideas are less good/aren't as good.*)

Mauvais has two comparative and superlative forms. You can say **plus mauvais** (*more bad*) or **pire** (*worse*):

> **Cette décision est plus mauvaise que l'autre.** or **Cette décision est pire que l'autre.** (*This decision is worse than the other one.*)

> **Ces problèmes sont les plus mauvais.** or **Ces problèmes sont les pires.** (*These problems are the worst.*)

> **Cette question est moins mauvaise.** (*This issue is less bad/not as bad.*)

French also has two special forms for the comparative and superlative adverbs. The French adverb **bien** (*well*) has special forms in the superior comparative and superlative. The comparative is **mieux** (*better*), and the superlative is **le mieux** (*the best*):

> **Philippe comprend mieux que moi.** (*Philippe understands better than I do.*)

> **C'est en France que je me sens le mieux.** (*It's in France that I feel best.*)

> **Tu écris moins bien.** (*You write less well, You don't write as well.*)

Your friend Élise is so competitive! Whenever you describe anything at all, she claims that hers is bigger, better, or just more of whatever. For each phrase, write what Élise's response would be. For numbers 31–35, use the comparative, and for 36–40, use the superlative. Be sure to consider whether you're comparing adjectives or adverbs when choosing the comparative and superlative forms.

0. Ma voiture est rouge.

A. Ma voiture est **plus rouge.** (*My car is redder!*)

41. Ce livre est intéressant. _____

42. Mes amis sont sportifs. _____

43. J'ai une bonne question. _____

44. Martin s'habille professionnellement. _____

45. Anne travaille consciencieusement. _____

46. Je regarde un film amusant. _____

47. Ma sœur est belle. _____

48. J'ai un grand problème. _____

49. Nicolas nage bien. _____

50. Ils parlent le français couramment. _____

Answer Key

1   **difficile, difficiles, difficiles** (*difficult*)

2   **grasse, gras, grasses** (*fatty*)

3   **gentille, gentils, gentilles** (*kind*)

4   **première, premiers, premières** (*first*)

5   **heureuse, heureux, heureuses** (*happy*)

6   **neuve, neufs, neuves** (*new*)

7   **anglaise, anglais, anglaises** (*English*)

8   **intéressante, intéressants, intéressantes** (*interesting*)

9   **nouvelle, nouveaux, nouvelles** (*new*)

10   **bonne, bons, bonnes** (*good*)

11   **une maison jaune**

12   **un beau pays**

13   **un film amusant**

14   **une jeune fille**

15   **une histoire intéressante**

16   **un nouvel appartement**

17   **un grand médecin**

18   **une petite voiture**

19   **une femme grande**

20   **un vieil ami**

21   **naturellement** (*naturally*)

22   **clairement** (*clearly*)

23   **lentement** (*slowly*)

24   **malheureusement** (*unfortunately*)

25   **vraiment** (*truly*)

26   **premièrement** (*firstly, in the first place*)

27 **abondamment** (*abundantly*)

28 **gentiment** (*kindly*)

29 **affreusement** (*terribly, horribly*)

30 **prudemment** (*prudently*)

31 Elle se tient **normalement** dans le bureau. (*It is normally held in the office.*)

32 Mais cette fois, nous pouvons trouver un endroit **plus** intéressant. (*But this time, we can find a more interesting spot.*)

33 À mon avis, un restaurant est un **très** bon choix. (*In my opinion, a restaurant is a very good choice.*)

34 Comme ça, nous mangeons **exactement** ce que nous voulons. (*That way, we eat exactly what we want.*)

35 **Hier,** j'ai téléphoné à plusieurs restaurants . . . (*Yesterday, I called several restaurants . . .*)

36 . . . et j'en ai trouvé trois qui semblent **presque** idéaux. (*. . . and I found three that seem almost perfect.*)

37 Le premier a **beaucoup** de charme. (*The first has a lot of charm.*)

38 Le deuxième est **près d'**ici. (*The second is near here.*)

39 Et le troisième est **souvent** fréquenté par des célébrités. (*And the third is often frequented by celebrities.*)

40 Répondez **immédiatement** pour me dire lequel vous préférez. (*Respond immediately to tell me which one you prefer.*)

41 Ce livre est **plus intéressant !** (*This book is more interesting!*)

42 Mes amis sont **plus sportifs !** (*My friends are more athletic!*)

43 J'ai une **meilleure** question ! (*I have a better question!*)

44 Je m'habille **plus professionnellement !** (*I dress more professionally!*)

45 Je travaille **plus consciencieusement !** (*I work more conscienciously!*)

46 Je regarde le film **le plus amusant !** (*I'm watching the funniest movie!*)

47 Ma sœur est **la plus belle !** (*My sister is the most beautiful!*)

48 J'ai **le plus grand problème !** (*I have the biggest problem!*)

49 Je nage **le mieux !** (*I swim the best!*)

50 Je parle le français **le plus couramment !** (*I speak French the most fluently!*)

Chapter 10

I Command You: The Imperative

In This Chapter

▶ Conjugating the imperative

▶ Understanding affirmative and negative commands

▶ Giving orders without using the imperative

*T*he *imperative* is the verb mood used for giving orders, making suggestions, and offering advice. It's the only personal French verb form that you don't use with a subject pronoun, but it's still *personal* because it has different forms for each of the three grammatical persons that you can give orders to: **tu, nous,** and **vous.**

The imperative is a mood, not a tense — it indicates something that you're telling someone to do, but because that person may or may not actually do it, you don't use the *indicative*. A *mood* is a verb form that indicates how the speaker feels about the action of the verb, whether it is real (the indicative mood), conditional (the conditional mood), subjective (the subjunctive mood), or a command (the imperative mood). This chapter explains how to conjugate the imperative, covers the differences between affirmative and negative commands, and provides some ways to give commands without the imperative.

Conjugating the Imperative

There are only three imperative conjugations: **tu** (*you* singular/familiar), **nous** (*we*), and **vous** (*you* plural/formal). With no subject pronoun to guide you, getting the conjugations right is extra important because they're the only thing that tells you who's being ordered to do something. The following sections show you how to conjugate the imperative of regular, irregular, and reflexive verbs.

Regular verbs

The imperative conjugations of many French verbs are exactly the same as the present tense — except that you don't use a subject pronoun with them. (Check out Chapter 4 for how to conjugate regular verbs in the present tense.)

Imperative of -er verbs

Regular **-er** verbs use the present tense conjugations for the **nous** and **vous** imperative. (Just drop the **-er,** and then add **-ons** to the **nous** form and **-ez** to the **vous** form.) For the **tu** form, however, **-er** verbs use the present tense conjugation minus the final **s.** See Table 10-1 for the present tense and imperative of **parler** (*to speak*) — the subject pronouns are in parentheses to remind you that you don't use them with the imperative.

Table 10-1	Imperative of Parler (*to talk, speak*), a Regular -er Verb
Present Tense	*Imperative*
Tu parles (*You talk, speak*)	(tu) **Parle** (*Talk, speak*)
Nous parlons (*We talk, speak*)	(nous) **Parlons** (*Let's talk, let's speak*)
Vous parlez (*You talk, speak*)	(vous) **Parlez** (*Talk, speak*)

Imperative of -ir and -re verbs

Imperative conjugations for regular **-ir** and **-re** verbs are the same as the present tense in all three forms. For **-ir** verbs, drop the **-ir** and add **-is** to the **tu** form, **-issons** to the **nous** form, and **-issez** to the **vous** form. For **-re** verbs, drop the **-re** and add **-s** to the tu form, **-ons** to the **nous** form, and **-ez** to the **vous** form. Table 10-2 shows the conjugation of a regular **-ir** verb.

Table 10-2	Imperative of Choisir (*to choose*), a Regular -ir Verb
Present Tense	*Imperative*
Tu choisis (*You choose*)	(tu) **Choisis** (*Choose*)
Nous choisissons (*We choose*)	(nous) **Choisissons** (*Let's choose*)
Vous choisissez (*You choose*)	(vous) **Choisissez** (*Choose*)

See Table 10-3 for the imperative form of a regular **-re** verb.

Table 10-3	Imperative of Vendre (*to sell*), a Regular -re Verb
Present Tense	*Imperative*
Tu vends (*You sell*)	(tu) **Vends** (*Sell*)
Nous vendons (*We sell*)	(nous) **Vendons** (*Let's sell*)
Vous vendez (*You sell*)	(vous) **Vendez** (*Sell*)

Note: The **tu** imperative of **-er** verbs doesn't end in **s**, but the **tu** imperative of **-ir** and **-re** verbs does.

Provide all three imperative forms for each of these verbs.

Q. marcher

A. **marche, marchons, marchez** (*walk, let's walk, walk*)

1. finir _____

2. étudier _____

3. danser _____

4. attendre _____

5. compter _____

6. réfléchir _____

7. chanter _____   **9.** répondre _____

8. couvrir _____   **10.** jouer _____

Irregular verbs

As long as you know how to conjugate irregular verbs in the present tense, you shouldn't have any trouble figuring out their imperative conjugations because most irregular verbs use the same conjugations for the present tense and the imperative. (Check out Chapter 4 to see how to conjugate irregular verbs in the present tense.) These sections show how to conjugate the different irregular verbs in the imperative.

Irregular -er verbs

Stem-changing and spelling-change verbs are conjugated like regular **-er** verbs in the imperative: They use the present tense conjugations for the **nous** and **vous** imperative and the present tense minus the final **s** for the **tu** form. Table 10-4 and Table 10-5 show the conjugations.

Table 10-4	Imperative of Acheter (*to buy*), a Stem-Changing Verb
Present Tense	*Imperative*
Tu achètes (*You buy*)	(tu) **Achète** (*Buy*)
Nous achetons (*We buy*)	(nous) **Achetons** (*Let's buy*)
Vous achetez (*You buy*)	(vous) **Achetez** (*Buy*)

Table 10-5	Imperative of Commencer (*to begin*), a Spelling-Change Verb
Present Tense	*Imperative*
Tu commences (*You begin*)	(tu) **Commence** (*Begin*)
Nous commençons (*We begin*)	(nous) **Commençons** (*Let's begin*)
Vous commencez (*You begin*)	(vous) **Commencez** (*Begin*)

Aller, the only irregular **-er** verb, also follows this pattern. See Table 10-6.

Table 10-6	Imperative of the Irregular Verb Aller (*to go*)
Present Tense	*Imperative*
Tu vas (*You go*)	(tu) **Va** (*Go*)
Nous allons (*We go*)	(nous) **Allons** (*Let's go*)
Vous allez (*You go*)	(vous) **Allez** (*Go*)

Irregular -ir and -re verbs

The imperative of most irregular **-ir** and **-re** verbs is the same as the present tense (without the subject pronoun). Take a look at Tables 10-7 and 10-8.

Table 10-7	Imperative of Partir (*to leave*), an Irregular -ir Verb
Present Tense	*Imperative*
Tu pars (*You leave*)	(tu) **Pars** (*Leave*)
Nous partons (*We leave*)	(nous) **Partons** (*Let's leave*)
Vous partez (*You leave*)	(vous) **Partez** (*Leave*)

Table 10-8	Imperative of Mettre (*to put*), an Irregular -re Verb
Present Tense	*Imperative*
Tu mets (*You put*)	(tu) **Mets** (*Put*)
Nous mettons (*We put*)	(nous) **Mettons** (*Let's put*)
Vous mettez (*You put*)	(vous) **Mettez** (*Put*)

The only **-ir** verbs that don't follow this pattern are verbs like **ouvrir** and the verbs **avoir, savoir,** and **vouloir.** The only **-re** verb that doesn't follow this pattern is **être.**

Ouvrir and other **-ir** verbs conjugated like it in the present tense (that is, with the same endings as regular **-er** verbs) follow the same pattern as **-er** verbs in the imperative: You use the present tense **nous** and **vous** forms and the **tu** form minus **s.** See Table 10-9.

Table 10-9	Imperative of Ouvrir (*to open*), Conjugated Like -er Verbs
Present Tense	*Imperative*
Tu ouvres (*You open*)	(tu) **Ouvre** (*Open*)
Nous ouvrons (*We open*)	(nous) **Ouvrons** (*Let's open*)
Vous ouvrez (*You open*)	(vous) **Ouvrez** (*Open*)

Four French verbs — **avoir** (Table 10-10), **être** (Table 10-11), **savoir** (Table 10-12), and **vouloir** (Table 10-13) — have irregular imperative conjugations. *Note:* The imperative conjugations for these four irregular verbs are similar to their subjunctive conjugations. You can read about the subjunctive in Chapter 8.

Table 10-10	Imperative of Avoir (*to have*)
Present Tense	*Imperative*
Tu as (*You have*)	(tu) **Aie** (*Have*)
Nous avons (*We have*)	(nous) **Ayons** (*Let's have*)
Vous avez (*You have*)	(vous) **Ayez** (*Have*)

Table 10-11	Imperative of Être (*to be*)
Present Tense	*Imperative*
Tu es (*You are*)	(tu) **Sois** (*Be*)
Nous sommes (*We are*)	(nous) **Soyons** (*Let's be*)
Vous êtes (*You are*)	(vous) **Soyez** (*Be*)

Table 10-12	Imperative of Savoir (*to know*)
Present Tense	*Imperative*
Tu sais (*You know*)	(tu) **Sache** (*Know*)
Nous savons (*We know*)	(nous) **Sachons** (*Let's know*)
Vous savez (*You know*)	(vous) **Sachez** (*Know*)

Vouloir in the imperative isn't a command for someone to *want* something but rather a way of making a very polite request: **Veuillez m'excuser** (*Please excuse me*). **Vouloir** has no **nous** imperative because it doesn't make sense to say, "Let's want!"or "Let's excuse ourselves!" See Table 10-13.

Table 10-13	Imperative of Vouloir (*to want*)
Present Tense	*Imperative*
Tu veux (*You want*)	(tu) **Veuille** (*Please*)
Nous voulons (*We want*)	(not applicable)
Vous voulez (*You want*)	(vous) **Veuillez** (*Please*)

Provide all three imperative forms for each of these verbs.

Q. prendre

A. **prends, prenons, prenez** (*take, let's take, take*)

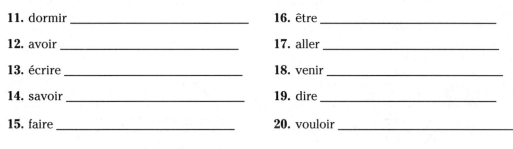

11. dormir _____

12. avoir _____

13. écrire _____

14. savoir _____

15. faire _____

16. être _____

17. aller _____

18. venir _____

19. dire _____

20. vouloir _____

Pronominal verbs

To use pronominal verbs (see Chapter 11) in the imperative, you start by conjugating the verb itself according to whichever of the preceding rules applies. Then you attach the correct form of the reflexive pronoun to the end of the verb with a hyphen, as in Tables 10-14 and 10-15.

Table 10-14 Imperative of Se Coucher (*to go to bed*), a Pronominal Verb	
Present Tense	*Imperative*
Tu te couches (*You go to bed*)	(tu) **Couche-toi** (*Go to bed*)
Nous nous couchons (*We go to bed*)	(nous) **Couchons-nous** (*Let's go to bed*)
Vous vous couchez (*You go to bed*)	(vous) **Couchez-vous** (*Go to bed*)

Table 10-15 Imperative of Se Taire (*to be quiet*), a Pronominal Verb	
Present Tense	*Imperative*
Tu te tais (*You are being quiet*)	(tu) **Tais-toi** (*Be quiet*)
Nous nous taisons (*We are being quiet*)	(nous) **Taisons-nous** (*Let's be quiet*)
Vous vous taisez (*You are being quiet*)	(vous) **Taisez-vous** (*Be quiet*)

Provide all three imperative forms for each of these pronominal verbs.

0. se coiffer

A. **coiffe-toi, coiffons-nous, coiffez-vous** (*fix your hair, let's fix our hair, fix your hair*)

21. se raser _____

22. se doucher _____

23. se reposer _____

24. s'amuser _____

25. se lever _____

Giving Affirmative and Negative Commands

You use affirmative commands to tell people to do something and negative commands to tell them not to do something. Other than the meaning, the only real difference between the affirmative and negative imperative is the word order you must use when the command includes reflexive, object, and/or adverbial pronouns. This section helps you keep everything straight.

For the to-do list: Affirmative commands

Affirmative commands tell someone to do something. Remember that the sentence has no subject pronoun, so the verb conjugation alone tells you who's being ordered to do the action. To create an affirmative command, just begin your statement with the verb in the imperative, and then add on anything else you need, such as an adverb or direct object.

> **Mange plus lentement.** (*Eat more slowly.*)
>
> **Fermez la porte.** (*Close the door.*)

The imperative doesn't always give commands; it can also offer suggestions or make requests, especially in the **nous** form:

> **Partons à midi.** (*Let's leave at noon.*)
>
> **Voyageons ensemble.** (*Let's travel together/Why don't we travel together?*)

The imperative can also make a very polite request in the **vous** form:

> **Veuillez m'excuser.** (*Please [be so kind as to] excuse me.*)
>
> **Ayez la bonté de fermer la porte.** (*Won't you please close the door?*)

Any reflexive, direct object, indirect object, and adverbial pronouns have to follow the affirmative imperative, attached by hyphens. The affirmative imperative is the only type of sentence in which reflexive, object, and adverbial pronouns follow the verb. In all other tenses and moods, including the negative imperative, these pronouns come before the verb. (See Chapter 13 for more info on object and adverbial pronouns, including what order they go in when you have two in the same sentence.)

> **Parle-nous !** (*Talk to us!*)
>
> **Montre-le-moi !** (*Show it to me!*)

When the **tu** form of the imperative of an **-er** verb is followed by **y** or **en,** the verb takes on an **s** like the present tense **tu** form of the verb.

> **Manges-en !** (*Eat some!*)
>
> **Vas-y !** (*Go ahead!*)

Translate these commands into French, in the conjugation for the pronoun in parentheses.

Q. Open the door. (tu)

A. **Ouvre la porte.**

26. Let's read the newspaper. (nous)

_____

27. Look at this painting. (vous)

_____

28. Buy some books. (tu)

_____

29. Let's go to the bakery. (nous)

_____

30. Please close the window. (vous)

_____

Don't do it! Negative commands

When you tell someone not to do something, you use a negative command by putting **ne** in front of the verb and the second part of the negative structure — **pas** (*not*), **rien** (*nothing*), **plus** (*no more*), **jamais** (*never*), and so on — after the verb. See Chapter 6 for info about making French verbs negative.

> **Ne parle pas comme ça.** (*Don't talk like that.*)

> **Ne reviendrons pas ici.** (*Let's not come back here.*)

If the verb requires a preposition, the word order depends on what kind of negation you're using. If you're using a negative adverb, the preposition goes after it, as in **Ne demandons pas à Pierre** (*Let's not ask Pierre*), but if it's a negative pronoun, the preposition goes before it, such as **N'aie peur de rien** (*Don't be afraid of anything*). See Chapter 6 to read about negation and Chapter 12 for information about verbs that have to be followed by a preposition.

As with all verb tenses and moods except affirmative commands, reflexive, object, and adverbial pronouns always precede the verb in the negative imperative (go to Chapter 13 to read about object and adverbial pronouns, including what order they go in when you have two in the same sentence):

> **Ne le dis pas.** (*Don't say it.*)

> **Ne nous mentez jamais !** (*Don't ever lie to us!*)

Translate these negative commands into French in the conjugation for the pronoun in parentheses.

Q. Don't eat this cake. (vous)

A. **Ne mangez pas ce gâteau.**

31. Don't talk during the movie. (tu)

_____

32. Let's not go out tonight. (nous)

_____

33. Don't read my letter. (vous)

_____

34. Don't forget to write. (tu)

35. Let's not be late. (nous)

Identifying Other Ways to Give Commands

The imperative is the most common way to give orders and make suggestions in French, but you have a few other options as well. This section gives you a quick overview.

Commanding with the infinitive

Use the infinitive for impersonal orders when you're giving instructions to an unknown audience, such as on signs and in books:

> **Fermer la porte et les fenêtres en quittant la nuit.** (*Close the door and windows upon/when leaving at night.*)

> **Couper les tomates et les ajouter à la soupe.** (*Cut the tomatoes and add them to the soup.*)

Chapter 7 has more information about the French infinitive.

Forbidding with "défense de"

The expression **défense de** (Literally: *prohibited from*), gives short, impersonal *do not do this* orders on signs. You probably won't use it yourself, unless you're in charge of making signs to post on doors and windows.

> **Défense d'entrer** (*Do not enter*)

> **Défense de fumer** (*No smoking*)

Requesting with the future

To make polite requests, you can use the future tense instead of using the **vous** imperative. For example, you may use this when giving instructions to people you don't know (as in a meeting or interview).

> **Vous travaillerez ensemble, s'il vous plaît.** (*Work together, please.*)

> **Vous le compléterez avant vendredi, s'il vous plaît.** (*Finish it by Friday, please.*)

Chapter 18 explains how to conjugate and use the French future tense.

Demanding with the subjunctive

Certain verbs and expressions that require the subjunctive are equivalent to giving commands or making requests. You can use these to soften the command while still making it clear that it's very much an order.

Here are some verbs and expressions that you can use to give commands or make requests.

- **il est essentiel que** (*it's essential that*)
- **il est nécessaire que** (*it's necessary that*)
- **il est urgent que** (*it's urgent that*)
- **exiger que** (*to demand that*)
- **ordonner que** (*to order that*)
- **préférer que** (*to prefer that*)

Here are some examples:

> **J'exige que vous vous taisiez !** (*I demand that you be quiet!*)

> **Il est essentiel que tout le monde fasse attention.** (*It's essential for everyone to pay attention.*)

Chapter 8 explains all about the subjunctive.

Rewrite each of these alternative commands using the **vous** form of the imperative.

Q. Défense d'entrer.

A. **N'entrez pas.** (*Do not enter.*)

36. Il exige que tu sois prêt à huit heures.

_____

37. Vous ouvrez la porte, s'il vous plaît.

_____

38. Mélanger la sauce et ajouter du sel.

_____

39. Défense de stationner.

_____

40. J'ordonne que vous écoutiez.

_____

Answer Key

1 **finis, finissons, finissez** (*finish, let's finish, finish*)

2 **étudie, étudions, étudiez** (*study, let's study, study*)

3 **danse, dansons, dansez** (*dance, let's dance, dance*)

4 **attends, attendons, attendez** (*wait, let's wait, wait*)

5 **compte, comptons, comptez** (*count, let's count, count*)

6 **réfléchis, réfléchissons, réfléchissez** (*reflect, let's reflect, reflect*)

7 **chante, chantons, chantez** (*sing, let's sing, sing*)

8 **couvre, couvrons, couvrez** (*cover, let's cover, cover*)

9 **réponds, répondons, répondez** (*respond, let's respond, respond*)

10 **joue, jouons, jouez** (*play, let's play, play*)

11 **dors, dormons, dormez** (*sleep, let's sleep, sleep*)

12 **aie, ayons, ayez** (*have, let's have, have*)

13 **écris, écrivons, écrivez** (*write, let's write, write*)

14 **sache, sachons, sachez** (*know, let's know, know*)

15 **fais, faisons, faites** (*do/make, let's do/make, do/make*)

16 **sois, soyons, soyez** (*be, let's be, be*)

17 **va, allons, allez** (*go, let's go, go*)

18 **viens, venons, venez** (*come, let's come, come*)

19 **dis, disons, dites** (*say, let's say, say*)

20 **veuille, —, veuillez** (*please, —, please*)

21 **rase-toi, rasons-nous, rasez-vous** (*shave, let's shave, shave*)

22 **douche-toi, douchons-nous, douchez-vous** (*shower, let's shower, shower*)

23 **repose-toi, reposons-nous, reposez-vous** (*rest, let's rest, rest*)

24 **amuse-toi, amusons-nous, amusez-vous** (*have fun, let's have fun, have fun*)

25 **lève-toi, levons-nous, levez-vous** (*get up, let's get up, get up*)

26 Lisons le journal.

27 Regardez cette peinture.

28 Achète des livres.

29 Allons à la boulangerie.

30 Veuillez fermer la fenêtre.

31 Ne parle pas pendant le film.

32 Ne sortons pas ce soir.

33 Ne lisez pas ma lettre.

34 N'oublie pas d'écrire.

35 Ne soyons pas en retard.

36 Soyez prêt à huit heures. (*Be ready at 8 a.m.*)

37 Ouvrez la porte s'il vous plait. (*Open the door please.*)

38 Mélangez la sauce et ajoutez du sel. (*Stir the sauce and add some salt.*)

39 Ne stationnez pas. (*Do not park.*)

40 Écoutez. (*Listen.*)

Chapter 11

Sorting Out Pronominal Verbs: Idioms, Oneself, and Each Other

Pronominal verbs may sound like something out of a grammatical horror story, but *pronominal* is just a fancy word that means *with a pronoun.* The pronoun in question is the reflexive pronoun, and its only job is to tell you that the verb you're using has a special meaning. You can also use most pronominal verbs without the reflexive pronoun, but then the meaning changes — sometimes slightly, sometimes significantly. Pronominal verbs are often mistakenly called *reflexive verbs,* when in fact, reflexive verbs are just one type of pronominal verb.

Pronominal verbs are different from other verbs in that they need a reflexive pronoun to tell you one of three things:

✔ The subject is performing the action of the verb on him- or herself.

✔ Two or more subjects are performing the action on one another.

✔ The verb has a special meaning, unrelated to the one it has without the pronoun.

This chapter explains the types of pronominal verbs, how to correctly use reflexive pronouns with pronominal verbs, and how to use pronominal verbs effectively.

Understanding the Types of Pronominal Verbs

Just like ice cream, pronominal verbs come in many different flavors (though they may not taste as good). *Pronominal verbs* are all the different verbs that you have to use with a reflexive pronoun (check out the section "Introducing the Relationship of Reflexive Pronouns to Pronominal Verbs," later in this chapter, to understand what reflexive pronouns are and how to use them correctly).

You can recognize a pronominal verb by the reflexive pronoun **se** that precedes the infinitive in the dictionary or your vocab lists: **se coucher** (*to go to bed*), **se laver** (*to wash oneself*), and so on. (Within sentences, you can tell a verb is pronominal when you see **se** or one of the other reflexive pronouns I discuss in "Eying the reflexive pronouns.") Although you can use most pronominal verbs without the reflexive pronoun, the meaning changes:

Alone, **coucher** means *to put (someone else) to bed,* and **laver** means *to wash (someone/something else).* So knowing when to use the reflexive pronoun and when not to is very important. This section covers the three types of pronominal verbs.

Reflexive verbs: Acting on oneself

Reflexive verbs tell you that someone is doing something to himself or herself. Table 11-1 shows some common reflexive verbs. Note that many of them have something to do with parts of the body or clothing, and the others have to do with personal circumstance or position.

Table 11-1		Common Reflexive Verbs	
Verb	*Translation*	**Verb**	*Translation*
s'approcher de	*to approach*	se laver (les mains, les cheveux)	*to wash (one's hands, hair)*
s'asseoir	*to sit down*	se lever	*to get up*
se baigner	*to bathe, swim*	se maquiller	*to put on makeup*
se brosser (les dents, les cheveux)	*to brush (one's teeth, hair)*	se marier (avec)	*to get married (to)*
se casser (le bras, le doigt)	*to break (one's arm, finger)*	se moucher	*to blow one's nose*
se coiffer	*to fix one's hair*	se peigner	*to comb one's hair*
se coucher	*to go to bed*	se promener	*to go for a walk*
se couper	*to cut oneself*	se raser	*to shave*
se déshabiller	*to get undressed*	se regarder	*to look at oneself*
se doucher	*to take a shower*	se reposer	*to rest*
se fâcher	*to get angry*	se réveiller	*to wake up*
s'habiller	*to get dressed*	se souvenir de	*to remember*
s'inquiéter	*to worry*		

Here are a couple of example sentences:

> **Je me marie avec Thérèse demain.** (*I'm marrying Thérèse tomorrow.*)

> **Il se rase une fois par semaine.** (*He shaves once a week.*)

Reflexive verbs don't really exist in English — you just use regular verbs, and if you want to stress that you're doing something to yourself, you can tack on *myself,* as in *I got dressed by myself* or *I dressed myself.* In French, though, the idea of *by myself,* represented by the reflexive pronoun **me,** is not optional — you have to use it to distinguish from the non-reflexive meaning. See "Deciding Whether to Make a Verb Pronominal," later in this chapter, for more information.

Reciprocal verbs: What you do to each other

Reciprocal verbs are any verbs that you use reflexively to mean that two or more subjects are doing something to, at, or with each other. Table 11-2 lists some common reciprocal verbs.

Table 11-2	Common Reciprocal Verbs		
Verb	*Translation*	**Verb**	*Translation*
s'aimer	*to love (each other)*	**se parler**	*to talk (to each other)*
se comprendre	*to understand (each other)*	**se promettre**	*to promise (each other)*
se connaître	*to know (each other)*	**se quitter**	*to leave (each other)*
se détester	*to hate (each other)*	**se regarder**	*to look (at each other)*
se dire	*to tell (each other)*	**se rencontrer**	*to meet (each other)*
se disputer	*to argue (with each other)*	**se sourire**	*to smile (at each other)*
s'écrire	*to write (each other)*	**se téléphoner**	*to call (each other)*
s'embrasser	*to kiss (each other)*	**se voir**	*to see (each other)*

The following sentence indicates reciprocal action:

> **Nous nous connaissons depuis 20 ans.** (*We've known each other for 20 years.*)

Many reciprocal verbs can also be used reflexively: **Je me parle** (*I'm talking to myself*), **Elle se regarde** (*She's looking at herself*), and so on.

Figuratively speaking: Idiomatic pronominal verbs

Idiomatic pronominal verbs sound exciting, but *idiomatic* just means that the meaning of these verbs is distinctly different from their meaning when you use them non-reflexively. (An *idiom* is an expression whose meaning you can't determine just by literally translating the individual words because at least one of them is used figuratively. See Chapter 1 for more info.) Table 11-3 shows some common idiomatic pronominal verbs and their non-pronominal equivalents.

Table 11-3	Idiomatic Pronominal Verbs		
Non-Pronominal French Verb	*Translation*	**Pronominal Verb**	*Translation*
amuser	*to amuse*	**s'amuser**	*to have a good time*
appeler	*to call*	**s'appeler**	*to be named*
débrouiller	*to untangle*	**se débrouiller**	*to manage, get by*

(continued)

Table 11-3 *(continued)*

Non-Pronominal French Verb	Translation	Pronominal Verb	Translation
décider	to decide	se décider	to make up one's mind
demander	to ask	se demander	to wonder
dépêcher	to send, to dispatch	se dépêcher	to hurry
endormir	to put to sleep	s'endormir	to fall asleep
ennuyer	to bother, to annoy	s'ennuyer	to be bored
entendre	to hear	s'entendre	to get along
installer	to install	s'installer	to settle in (a home)
mettre	to place, put	se mettre à	to begin to
rappeler	to call back	se rappeler	to recall, remember
rendre compte de	to account for	se rendre compte de	to realize, take into account
réunir	to gather, collect	se réunir	to meet, get together
tromper	to deceive	se tromper	to be mistaken
trouver	to find	se trouver	to be located

Here's what these verbs look like pronominally:

Je m'appelle Laura. (*My name is Laura.*)

Il s'est bien amusé. (*He had a really good time.*)

Introducing the Relationship of Reflexive Pronouns to Pronominal Verbs

Pronominal verbs are just like other verbs in that they describe actions and have to be conjugated for different tenses and moods. The difference is that pronominal verbs also have to use reflexive pronouns. This section gives you a quick overview on what reflexive pronouns are and how to use them correctly.

Eyeing the reflexive pronouns

Reflexive pronouns are the pronouns that you have to use with pronominal verbs. They're *personal*, meaning that you use a different one for each grammatical person (Chapter 4 explains grammatical person in more detail). See Table 11-4 for the French reflexive pronouns in all their forms.

Table 11-4	Reflexive Pronouns		
Subject Pronoun	*Reflexive Pronoun*	*Before a Vowel or Mute h*	*In the Imperative*
je	me	m'	
tu	te	t'	toi
il, elle, on	se	s'	
nous	nous	nous	nous
vous	vous	vous	vous
ils, elles	se	s'	

In the present tense (see Chapter 4), the reflexive pronoun goes in front of the verb, and the verb is conjugated according to its status as a regular, irregular, stem-changing, or spelling-change verb. (For info on different word-order situations, check out the next section.) For example, the pronominal verb **se doucher** means *to take a shower*. **Doucher** is a regular **-er** verb, so you'd conjugate the pronominal form like this.

se doucher (*to take a shower*)	
je **me** douche	nous **nous** douchons
tu **te** douches	vous **vous** douchez
il/elle/on **se** douche	ils/elles **se** douchent
Je **me douche** le soir. (*I shower at night.*)	

Don't let the **nous** and **vous** forms of pronominal verbs weird you out. Yes, the subject and object pronoun are identical, but they're both required.

When **me, te,** or **se** is followed by a word that begins with a vowel or mute *h,* you have to drop the **-e** and make a contraction. For instance, the pronominal verb **s'habiller** (*to get dressed*) is also a regular **-er** verb, so your conjugations would look like this.

s'habiller (*to get dressed*)	
je **m'**habille	nous **nous** habillons
tu **t'**habilles	vous **vous** habillez
il/elle/on **s'**habille	ils/elles **s'**habillent
Elle **s'habille** dans ta chambre. (*She's getting dressed in your room.*)	

The reflexive pronoun always has to agree with the subject in all tenses and moods, including the present participle and the infinitive (see Chapter 7). Table 11-5 gives some examples in which **je** is the subject.

Table 11-5	Reflexive Pronoun with Different Verb Forms	
Verb Form	**French**	**Translation**
Present tense	Je **me couche.**	*I'm going to bed.*
Past tense	Je **me** suis **douché.**	*I took a shower.*
Present participle	En **m'habillant,** je suis tombé.	*While getting dressed, I fell.*
Infinitive	Je vais **me fâcher.**	*I'm going to get angry.*

Fill in the blanks with the correct reflexive pronoun.

O. Il _____ lève.

A. Il **se** lève. (*He's getting up.*)

1. Je _____ baigne.

2. Marc _____ couche.

3. Ils _____ rasent.

4. Vous _____ reposez.

5. Tu _____ maquilles.

6. Nous _____ déshabillons.

7. Tu _____ approches du banc.

8. Elles _____ souviennent de ce film.

9. Je _____ habille.

10. Annette _____ regarde.

Knowing where the words go

When using pronominal verbs, you need to make sure you use the correct word order with the reflexive pronoun. If you don't, the person you're talking to may not understand who's doing what to whom. Word order with the reflexive pronoun is very simple: You put the pronoun directly in front of the pronominal verb in nearly all tenses, moods, and constructions. For example, **Je me lève à 9h00** (*I get up at 9 a.m.*)

When you have a conjugated verb followed by an infinitive, the reflexive pronoun goes in front of the infinitive because the infinitive is the pronominal verb. For example, **Nous allons nous acheter de la glace.** (*We're going to buy ourselves some ice cream.*)

The only times you don't put the reflexive pronoun right in front of the pronominal verb are in the following situations:

✔ **Affirmative imperative:** In the affirmative imperative (commands), you place the reflexive pronoun *after* the verb and connect the two words with hyphens. Note that **te** changes to **toi.** (See Chapter 10 for more information about the imperative.)

> **Lève-toi.** (*Get up.*)

> **Dépêchez-vous.** (*Hurry up.*)

✔ **Compound tenses:** In the **passé composé** and other *compound tenses* (that is, tenses that use a helping verb plus the past participle), the reflexive pronoun precedes the helping verb **être.** (Go to Chapter 15 to read up on the **passé composé.**)

> **Je me suis levé très tôt.** (*I got up really early.*)

> **Vous vous êtes trompés.** (*You made a mistake.*)

> ✔ **Questions with inversion:** When you use inversion to ask questions with pronominal verbs, the reflexive pronoun precedes the inverted verb-subject, which means it usually goes at the beginning of the sentence. (See Chapter 5 for information about asking questions with inversion.)
>
> **Te douches-tu le matin ou le soir ?** (*Do you shower in the morning or at night?*)
>
> **Vous êtes-vous levés avant 7h00 ?** (*Did you get up before 7 a.m.?*)

Determine which reflexive pronoun is needed for each sentence and where it goes; then rewrite these sentences. Remember that the pronoun may have different forms, depending on where it goes in the sentence.

Q. Jacques peigne les cheveux.

A. Jacques **se** peigne les cheveux. (*Jacques is combing his hair.*)

11. Nous demandons pourquoi.

_____

12. Elle va habiller après le petit-déjeuner.

_____

13. Tu regardes trop.

_____

14. Je vais laver les cheveux.

_____

15. Ils approchent lentement.

_____

Deciding Whether to Make a Verb Pronominal

Pronominal verbs tell you that the verb has a special meaning: The action is being done to the subject, two or more subjects are doing something to each other, or the verb has an idiomatic meaning. You can use pronominal verbs in all tenses and moods, and you conjugate them just like any other verb — the only difference between pronominal verbs and non-pronominal verbs is that pronominal verbs need a reflexive pronoun.

The important thing to understand about pronominal verbs is that you can use the great majority of them without the reflexive pronoun, but they'll have a different meaning. The extent of the difference in meaning depends on the type of pronominal verb. This section discusses the correct ways to use pronominal verbs.

Reflexive verbs: Oneself or something else?

Reflexive verbs indicate that the subject is doing something to itself — usually something to do with parts of the body (washing, brushing), clothing (dressing, undressing), personal circumstance (marriage, divorce), or position (sitting, waking up). Using those verbs without the reflexive pronoun means that the subject is doing something to someone or something else. Compare the following sentences:

> **Yvette se marie avec François demain.** (*Yvette is marrying François tomorrow.*)
>
> **Le prêtre marie trois couples par semaine.** (*The priest marries three couples a week.*)

In the first sentence, Yvette herself is getting married, but in the second, the priest is performing the ceremony that joins two people — not including himself — to one another.

> **Je me lave les mains.** (*I'm washing my hands.*)
>
> **Je lave la voiture.** (*I'm washing the car.*)

In the reflexive sentence, the subject is washing a part of himself or herself; in the non-reflexive sentence, the subject is washing something else. So the difference in meaning has nothing to do with the verb, which describes the same action in both sentences — the difference is just in who or what is affected by the verb.

When you use reflexive verbs like **se laver** (*to wash*), **se brosser** (*to brush*), and **se casser** (*to break*) with body parts, you use the definite article — not the possessive adjective — in front of the body part because the reflexive pronoun tells you whom it belongs to:

> **Je me suis cassé la jambe.** (*I broke my leg.*)
>
> **Il se brosse les dents.** (*He's brushing his teeth.*)

If you've broken someone else's leg or broken something non-human, you don't use the verb reflexively:

> **J'ai cassé la jambe de mon frère.** (*I broke my brother's leg.*)
>
> **J'ai cassé une assiette.** (*I broke a plate.*)

You can't use all pronominal verbs without the reflexive pronoun. **Se souvenir** (*to remember*), for example, is always reflexive. There's no non-reflexive equivalent.

Translate these sentences into French, paying careful attention to whether the verbs need to be reflexive.

Q. He's cutting his hair.

A. **Il se coupe les cheveux.**

16. I'm getting dressed.

_____

17. You (tu) are combing your hair.

_____

18. We're walking the dog.

_____

19. Thierry is shaving.

_____

20. Sandrine is bathing her little brother.

_____

Reciprocal verbs: Returning the favor?

Reciprocal verbs tell you that two or more people are doing something to each other, sort of a grammatical mutual admiration society. Reciprocal verbs usually have to do with communication (reading/writing to each other), feeling (loving/hating each other), and being together or apart. You use them when you want to be clear that the subjects are both doing the same thing to each other. All reciprocal verbs can be used without the reflexive pronoun. Compare these sentences:

- **Nous nous promettons.** (*We promise each other.*)

  Je te promets. (*I promise you.*)

- **Ils se sourient.** (*They're smiling at each other.*)

  Il a souri en voyant le chiot. (*He smiled upon seeing the puppy.*)

The difference in meaning here isn't huge. The reciprocal verb indicates that multiple subjects are all treating each other the same way: They're making promises to each other, smiling at each other, and so on. The nonreciprocal verb indicates the same activity, but it's not returned.

Your friend Charles hates inequality. He thinks these sentences are unfair because only one person is doing something. Rewrite them so that the two subjects are reciprocating. Note that you need to replace the singular subjects with plural subjects and then conjugate the verbs for the new subject.

Q. Je t'écris. (*I'm writing you.*)

A. **Nous nous écrivons.** (*We're writing each other.*)

NOTE DE SERVICE

À:

De:

21. Il m'aime. _____

22. Tu lui téléphones. _____

23. Elle l'embrasse. _____

24. Géraldine voit Michèle. _____

25. Elle me regarde. _____

26. Ils vous comprennent. _____

27. Je lui dis la vérité. _____

28. Tu me parles. _____

29. Elles me connaissent. _____

30. Il la déteste. _____

Idiomatic verbs: What's the meaning of all this?

Idiomatic pronominal verbs have the biggest difference in meaning between the pronominal and non-pronominal forms. Although reflexive and reciprocal verbs used without the reflexive pronoun just change who receives the action of the verb and whether the action is reciprocated, idiomatic pronominal verbs have a meaning that's completely different from that of their non-pronominal counterparts. Therefore, you need to memorize the list in the earlier section "Figuratively speaking: Idiomatic pronominal verbs" to be sure you're saying the right thing. Compare these sentence pairs:

> ✔ **Je m'entends bien avec mes parents.** (*I get along well with my parents.*)
>
> **J'entends du bruit.** (*I hear some noise.*)
>
> ✔ **Te rappelles-tu de son prénom ?** (*Do you remember his name?*)
>
> **Tu peux me rappeler demain.** (*You can call me back tomorrow.*)

Even though the verb itself is the same, the meanings of these sentence pairs have nothing in common because the reflexive pronoun changes the literal meaning of the verb into an idiomatic meaning.

Translate these sentences into French, paying special attention to the meanings of the words in italics and to whether you have to use normal verbs or idiomatic pronominal verbs.

Q. *His name is* Jean.

A. **Il s'appelle Jean.**

31. You (tu) have to *hurry*!

_____

32. I'm *bored*.

_____

33. He can't *find* his keys.

_____

34. She's *deceiving* everyone.

_____

35. We're *settling* in our new apartment.

_____

Answer Key

1 Je **me** baigne. (*I'm bathing.*)

2 Marc **se** couche. (*Marc is going to bed.*)

3 Ils **se** rasent. (*They're shaving.*)

4 Vous **vous** reposez. (*You're resting.*)

5 Tu **te** maquilles. (*You're putting on makeup.*)

6 Nous **nous** déshabillons. (*We're getting undressed.*)

7 Tu **t'**approches du banc. (*You're approaching the bench.*)

8 Elles **se** souviennent de ce film. (*They remember this movie.*)

9 Je **m'**habille. (*I'm getting dressed.*)

10 Annette **se** regarde. (*Annette is looking at herself.*)

11 Nous **nous** demandons pourquoi. (*We wonder why.*)

12 Elle va **s'**habiller après le petit-déjeuner. (*She's going to get dressed after breakfast.*)

13 Tu **te** regardes trop. (*You look at yourself too much.*)

14 Je vais **me** laver les cheveux. (*I'm going to wash my hair.*)

15 Ils **s'**approchent lentement. (*They are approaching slowly.*)

16 **Je m'habille.**

17 **Tu te peignes.**

18 **Nous promenons le chien.**

19 **Thierry se rase.**

20 **Sandrine baigne son petit frère.**

21 **Nous nous aimons.** (*We love each other.*)

22 **Vous vous téléphonez.** (*You call each other.*)

23 **Ils s'embrassent.** (*They're kissing each other.*)

24 **Elles se voient.** (*They see each other.*)

25 **Nous nous regardons.** (*We're looking at each other.*)

26 **Vous vous comprenez.** (*You understand each other.*)

27 **Nous nous disons la vérité.** (*We tell each other the truth.*)

28 **Nous nous parlons.** (*We're talking to each other.*)

29 **Nous nous connaissons.** (*We know each other.*)

30 **Ils se détestent.** (*They hate each other.*)

31 **Tu dois te dépêcher !**

32 **Je m'ennuie.**

33 **Il ne peut pas trouver ses clés.**

34 **Elle trompe tout le monde.**

35 **Nous nous installons dans notre nouvel appartement.**

Chapter 12

An Ode to Prepositions

Prepositions are *joining* words — they connect nouns to other nouns or to verbs in order to show the relationship between those words, such as what something is *about*, whom someone is working *for*, or how your keys always manage to hide *from* you. Prepositions can be tricky in foreign languages because you can't memorize them like you do vocabulary lists.

Many French prepositions have more than one English translation — and vice versa — because it's not a simple matter of knowing what they mean but rather how you use them in each language. The job of prepositions is to explain how one word affects another, such as by talking *to, about,* or *over* it, and those uses can vary widely between French and English. This chapter explains the most common French prepositions and how to use them with places, time, and verbs, as well as how and when to form contractions.

Identifying Common Prepositions

The most common French prepositions are **à** and **de,** but knowing how to use them is not a simple matter of translation. **À** often means *to, at,* or *in,* and **de** usually means *of, from,* or *about,* but you also use these prepositions to indicate other concepts, such as possession or purpose; therefore, you have to understand not only what they mean but also how you use them in French. No need to worry, though — this section identifies the most common prepositions.

The preposition à

À is the French equivalent of *to, at,* or *in* — at least most of the time. It often indicates current location or future destination:

> **Je vais à la banque.** (*I'm going to the bank.*)

> **Je suis à l'hôpital.** (*I'm at/in the hospital.*)

English makes a distinction between whether you're going *to* a place or are currently *at* or *in* it, but French doesn't. **À** covers both of those concepts.

You can also use **à** to mean *at* a point in time (see Chapter 3 for more on time):

> **Notre vol est à 14h00.** (*Our flight is at 2 p.m.*)
>
> **Je suis parti à 5h30.** (*I left at 5:30 a.m.*)

The preposition **à** has some other uses as well — you can read about them in the sections "When to use à or de" and "Looking at Verbs That Need Prepositions," later in this chapter.

The preposition de

De is the French equivalent of *of, from,* and *about* — usually. You use **de** for all these meanings:

- ✔ Cause: **Je meurs de soif !** (*I'm dying of thirst!*)
- ✔ Description: **un guide de voyage** (*a travel guide*)
- ✔ Origin: **Il est de Dakar.** (*He is from Dakar.*)
- ✔ Possession: **le voyage de Simone** (*Simone's trip*)
- ✔ Way of doing something: **un choc de front** (*head-on crash*)

In English, you use *'s* or *s'* for possession: Jean's book, the kids' bedroom. To translate this into French, you have to reverse the words and join them with the preposition **de: le livre de Jean, la chambre des enfants.** See Chapter 2 for more information about expressing possession in French.

The **de** contracts to **d'** in front of a vowel or mute *h*, such as **la voiture d'Anne** (*Anne's car*).

You need the preposition **de** in other constructions as well — see the sections "Distinguishing between Prepositions" and "Looking at Verbs That Need Prepositions," later in this chapter.

Forming contractions with prepositions

When you follow the prepositions **à** and **de** with the definite articles **le** and **les,** you have to form contractions. But you don't form contractions with the definite articles **la** and **l'** — see Table 12-1.

Table 12-1		Preposition Contractions	
à + Article	*Contraction*	*de + Article*	*Contraction*
à + le	Yes: **au**	**de + le**	Yes: **du**
à + la	No: **à la**	**de + la**	No: **de la**

à + Article	Contraction	de + Article	Contraction
à + l'	No: **à l'**	**de + l'**	No: **de l'**
à + les	Yes: **aux**	**de + les**	Yes: **des**

Je vais au marché. (*I'm going to the store.*)

Il se plaint des mouches. (*He's complaining about the flies.*)

À and **de** contract only with the definite articles **le** and **les.** They don't contract with the direct objects **le** and **les** (see Chapters 2 and 13 for information about definite articles and direct objects):

Je parle du problème. (*I'm talking about the problem.* — **du** + [**de** + **le**] means *about the*)

Il m'a dit de le faire. (*He told me to do it.* — *it* is what's being done, so **le** is the direct object of **faire**)

Translate these sentences into French. Pay attention to which preposition you need, either **à** or **de,** and whether it needs to contract.

0. I'm talking to Guillaume.

A. Je parle **à** Guillaume.

1. Let's leave at noon.

_____

2. They're from Rabat.

_____

3. He's going to the bank.

_____

4. Dominique's car is at the beach.

_____

5. She wants to go to the museum.

_____

6. I don't like my friends' cat.

_____

7. We bought a history book.

_____

8. I'm using my colleague's computer.

_____

9. Are you going to the clubs with (avec) Timothy?

_____

10. She arrived from Montreal.

_____

Identifying other useful prepositions

Though **à** and **de** are the most common French prepositions, you may hear, read, and use many others on a daily basis. The following are a couple of other useful prepositions that you need to know:

- ✔ **Chez** is one of the most interesting French prepositions. It has several meanings and no simple English equivalent — in different contexts, you can translate it as *at/to the home of, at/to the office of, in the mind of,* or *among:*

    Je suis rentré chez moi. (*I went back [to my] home.*)

    Elle va chez le dentiste. (*She's going to the dentist's office.*)

    Chez Sartre, l'enfer, c'est les autres. (*In Sartre's mind/According to Sartre, hell is other people.*)

    Manger en famille est très important chez les Français. (*Eating as a family is very important to/among the French.*)

- ✔ **En** is another preposition with multiple meanings — you may translate it as *in* or *to* (for more-detailed information about **en,** see "When to use dans or en," later in this chapter):

    Je l'ai fait en 5 minutes. (*I did it in 5 minutes.*)

    Je suis en France. (*I'm in France.*)

    Nous allons en Algérie. (*We're going to Algeria.*)

The other important French prepositions have simpler, more one-to-one meanings — see Table 12-2.

Table 12-2	French Prepositions		
French Preposition	*English Preposition*	*Example*	*Translation*
après	*after*	Je suis parti **après** minuit.	I left *after* midnight.
avant	*before*	J'ai mangé **avant** la fête.	I ate *before* the party.
avec	*with*	Il voyage **avec** sa copine.	He's traveling *with* his girlfriend.
contre	*against*	J'ai voté **contre** lui.	I voted *against* him.
dans	*in*	Mets-le **dans** le tiroir.	Put it *in* the drawer.
pour	*for*	Je l'ai acheté **pour** vous.	I bought it *for* you.
sans	*without*	Elle mange **sans** parler.	She eats *without* speaking.
sous	*under*	Cet animal habite **sous** terre.	This animal lives *under* the ground.

French Preposition	English Preposition	Example	Translation
sur	*on*	Il y a un carton **sur** mon lit.	There's a box *on* my bed.
vers	*toward*	Conduisons **vers** la plage.	Let's drive *toward* the beach.

Translate these sentences into French.

Q. He's walking toward the park.

A. Il marche **vers** le parc.

11. It's in a box.

_____

12. The dog is on the table.

_____

13. I'm leaving with or without you.

_____

14. Are you for or against this solution?

_____

15. You can eat before or after the party.

_____

Distinguishing between Prepositions

Part of the difficulty with French prepositions is that some of them have more than one meaning, and some of them share a meaning with other prepositions — at least when you translate them into English. In fact, French prepositions are very precise. The ones that seem to share a meaning have specific rules governing their uses. The following sections help you determine how to use the right preposition in the correct manner.

When to use à or de

The French prepositions **à** and **de** have overlapping or complementary meanings, which can be confusing. The key is to understand what they mean in French before you try to translate them into English. The following spells out when to use each one:

✔ **Location:** **À** tells you where something is or will be, and **de** tells you where it was.

Je suis à Paris. (*I'm in Paris.*)

Je vais à Marseille. (*I'm going to Marseilles.*)

Il est de Québec. (*He is from Quebec City.*)

Il arrive de Montréal. (*He is arriving from Montreal.*)

✔ **Description:** When you use **à** between two nouns, the second noun explains what the first noun is *for*. In comparison, when **de** goes between two nouns, the second noun tells you what is *in* the first noun.

> **une cuiller à thé** (*teaspoon*)
>
> **un verre à eau** (*water glass, glass for water*)
>
> **une cuiller de thé** (*spoonful of tea*)
>
> **un verre d'eau** (*glass of water*)

In addition, many French verbs require either **à** or **de** — see "Looking at Verbs That Need Prepositions," later in this chapter.

When to use dans or en

Dans and **en** both mean *in,* but they're not interchangeable. **Dans** means *in* in both location and time. In terms of location, **en** can only mean *in* or *to* a country. In reference to time, **en** means *in a certain amount of time* or *in a given time period.* The following spells out when to use **dans** or **en:**

✔ **Location: Dans** means inside of something, such as a box, bag, or house.

> **Il y a une souris dans ma chambre !** (*There's a mouse in my bedroom!*)
>
> **As-tu un stylo dans ton sac ?** (*Do you have a pen in your bag?*)

En can't mean *in* something concrete, like a box or a bag. It can only mean in a country, which you can read about in the next section, "Prepositions with countries."

✔ **Time:** When you use **dans** followed by a period of time, it means that you'll do something that far in the future.

> **Je le ferai dans dix minutes.** (*I'll do it in ten minutes.* — I'll do it ten minutes from now.)
>
> **Nous partons dans un mois.** (*We're leaving in a month.*)

In reference to time, **en** explains how long something takes.

> **Je l'ai fait en dix minutes.** (*I did it in ten minutes.* — It took me ten minutes to do it.)
>
> **Je peux écrire cet article en un mois.** (*I can write this article in a month.* — It will take me a month to write this article.)

En can also tell you when something happens — in which month, season, or year.

> **Nous ne travaillons pas en été.** (*We don't work in the summer.*)
>
> **Il a écrit cet article en 2007.** (*He wrote this article in 2007.*)

Your boss wrote you an e-mail about an upcoming meeting with employees — some of whom have very particular requirements — from other branch offices. Unfortunately, your printer has been acting up, and it left out all the prepositions when you printed it off. Fill in the blanks with the correct preposition: **à, de, dans,** or **en.**

Q. La réunion commencera _____ 14h00.

A. La réunion commencera **à** 14h00. (*The meeting will begin at 2 p.m.*)

New Message

| File | Edit | View | Insert | Format | Tools | Message | Help |

| Send | Cut | Copy | Paste | Undo | **abc✔** Check |

From:	Françoise Dupré
To:	Juliette LaCroix
Cc:	
Subject	

M. Boumani arrivera (16) _____ (from) Tanger (17) _____
13h00. Il préfère boire son café dans une tasse (18) _____
thé. Sa collègue, Mme Labiya, a besoin d'un verre (19) _____
eau dans un verre (20) _____ vin. Mlle Leblanc, venant
(21) _____ Genève, peut manger tous les hors-d'œuvre
(22) _____ cinq minutes, donc elle ne devrait pas être
assise à côté du buffet. Les trois employés (23) _____
Paris, qui sont déjà venus ici (24) _____ mai, n'ont pas
de besoins particuliers. Venez à mon bureau (25) _____
une heure et je vous donnerai les autres détails.

Using Prepositions with Places

In French, you use all kinds of different prepositions with places, depending on whether you're talking about a city or a country — and in the case of a country, depending on the gender, number, and first letter of that country. This section clarifies the rules so you can figure out which preposition to use the next time you're traveling or talking about a specific place.

Prepositions with countries

When choosing between the prepositions to use with countries, you can't just put your hand in the preposition grab bag and pull one out. You have to look at the following three things to determine which preposition to use:

✔ **The gender of the country**

Determining the gender of countries is simple. Countries that end in **-e** are feminine: **la France, l'Italie,** and so on. There are only four exceptions:

> • **le Cambodge** (*Cambodia*)
>
> • **le Mexique** (*Mexico*)
>
> • **le Mozambique** (*Mozambique*)
>
> • **le Zimbabwe** (*Zimbabwe*)
>
> The four countries listed here plus all countries that don't end in **-e** are masculine: **le Canada, l'Iran,** and so on.
>
> ✔ **The first letter of the country**
>
> ✔ **Whether the country is singular or plural**

After you know your country's gender, you can use the info in the following sections to help you determine which preposition to use in the right situation.

Going to or being in a country

To say *in* or *to* a singular feminine country, you use the preposition **en** with no article:

> **Je vais en France.** (*I'm going to France.*)
>
> **Il habite en Côte d'Ivoire.** (*He lives in Côte d'Ivoire.*)

English has different prepositions depending on whether you're on you way somewhere or you're already there, but French doesn't. The same preposition expresses both of these ideas.

To say *in* or *to* a singular masculine country, you use the preposition **à** plus the definite article **le.** So for countries that begin with a consonant or aspirate *h,* use the contraction **au:**

> **Nous voyageons au Maroc.** (*We're traveling to Morocco.*)
>
> **Il veut rester au Sénégal.** (*He wants to stay in Senegal.*)

But if the masculine country begins with a vowel, you use the preposition **à l':**

> **Quand vas-tu à l'Angola ?** (*When are you going to Angola?*)
>
> **Je veux bien voyager à l'Ouganda.** (*I'd really like to travel to Uganda.*)

For plural countries of either gender, you use **à** plus the plural definite article **les,** which contracts to **aux:**

> **Nous habitons aux États-Unis.** (*We live in the United States.*)
>
> **Il va aux Seychelles.** (*He's going to the Seychelles.*)

Coming from or being from a country

To say that you are arriving *from,* or are originally from, a singular feminine country, use the preposition **de** with no article:

> **Nous sommes de Suisse.** (*We are from Switzerland.*)
>
> **Il arrive de Belgique.** (*He's arriving from Belgium.*)

If the feminine country begins with a vowel or mute *h,* **de** contracts to **d':**

Êtes-vous d'Égypte ? (*Are you from Egypt?*)

Il vient d'Hongrie. (*He's coming from Hungary.*)

When you're arriving or are originally from a masculine country, use **de** plus the definite article **le (du** or **de l'):**

Elle est du Canada. (*She is from Canada.*)

J'arrive de l'Oman. (*I'm arriving from Oman.*)

To say that you're arriving from or are originally from a plural country, use **des (de** plus the plural definite article **les):**

Nous sommes des États-Unis. (*We are from the United States.*)

Elle vient des Fidji. (*She comes from Fiji.*)

Prepositions with cities

The prepositions you use with cities are much more straightforward. You use **à** to mean *in* or *to* a city and **de** to mean *from:*

Nous allons à Genève. (*We're going to Geneva.*)

Ils sont à Casablanca. (*They're in Casablanca.*)

Elle est de Bruxelles. (*She's from Brussels.*)

Je suis arrivé d'Alger. (*I arrived from Algiers.*)

Fill in the blanks with the correct preposition for the meaning in parentheses.

0. Je suis _____ (from) France.

A. Je suis **de** France. (*I am from France.*)

26. Il va _____ (to) Australie.

27. Nous voyageons _____ (in) Canada.

28. Elle vient _____ (from) Italie.

29. Ils arrivent _____ (from) Mali.

30. Je vais _____ (to) Londres.

Looking at Verbs That Need Prepositions

Many French verbs need a preposition when they're followed by an object or an infinitive. English has some verbs that need prepositions, called *phrasal verbs*, but they're not at all the same thing as in French. Phrasal verbs require different prepositions depending on meaning, such as *to move on* and *to move in.*

French has a few verbs that have different meanings depending on which preposition follows, but most verbs just require a certain preposition that, confusingly, often has no English translation or has a meaning that doesn't correspond to the "normal" meaning of the preposition. This section points out some of the more common verbs and the prepositions that go with them.

Verbs with à

Hundreds of French verbs require the preposition **à**; Table 12-3 shows some of the most common. The preposition doesn't make any difference in the verb conjugation, so to use these verbs, just conjugate each verb according to its status as a regular, stem-changing, irregular, or pronominal verb, and then follow with the preposition.

Table 12-3		Verbs That Require à	
Verb + à	*Translation*	*Verb + à*	*Translation*
aider à + infinitive	*to help to do something*	**s'intéresser à** + noun	*to be interested in something*
s'amuser à + infinitive	*to enjoy doing*	**inviter** (someone) **à** + noun	*to invite (someone) to something*
arriver à + infinitive	*to manage to do/ succeed in doing*	**se mettre à** + infinitive	*to start, set about doing*
assister à + noun	*to attend something*	**persister à** + infinitive	*to persist in doing*
s'attendre à + infinitive	*to expect to do*	**plaire à** + person	*to please someone*
chercher à + infinitive	*to attempt to do*	**se préparer à** + infinitive	*to prepare oneself to*
conseiller à + person	*to advise someone*	**réfléchir à** + noun	*to think about something*
consentir à + infinitive	*to consent to doing*	**renoncer à** + infinitive	*to give up doing*
se décider à + infinitive	*to decide to do, make up one's mind to do*	**répondre à** + person or noun	*to answer someone/ something*
demander à + person	*to ask someone*	**résister à** + infinitive	*to resist doing*
dire à + person	*to tell someone*	**réussir à** + infinitive	*to succeed in doing*
emprunter à + person	*to borrow from someone*	**serrer la main à** + person	*to shake someone's hand*
encourager à + infinitive	*to encourage to do*	**servir à** + infinitive	*to serve to do*
faire attention à + noun	*to pay attention to*	**tarder à** + infinitive	*to delay / be late in doing*
s'habituer à + noun or infinitive	*to get used to something*	**téléphoner à** + person	*to call someone*
hésiter à + infinitive	*to hesitate to do*	**voler à** + person	*to steal from someone*

Fais attention aux instructions. (*Pay attention to the instructions.*)

Vas-tu m'inviter à la fête ? (*Are you going to invite me to the party?*)

Il a volé cette idée à son collègue. (*He stole this idea from his colleague.*)

Note that the French infinitive after **à** often translates more naturally as the present participle in English (you can read more about the difference between French and English infinitives and present participles in Chapter 7): **Je m'amuse à regarder les touristes.** (*I enjoy watching the tourists.*)

Verbs with de

Hundreds more French verbs require the preposition **de**, including these in Table 12-4. To use these verbs, just conjugate them and follow them with the preposition **de.**

Table 12-4		Verbs Followed by de	
Verb + de	*Translation*	*Verb + de*	*Translation*
accepter de + infinitive	*to accept, agree to*	**finir de** + infinitive	*to finish doing*
s'agir de + infinitive/noun	*to be a question of doing/something*	**se méfier de** + infinitive	*to beware of*
avoir besoin de + noun	*to need*	**mériter de** + infinitive	*to deserve to*
avoir envie de + noun	*to want*	**se moquer de** + noun	*to make fun of*
avoir peur de + infinitive/noun	*to be afraid of doing/something*	**offrir de** + infinitive	*to offer to*
cesser de + infinitive	*to stop, cease doing*	**oublier de** + infinitive	*to forget to*
choisir de + infinitive	*to choose to*	**persuader de** + infinitive	*to persuade to*
conseiller de + infinitive	*to advise to*	**se plaindre de** + noun	*to complain about*
craindre de + infinitive	*to fear doing*	**prier de** + infinitive	*to beg to*
décider de + infinitive	*to decide to*	**promettre de** + infinitive	*to promise to*
défendre à quelqu'un de + infinitive	*to forbid (someone) to do*	**proposer de** + infinitive	*to suggest doing*
demander à quelqu'un de + infinitive	*to ask (someone) to do*	**refuser de** + infinitive	*to refuse to*
se dépêcher de + infinitive	*to hurry to*	**regretter de** + infinitive	*to regret doing*

(continued)

Table 12-4 *(continued)*

Verb + de	Translation	Verb + de	Translation
dire à quelqu'un de + infinitive	to tell (someone) to do something	**remercier de** + infinitive	to thank for doing
empêcher de + infinitive	to prevent, keep from doing	**risquer de** + infinitive	to risk doing
essayer de + infinitive	to try to	**se souvenir de** + infinitive/noun	to remember doing/something
s'excuser de + infinitive	to apologize for doing	**venir de** + infinitive	to have just done something
féliciter de + infinitive	to congratulate for doing		

Nous refusons de partir. (*We're refusing to leave.*)

Il a oublié de se raser. (*He forgot to shave.*)

Je viens de manger. (*I just ate.*)

Your boss's computer is at it again! All the prepositions dropped out. Fill in the blanks with the correct preposition, either **à** or **de**.

Q. Je vous demande _____ m'excuser.

A. Je vous demande **de** m'excuser. (*I ask you to excuse me/Please excuse me.*)

🖼 New Message

| File | Edit | View | Insert | Format | Tools | Message | Help |

✉ Send   ✂ Cut   📄 Copy   📋 Paste   ↩ Undo   **abc✔** Check

From: Marc Laullete
To: Elisabeth Bleu
Cc:
Subject:

Mon ordinateur refuse (31) _____ marcher correctement.
Il persiste (32) _____ effacer les prépositions. Je
viens (33) _____ commander un nouvel ordinateur. En
attendant, je vais emprunter un portable (34)_____
quelqu'un. Veuillez téléphoner (35)_____ notre service
de soutien technique.

Verbs with other prepositions

Though **à** and **de** are the most common prepositions after verbs, other French prepositions are also required with certain verbs. Just conjugate them, add the preposition, and go! See Table 12-5.

Table 12-5	Verbs That Need Other Prepositions		
Verb	*Translation*	*Verb*	*Translation*
Verbs with *contre*			
s'asseoir contre + person	*to sit next to someone*	**échanger** (noun) **contre** (noun)	*to exchange something for something else*
se battre contre + noun/person	*to fight against something/someone*	**se fâcher contre** + person	*to get mad at someone*
Verbs with dans			
boire quelque chose dans + noun	*to drink something out of something*	**lire dans** + noun	*to read in (a publication)*
courir dans + noun	*to run through something*	**manger dans** + noun	*to eat out/off of*
coûter dans + amount	*to cost about*	**prendre quelque chose dans** + noun	*to take something from something*
entrer dans + noun	*to enter something*	**regarder dans** + noun	*to look in something*
fouiller dans + noun	*to look through something*	**vivre dans** + noun	*to live in something*
Verbs with en			
agir en + noun	*to act like something*	**écrire en** + language	*to write in a language*
casser en + noun/ number	*to break in(to) something or a certain number of pieces*	**transformer** (noun) **en** + noun	*to change something into something else*
se changer en + noun	*to change/turn into something*	**se vendre en** + noun	*to be sold in/by (bottle, kilo)*
couper en + number	*to cut in some number of pieces*	**voyager en** + noun	*to travel by (train, car)*
croire en + noun	*to believe in something*		
Verbs with *par*			
commencer par + infinitive	*to begin by doing*	**jurer par** + noun	*to swear by something*
finir par + infinitive	*to end up doing / to finally do something*	**obtenir quelque chose par** + infinitive	*to obtain something by doing*

(continued)

Table 12-5 *(continued)*

Verb	Translation	Verb	Translation
sortir par + noun	*to leave by way of something*		
*Verbs with **pour***			
creuser pour + noun	*to dig for something*	**payer pour** + person	*to pay for someone*
être pour + noun	*to be in favor of*	**signer pour** + person	*to sign on behalf of someone*
parler pour + person	*to speak on behalf of*		
*Verbs with **sur***			
acheter (noun) **sur le marché**	*to buy (something) at the market*	**s'étendre sur** + noun	*to spread out over something*
appuyer sur + noun	*to press something*	**interroger** (someone) **sur** + noun	*to question someone about something*
arriver sur + time	*to arrive around*	**se jeter sur** + person	*to throw oneself upon someone*
compter sur + noun/person	*to count on something/someone*	**prendre modèle sur** + person	*to model oneself on someone*
concentrer sur + noun	*to concentrate on something*	**réfléchir sur** + noun	*to study, to examine something*
copier sur + person	*to copy from someone*	**revenir sur** + noun	*to go back over something*
s'endormir sur + noun	*to fall asleep over something*		
*Verbs with **vers***			
se diriger vers + noun	*to move toward/ make/head for something*	**tourner vers** + noun	*to turn toward something*
regarder vers + noun	*to face/look toward something*		

Verbs with different prepositions

Although most verbs always require one specific preposition, a few have different meanings according to which preposition you use. See Table 12-6 for some examples. Just conjugate these verbs and follow with the appropriate preposition. No simple shortcut exists to know which verb uses which preposition, but you'll have an easier time remembering them if you make your vocabulary lists with the prepositions each verb needs and the different translations.

Table 12-6	Verbs with Different Prepositions		
Verb + à	*Translation*	*Verb + Another Preposition*	*Translation*
aller à	*to go to*	**aller vers**	*to go toward, in the direction of*
donner à	*to give to*	**donner contre**	*to trade for, exchange*
être à	*to be at, to belong to*	**être vers**	*to be near, around*
jouer à	*to play a game or sport*	**jouer de**	*to play an instrument*
manquer à	*to miss someone*	**manquer de**	*to fail to do something, to lack*
parler à	*to talk to*	**parler de**	*to talk about*
penser à	*to think about, reflect upon*	**penser de**	*to have an opinion on*
profiter à	*to benefit, be profitable to*	**profiter de**	*to make the most of*
téléphoner à	*to call someone*	**téléphoner pour**	*to phone about/ regarding something*
tenir à	*to insist on*	**tenir de**	*to resemble*

> **Je parle à mon frère.** (*I'm talking to my brother.*)
>
> **Nous parlons de la France.** (*We're talking about France.*)
>
> **Il va à Paris.** (*He's going to Paris.*)
>
> **Elle va vers le musée.** (*She's going toward the museum.*)

You can translate both **penser à** and **penser de** as *to think about,* but there's a big difference. **Penser à** means *to have in mind, to consider,* and **penser de** means *to have an opinion on:*

> **Je pense à mes vacances.** (*I'm thinking about my vacation.*)
>
> **Que penses-tu de cette idée ?** (*What do you think about this idea?*)

A few French verbs can be used with two different prepositions with no difference in meaning:

- **commencer à, commencer de** + infinitive (*to begin doing*)
- **continuer à, continuer de** + infinitive (*to continue doing*)
- **rêver à, rêver de** + noun or infinitive (*to dream of/about [doing] something*)
- **traduire en, traduire vers le** + language (*to translate into a language*)

Verbs with no preposition

Some French verbs are followed directly by the infinitive or direct object, even though their English equivalents need a preposition. For example, **attendre** means *to wait for* + noun, not *to wait.* To remember these verbs (see Table 12-7), be sure to include the English preposition and whether it's followed by a noun or verb in your vocabulary list.

Table 12-7	Verbs with Prepositions in English but Not in French		
Verb	**Translation**	**Verb**	**Translation**
aller + infinitive	to be going to do something	**être censé** + infinitive	to be supposed to do something
approuver + noun	to approve of something	**habiter** + noun	to live in some place
attendre + noun	to wait for something	**ignorer** + noun	to be unaware of something
chercher + noun	to look for something	**mettre** + noun	to put something on
demander + noun	to ask for something	**payer** + noun	to pay for something
devoir + infinitive	to have to, be obliged to do something	**pouvoir** + infinitive	to be able to
écouter + noun	to listen to something	**regarder** + noun	to look at something
envoyer chercher + noun	to send for something	**sentir** + noun	to smell of something
essayer + noun	to try something on	**soigner** + person	to take care of someone

Je cherche mon sac à dos. (*I'm looking for my backpack.*)

Il ignore mon dilemme. (*He is unaware of my dilemma.*)

Tu es censé travailler aujourd'hui. (*You're supposed to work today.*)

Translate these sentences into French.

Q. I'm listening to the radio.

A. **J'écoute la radio.**

36. He's going to visit Versailles.

_____

37. Did you pay for the work?

_____

38. I want to try on this dress.

_____

39. She's looking at some paintings.

_____

40. They're looking for an apartment.

_____

Answer Key

1 Partons **à** midi.

2 Ils sont **de** Rabat.

3 Il va **à** la banque.

4 La voiture **de** Dominique est **à** la plage.

5 Elle veut aller **au** musée.

6 Je n'aime pas le chat **de** mes amis.

7 Nous avons acheté un livre **d'**histoire.

8 J'utilise l'ordinateur **de** mon collègue.

9 Vas-tu/Allez-vous **aux** boîtes avec Timothy?

10 Elle est arrivée **de** Montréal.

11 C'est **dans** un carton.

12 Le chien est **sur** la table.

13 Je pars **avec** ou **sans** toi/vous.

14 Es-tu/Êtes-vous **pour** ou **contre** cette solution ?

15 Tu peux/Vous pouvez manger **avant** ou **après** la fête.

New Message

File   Edit   View   Insert   Format   Tools   Message   Help

Send   Cut   Copy   Paste   Undo   abc✔ Check

From: Françoise Dupré

To: Juliette LaCroix

Cc:

Subject:

M. Boumani arrivera (16) **de** Tanger (17) à 13h00. Il préfère boire son café dans une tasse (18) **à** thé. Sa collègue, Mme Labiya, a besoin d'un verre (19) **d'**eau dans un verre (20) **à** vin. Mlle Leblanc, venant (21) **de** Genève, peut manger tous les hors-d'œuvre (22) **en** cinq minutes, donc elle ne devrait pas être assise à côté du buffet. Les trois employés (23) **de** Paris, qui sont déjà venus ici (24) **en** mai, n'ont pas de besoins particuliers. Venez à mon bureau (25) **dans** une heure et je vous donnerai les autres détails.

(Mr. Boumani will arrive from Tangiers at 1 p.m. He prefers to drink his coffee from a teacup. His colleague, Mrs. Labiya, needs a glass of water in a wine glass. Miss Leblanc, coming from Geneva, can eat all the hors díoeuvres in five minutes, so she should not be seated next to the buffet. The three employees from Paris, who already came here in May, don't have any special needs. Come to my office in an hour and I'll give you the other details.)

26   Il va **en** Australie. (*He's going to Australia.*)

27   Nous voyageons **au** Canada. (*We're traveling in Canada.*)

28   Elle vient **d'**Italie. (*She's coming from Italy.*)

29   Ils arrivent **du** Mali. (*They're arriving from Mali.*)

30   Je vais **à** Londres. (*I'm going to London.*)

✉ New Message

| File | Edit | View | Insert | Format | Tools | Message | Help |

Send   Cut   Copy   Paste   Undo   **abc✔** Check

From: Marc Laullete

To: Elisabeth Bleu

Cc:

Subject:

Mon ordinateur refuse (31) **de** marcher correctement. Il persiste (32) **à** effacer les prépositions. Je viens (33) **de** commander un nouvel ordinateur. En attendant, je vais emprunter un portable (34) **à** quelqu'un. Veuillez téléphoner (35) **à** notre service de soutien technique.

(My computer refuses to work correctly. It keeps erasing the prepositions. I just ordered a new computer. In the meantime, I'm going to borrow a laptop from someone. Please call our technical support team.)

---

36   **Il va visiter Versailles.**

37   **As-tu/Avez-vous payé le travail ?**

38   **Je veux essayer cette robe.**

39   **Elle regarde des peintures.**

40   **Ils cherchent un appartement.**

Chapter 13

Getting a Hold on Pronouns

*O*bject and adverbial pronouns are little words that provide a lot of information. Direct and indirect objects tell you *who* or *what* is being looked at, spoken to, or otherwise acted upon, such as in *I gave Tim the book* (*book* is the direct object and *Tim* is the indirect object); *object pronouns* replace them to keep you from repeating the same words over and over (and over and over), as in *I gave him it* (*it* and *him* are object pronouns). Similarly, adverbial pronouns replace certain phrases to give you the same amount of information in less space. For instance, in *We went to France and lived there for two months,* the word *there* would be translated as the adverbial pronoun **y** in French.

To use object and adverbial pronouns effectively, you have to understand what they mean and where they go in the sentence, as well as what order they go in when you use two at once. This chapter explains direct object, indirect object, and adverbial pronouns, as well as the correct order for two pronouns working together.

Using Object Pronouns

Just as pronouns replace nouns, *object pronouns* replace objects. In a rare case of linguistic logic, direct-object pronouns replace direct objects, and indirect-object pronouns replace indirect objects. Despite the objectified nature of the word, *objects* aren't always just things like books and trees — they can, and often do, refer to people and animals. If you don't know your French object pronouns, you may end up saying something like "I ate you" instead of "I ate it"!

This section spells out how to use direct-object and indirect-object pronouns so everyone clearly knows what you're writing or talking about.

Presenting direct-object pronouns

A *direct object* is a person or thing that a verb is acting on. When not in the form of a pronoun, the direct object usually comes after the verb in both French and English, and you can tell it's a direct object because there's no preposition in front of it.

To use a direct-object pronoun, you first need to be able to identify the object. To figure out the direct object, you can ask the question, "Who or what is + [whatever the verb is]?" For example, in the sentence, **Lise connaît les athlètes** (*Lise knows the athletes*), *Lise* is the subject of the sentence — she's the person who knows. To find the direct object, you'd ask, "Who is known?" **Athlètes** is the object — the people she knows. Or in this sentence, **Mon frère déteste la glace** (*My brother hates ice cream*), **mon frère** is the subject — the person who hates. Ask, "What does he hate?" **La glace** is the object — the thing that he hates. Asking "who or what is . . ." with these two examples, you discover the direct objects: Who is known? The athletes. What is hated? Ice cream. (And who is clearly insane? The brother who hates ice cream.)

Just as you can replace the subjects **Lise** and **mon frère** with subject pronouns (see Chapter 4), you can replace the direct objects **les athlètes** and **la glace** with direct-object pronouns. However, French direct-object pronouns precede the verb, while English direct-object pronouns follow it. When you choose a direct-object pronoun, you have to consider the gender and number of the object you're replacing, as well as the grammatical person, because there are different forms for each of these.

See Table 13-1 for the French direct-object pronouns.

Table 13-1	Direct-Object Pronouns	
Subject Pronoun	*Direct-Object Pronoun*	*Translation*
je	me (m', moi)	*me*
tu	te (t', toi)	*you*
il	le (l')	*him, it*
elle	la (l')	*her, it*
nous	nous	*us*
vous	vous	*you*
ils, elles	les	*them*

Lise les connaît. (*Lise knows them.*)

Mon frère la déteste. (*My brother hates it.*)

Je vous écoute. (*I'm listening to you.*)

When there are two verbs in French, the pronoun precedes the second one, such as with **Je dois le faire** (*I have to do it*). In the **passé composé** and other compound tenses (see Chapter 15), the direct-object pronoun precedes the auxiliary verb, as with **Je l'ai fait** (*I did it.*).

Transitive verbs are verbs that need direct objects, verbs such as *to like* and *to watch*. You can't say *I like* without a direct object — the sentence isn't complete. You have to say *I like you, I like chocolate, I like polka-dot slippers.* Verbs that don't need direct objects, such as *to walk* and *to travel,* are *intransitive* verbs. Of course, some verbs, like *to read,* can be both transitive and intransitive: *I read the newspaper* (transitive) versus *I read every day* (intransitive). Knowing the difference between transitive and intransitive helps you choose the right translation when you look up verbs in a dictionary (see Chapter 1).

Some verbs that have direct objects in French have an object of the preposition in English, and some English verbs that have direct objects have indirect objects in French. You don't use a preposition after **écouter,** for example, so the person or thing being listened to is a direct object in French. But in English, you say *listen to,* which means the person or thing being listened to isn't a direct object. See Chapter 12 for more information about verbs with prepositions.

Me, te, le, and **la** contract to **m', t',** and **l'** whenever they precede a vowel, a mute *h,* or the adverbial pronoun **y.**

In the affirmative imperative (see Chapter 10), the word order is different: Like reflexive pronouns, direct-object pronouns follow the verb and are attached to it with hyphens; in addition, **me** changes to **moi** and **te** changes to **toi:**

> **Trouvez-le.** (*Find it.*)
>
> **Écoute-moi !** (*Listen to me!*)

Rewrite sentences 1–5, replacing the underlined phrase with a direct-object pronoun. Then translate sentences 6–10 into French.

Q. Je vois <u>mon frère</u>.

A. Je **le** vois. (*I see him.*)

1. Il cherche <u>ses clés</u>.

_____

2. Nous avons <u>la voiture</u>.

_____

3. Avez-vous <u>l'heure</u> ?

_____

4. J'ai fini <u>notre itinéraire</u>.

_____

5. Qui connaît <u>Anne</u> ?

_____

6. I can see you guys.

_____

7. My friends don't understand me.

_____

8. Look at me.

_____

9. Are they listening to us?

_____

10. I love you.

_____

Giving you indirect-object pronouns

Indirect objects are the people that a verb is happening to or for. Indirect objects usually follow a preposition, such as **à** (_to_) or **pour** (_for_). (See Chapter 12 to read more about prepositions.)

Before you can correctly use an indirect-object pronoun, you first need to have a firm grasp of what an indirect-object pronoun is. To figure out the French indirect object, you can ask, "To whom?" or "For whom?" In this example, **Elle parle à ses amis** (_She's talking to her friends_), **elle** is the subject of the sentence — she's the person who's talking. **Ses amis** is the indirect object — the people she's talking to. In this example, **J'achète des livres pour ma nièce** (_I'm buying some books for my niece/I'm buying my niece some books_), **je** is the subject — the person who's buying. **Ma nièce** is the indirect object — the person I'm buying books for. Ask your questions to find the indirect object: To whom is she talking? Her friends. For whom am I buying books? My niece.

In English, the indirect object always follows the verb. In the sentence _I gave him the money, him_ is the indirect object, but in _I gave the money to John, John_ is the object of the preposition _to_. In French, both of these sentences have an indirect object: **Je lui ai donné l'argent** (**lui** is the indirect object) and **J'ai donné l'argent à John** (_John_ is the indirect object). In French, an indirect object is any noun or pronoun that tells you _to/for whom/what_ something is happening, whether it's preceded by a preposition or not.

Most of the French indirect-object pronouns are the same as the direct ones — only the third-person singular and plural change. To use an indirect-object pronoun correctly, you need to figure out the gender, number, and grammatical person of the object you want to replace, and then choose the corresponding indirect-object pronoun.

The word order for indirect-object pronouns is exactly the same as for direct-object pronouns:

✔ Object pronouns go in front of the verb.

✔ When there are two verbs, the pronouns go in front of the second verb.

✔ In the **passé composé,** they go in front of the auxiliary verb.

✔ In the affirmative imperative, they go after the verb, joined by a hyphen.

See Table 13-2 for the French indirect-object pronouns.

Table 13-2	Indirect-Object Pronouns	
Subject Pronoun	*Indirect-Object Pronoun*	*Translation*
je	me (m', moi)	*me*
tu	te (t', toi)	*you*
il, elle	lui	*him, her*
nous	nous	*us*
vous	vous	*you*
ils, elles	leur	*them*

Note that the third-person plural indirect object is **leur,** not to be confused with the possessive adjective **leur/leurs** (see Chapter 2).

> **Elle leur parle.** (*She's talking to them.*)

> **Je lui achète des livres.** (*I'm buying her some books.*)

Lui is the indirect-object pronoun for both men and women:

> **Il téléphone à David.** → **Il lui téléphone.** (*He's calling David.* → *He's calling him.*)

> **Je parle à ma mère.** → **Je lui parle.** (*I'm talking to my mother.* → *I'm talking to her.*)

Rewrite sentences 11–15, replacing the underlined phrase with an indirect-object pronoun. Then translate sentences 16–20 into French.

Q. Je parle <u>à mes parents</u>.

A. Je **leur** parle. (*I'm talking to them.*)

11. Il téléphone <u>à Pierre</u>.

_____

12. Nous demandons de l'argent <u>à notre entraîneur</u>.

_____

13. Vas-tu acheter cette bicyclette <u>pour moi</u> ?

_____

14. Faites attention <u>à vos collègues</u>.

_____

15. J'ai emprunté un stylo <u>à Sylvie</u>.

_____

16. He told me to leave.

_____

17. That pleases us.

_____

18. They stole some money from us.

_____

19. She didn't shake my hand.

_____

20. I'm asking you guys to help.

_____

Understanding Adverbial Pronouns

Adverbial pronouns are similar to indirect-object pronouns in that they replace a preposition + noun. However, the nouns that adverbial pronouns replace aren't indirect objects — they're _prepositional phrases_. (For example, in English, _to the movies_ is a prepositional phrase.) Prepositional phrases provide additional information about the verb, but they're not acted upon by the verb like indirect objects are. This section gives you the lowdown on the different adverbial pronouns and how to use them correctly.

Getting there with the adverbial pronoun y

You can use the adverbial pronoun **y** to replace the prepositions **à, chez, dans,** or **en** + [a place] to mean _there_. The adverbial pronoun **y** goes in exactly the same place as direct- and indirect-object pronouns:

> **Je vais à la plage. → J'y vais.** (_I'm going to the beach. → I'm going there._)

> **Elle a passé deux jours en France. → Elle y a passé deux jours.** (_She spent two days in France. → She spent two days there._)

You can also use **y** to replace **à** + [a thing] with verbs that require the preposition **à.** Earlier in this chapter, I explain that you can replace **à** + [a noun] with an indirect-object pronoun, so what's the difference? The indirect object tells you *whom* something is being done to or for, but **y** tells you *what* something is being done to. In French, indirect-object pronouns can replace only people; you have to replace places and things with the adverbial pronoun **y.** (See Chapter 12 to read about verbs that need a preposition.)

> **Je pense à l'amour. → J'y pense.** (*I'm thinking about love. → I'm thinking about it.*)

> **Nous obéissons aux lois. → Nous y obéissons.** (*We obey the laws. → We obey them.*)

But . . .

> **Je pense à mon ami. → Je pense à lui.** (*I'm thinking about my friend. → I'm thinking about him.*)

> **Nous obéissons à nos parents. → Nous leur obéissons.** (*We obey our parents. → We obey them.*)

Just as transitive verbs need a direct object to be complete, French verbs that need the preposition **à,** such as **aller** (*to go*), need either **à** + [a noun] or the adverbial pronoun **y** to be complete. In English, you can simply say, "I'm going," but in French, you can't — you either have to say where you're going, as in **Je vais chez moi,** or you have to use **y: J'y vais.**

Rewrite sentences 21–25, replacing the underlined phrase with **y.** Then translate sentences 26–30 into French.

Q. Nous allons <u>à Montréal</u>.

A. **Nous y allons.** (*We're going [there].*)

21. Il travaille <u>dans la bibliothèque</u>.

_____

22. Je réfléchis <u>à ma vie</u>.

_____

23. Vas-tu voyager <u>en Europe</u> tout seul ?

_____

24. Je suis <u>à la banque</u>.

_____

25. Je ne suis jamais allé <u>aux îles Caraïbes</u>.

_____

26. Did you guys attend it?

_____

27. He entered it.

_____

28. They'll answer it.

_____

29. We're thinking about them (the books).

_____

30. I'm going now.

_____

Adverbial grammar: Picking up more of it with the pronoun en

The adverbial pronoun **en** usually translates to _some_ or _of it/them_. To use the adverbial pronoun **en,** you replace one or more words with **en.** The word order for **en** is the same as for object pronouns and the adverbial pronoun **y** (see "Presenting direct-object pronouns" for details). Remember that **en** is also a preposition — see Chapter 12.

You can use **en** to replace

- **De** + noun
- Partitive article **du, de la,** or **des** + noun
- A noun after a number
- A noun after an adverb of quantity
- A noun after an indefinite or negative adjective

En replaces de + noun

With the preposition **de** and the partitive article (**du, de la, de l',** or **des**), **en** replaces the article as well as the noun following it:

> **Nous parlons d'amour.** → **Nous en parlons.** (_We're talking about love._ → _We're talking about it._)

> **Je veux des fraises.** → **J'en veux.** (_I want some strawberries._ → _I want some [of them]._)

In English, _of them_ or _of it_ is usually optional — as long as everyone knows you're talking about strawberries, you can just say, "I want some." In French, however, **Je veux** is incomplete — if you don't include **des fraises,** you have to replace it with **en.**

En with numbers

When you use **en** with a number, it replaces only the noun — you still need to put the number after the verb:

> **Il a trois voitures.** → **Il en a trois.** (*He has three cars.* → *He has three [of them].*)

> **J'ai acheté une douzaine de livres.** → **J'en ai acheté une douzaine.** (*I bought a dozen books.* → *I bought a dozen [of them].*)

En with adverbs of quantity

With adverbs of quantity, **en** replaces **de** and the noun, but you still need the adverb, so you tack it on the end (see Chapter 9 for more info on adverbs):

> **Avez-vous beaucoup de temps ?** → **En avez-vous beaucoup ?** (*Do you have a lot of time?* → *Do you have a lot [of it]?*)

> **Je mange très peu d'avocats.** → **J'en mange très peu.** (*I eat very few avocados.* → *I eat very few [of them].*)

En with indefinite and negative adjectives

You can also use **en** with indefinite and negative adjectives. Indefinite adjectives express an unspecific quantity, such as **quelques** (*some*) and **plusieurs** (*several*). Negative adjectives negate a noun — they're terms like **ne . . . aucun** (*not any*) and **ne . . . nul** (*none*). As with adverbs of quantity, you replace the noun with **en** and tack the indefinite adjective or the second part of the negative adjective on the end of the sentence. When you do this, the adjective becomes a pronoun, but because indefinite and negative adjectives and pronouns are identical, you don't need to change anything.

> **J'ai d'autres idées.** → **J'en ai d'autres.** (*I have other ideas.* → *I have others.*)

> **Il cherche plusieurs amis.** → **Il en cherche plusieurs, mais il n'en a trouvé aucun.** (*He's looking for several friends.* → *He's looking for several [of them], but he hasn't found any [of them].*)

PRACTICE

Rewrite these sentences, replacing all or part of the underlined phrase with **en.**

0. Je veux <u>de la salade</u>.

A. **J'en veux.** (*I want some.*)

31. Nous connaissons <u>beaucoup d'artistes</u>.

_____

32. Elle a <u>plusieurs idées</u>.

_____

33. J'ai besoin de <u>six chaises</u>.

_____

34. Avez-vous <u>un stylo</u> ?

_____

35. Il a bu <u>du thé</u>.

_____

36. Que penses-tu <u>du résultat</u> ?

_____

37. Je <u>n'</u>ai <u>aucun doute</u>.

_____

38. Elle connaît <u>quatre mécaniciens</u>.

_____

39. Nous cherchons <u>des chaussures</u>.

_____

40. <u>N'</u>as-tu <u>nulle foi</u> ?

_____

Positioning Double Pronouns

In English, you can't say, "I bought for him it" — you have to say, "I bought it for him." This word order is nonnegotiable. The same is true in French: Pronouns have to go in a certain order.

Object pronouns and adverbial pronouns, as well as reflexive pronouns (see Chapter 11), all go in the same place: in front of the verb — except in the affirmative imperative. But something else happens when you have two of these pronouns in the same sentence. They both go in front of the verb, but in which order? This section clarifies the order.

Lining up: Standard pronoun order

Using any two object, adverbial, or reflexive pronouns together requires a very specific word order, but before I tell you, check out Table 13-3 for the personal pronouns.

Table 13-3		Object and Reflexive Pronouns	
Subject Pronoun	*Reflexive Pronoun*	*Direct-Object Pronoun*	*Indirect-Object Pronoun*
je	me	me	me
tu	te	te	te
il	se	le	lui
elle	se	la	lui
nous	nous	nous	nous
vous	vous	vous	vous
ils, elles	se	les	leur

Here's the order:

1. **Me, te, se, nous,** or **vous** always comes first.

2. **Le, la,** or **les** comes second.

3. **Lui** or **leur** is next.

4. **Y** comes later.

5. **En** is last.

Of course, you can't have five pronouns in the same sentence — two is the maximum. Check out the following examples of correctly placed pronouns:

Il m'a donné le livre. → **Il me l'a donné.** (*He gave me the book.* → *He gave it to me.*)

Elle nous en parle. (*She's talking to us about it.*)

Je vais le lui montrer. (*I'm going to show it to him.*)

Il y en a trois. (*There are three [of them].*)

Me, te, nous, and **vous** are identical as direct, indirect, and reflexive pronouns, and they all come first when you have double pronouns. If you do have a sentence with more than two things that could potentially be replaced with object or adverbial pronouns, you can just pick two to replace and leave the other as is:

J'ai acheté des vêtements pour moi-même en France. → **Je m'y suis acheté des vêtements** or **Je m'en suis acheté en France** (*I bought some clothes for myself in France.* → *I bought myself some clothes there* or *I bought myself some in France.*)

Using pronouns in commands

You use that set word order for all verb tenses, moods, and constructions except the affirmative imperative (see Chapter 10 for more on commands). In the affirmative imperative, the pronouns follow the verb and are joined to it with hyphens; here's the slightly different double-pronoun order that applies:

1. **Le, la,** or **les** comes first.

2. **Moi, toi, lui, nous, vous,** or **leur** is next.

3. **Y** comes later.

4. **En** is last.

Remember that the pronouns **me** and **te** change to **moi** and **toi** in affirmative commands (see Chapter 10). The important change is that the direct objects **le, la,** and **les** now come first instead of second.

> **Donnez-nous-en.** (*Give us some.*)
>
> **Va-t'en !** (*Go away!*)
>
> **Montrez-le-moi.** (*Show it to me.*)

Answer these questions using double pronouns. You can answer however you like; I provide possible responses in the Answer Key so you can check your choice and placement of pronouns.

0. Combien d'amis as-tu en France?

A. **J'y en ai trois.** (*I have three there.*)

41. Vas-tu t'habituer à la pluie ?

_____

42. Peut-elle m'envoyer le paquet à mon bureau ?

_____

43. Quand vont-ils montrer le film aux enfants ?

_____

44. Pouvez-vous me donner les clés ?

_____

45. Veux-tu prendre un verre chez moi ?

_____

Answer Key

1 Il **les** cherche. (*He's looking for them.*)

2 Nous **l'**avons. (*We have it.*)

3 **L'**avez-vous ? (*Do you have it?*)

4 Je **l'**ai fini. (*I finished it.*)

5 Qui **la** connaît ? (*Who knows her?*)

6 Je peux **vous** voir.

7 Mes amis ne **me** comprennent pas.

8 Regarde-**moi**/Regardez-**moi.**

9 Est-ce qu'ils **nous** écoutent ?/**Nous** écoutent-ils ?

10 Je **t'**aime./Je **vous** aime.

11 Il **lui** téléphone. (*He's calling him.*)

12 Nous **lui** demandons de l'argent. (*We are asking him for some money.*)

13 Vas-tu **m'**acheter cette bicyclette ? (*Are you going to buy me this bike?*)

14 Faites-**leur** attention. (*Pay attention to them.*)

15 Je **lui** ai emprunté un stylo. (*I borrowed a pen from her.*)

16 **Il m'a dit de partir. Me** is the indirect object because in French you tell something to someone (**dire à quelqu'un**).

17 **Cela nous plaît. Plaire** requires the preposition **à** in front of the person who is pleased.

18 **Ils nous ont volé de l'argent. Voler** requires the preposition **à**: The construction is **voler quelque chose à quelqu'un.**

19 **Elle ne m'a pas serré la main.** The French expression is **serrer la main à quelqu'un,** which means **main** (*hand*) is the direct object and **me** (*of me*) is the indirect object.

20 **Je vous demande d'aider.** The French is **demander à quelqu'un de faire quelque chose,** so **vous** is an indirect object.

21 **Il y travaille.** (*He works there.*)

22 **J'y réfléchis.** (*I'm thinking about it.*)

23 **Vas-tu y voyager tout seul ?** (*Are you going to travel there all alone?*)

24 **J'y suis.** (*I'm there.*)

25 **Je n'y suis jamais allé.** (*I've never been there.*)

26 **Est-ce que vous y avez assisté ?/Y avez-vous assisté ?**

27 **Il y est entré.**

28 **Ils vont y répondre.**

29 **Nous y pensons.**

30 **J'y vais maintenant.**

31 **Nous en connaissons beaucoup.** (*We know a lot [of them].*)

32 **Elle en a plusieurs.** (*She has several [of them].*)

33 **J'en ai besoin de six.** (*I need six [of them].*)

34 **En avez-vous un ?** (*Do you have one?*)

35 **Il en a bu.** (*He drank some.*)

36 **Qu'en penses-tu ?** (*What do you think about it?*)

37 **Je n'en ai aucun.** (*I don't have any.*)

38 **Elle en connaît quatre.** (*She knows four [of them].*)

39 **Nous en cherchons.** (*We're looking for some.*)

40 **N'en as-tu nulle ?** (*Don't you have any?*)

41 **Oui, je vais m'y habituer.** or **Non, je ne vais pas m'y habituer.** (*Yes, I'm going to get used to it.* or *No, I'm not going to get used to it.*)

42 **Oui, elle peut t'y envoyer le paquet.** or **Oui, elle peut te l'envoyer à ton bureau.** or **Non, elle ne peut pas t'y envoyer le paquet.** or **Non, elle ne peut pas te l'envoyer à ton bureau.** (*Yes, she can send you the package there.* or *Yes, she can send it to you at your office.* or *No, she can't send you the package there.* or *No, she can't send it to you at your office.*)

43 **Ils vont le leur montrer demain.** (*They're going to show it to them tomorrow.*)

44 **Oui, je peux vous les donner.** or **Non, je ne peux pas vous les donner.** (*Yes, I can give them to you.* or *No, I can't give them to you.*)

45 **Oui, je veux y en prendre un.** or **Non, je ne veux pas y en prendre un.** (*Yes, I want to have one there.* or *No, I don't want to have one there.*)

Chapter 14

Grasping Conjunctions and Relative Pronouns

Conjunctions and relative pronouns help you join words and sentences. They can make your speech and writing much more elegant, so that instead of saying, "I like coffee. I like tea. I drink coffee in the morning. I drink tea at night," you can say, "I like coffee, which I drink in the morning, and tea, which I drink at night."

Conjunctions make some kind of a connection between two words, phrases, or clauses. When the words, phrases, or clauses are equal, you join them with coordinating conjunctions, as in "coffee or tea" or "funny stories and good food." When you have two clauses that aren't equal, you use subordinating conjunctions, as in "I think that you're right." *Relative pronouns* are like subordinating conjunctions in that they join two unequal clauses, but relative pronouns, like all pronouns, replace nouns, which means they can be subjects or objects in the joined clause. This chapter discusses the most common conjunctions and relative pronouns and how to use them effectively.

Joining with Conjunctions

Conjunctions are joining words, and the type of conjunction you use depends on equality. I'm not talking about equal rights for parts of speech but rather an equality of purpose for the words you're joining. If you have a verb with two direct objects, or a noun with two adjectives, or even an adjective describing two nouns, those "twos" are equal because they're modifying or being modified by the same word, so you connect them with a coordinating conjunction. If, on the other hand, you have one phrase that depends on another, those phrases aren't equal, so you need a subordinating conjunction. This section spells out the different ways to use coordinating and subordinating conjunctions.

Coordinating conjunctions

Coordinating conjunctions join two words, phrases, or clauses that are equal — they're the same part of speech and are modifying the same thing, or they're two similarly constructed and equally important words, phrases, or clauses. To correctly use a coordinating conjunction, just place it between the words you want to join. The items linked by coordinating conjunctions can usually be reversed with little or no difference in meaning.

> **Nous aimons bien la plage et les montagnes.** (*We love the beach and the mountains.*)

In this example, the coordinating conjunction **et** (*and*) joins two nouns, **la plage** and **les montagnes.** The nouns are equal because they serve the same purpose in the sentence — they're both direct objects of the verb **aimer.** We love the beach, and we love the mountains. And they can be reversed. There's no difference between *We love the beach and mountains* and *We love the mountains and the beach.*

> **Je veux une robe bleue ou verte.** (*I want a blue or green dress.*)

Here, the coordinating conjunction **ou** (*or*) joins two adjectives, **bleue** and **verte,** which are both modifying **robe.** Both colors are equally important — I want a blue dress or I want a green dress; it doesn't matter which.

> **J'ai acheté une ceinture noire et grise.** (*I bought a black and gray belt.*)

This time, **et** is joining two adjectives, **noire** and **grise,** both of which are modifying **ceinture.** The belt is both black and gray; neither color matters more or less than the other.

> **Le chat a miaulé, et puis le chien a aboyé.** (*The cat meowed, and then the dog barked.*)

In this case, the coordinating conjunction **et puis** is joining two clauses. The cat meowed, the dog barked — both of these can stand alone as complete sentences, and neither one is modifying the other, so they, too, are equal.

See Table 14-1 for a list of the most common French coordinating conjunctions.

Table 14-1	Coordinating Conjunctions
French Conjunction	*Translation*
donc	*so*
et	*and*
et . . . et	*both . . . and*
et/ou	*and/or*
et puis	*and then*
mais	*but*
ne . . . ni . . . ni	*neither . . . nor*
ou	*or*
ou bien	*or else*
ou . . . ou	*either . . . or*
soit . . . soit	*either . . . or*

You use the conjunctions **et . . . et, ou . . . ou, ne . . . ni . . . ni,** and **soit . . . soit** when you want to emphasize the relationship between the joined items, as in the following three examples:

> **Il veut et un vélo et une mobylette.** (*He wants both a bike and a moped.*)

This stresses the fact that he wants not just one or the other but both.

> **Je peux voyager ou en France ou en Suisse./Je peux voyager soit en France soit en Suisse.** (*I can travel either to France or to Switzerland.*)

With **ou . . . ou** and **soit . . . soit** rather than just **ou,** I'm emphasizing that I can't go to both places, only one or the other.

> **Elle ne peut ni lire ni écrire.** (*She can neither read nor write.*)

The negative conjunction **ne . . . ni . . . ni** stresses the negative aspect of both verbs — she can't read, nor can she write.

Translate these sentences into French, using coordinating conjunctions.

Q. I like to sing and dance.

A. **J'aime chanter et danser.**

1. You can use a pen or pencil.

_____

2. Do they want cream and/or sugar?

_____

3. I have to work, then we can go out.

_____

4. She is either brave or crazy.

_____

5. Are you going to help us, or [else] are you going to leave?

_____

6. We saw both Hélène and Marie.

_____

7. Did you find my keys or my wallet?

_____

8. I'd like to go, but I need to wait for Paul.

_____

9. It was either him or me.

_____

10. I've visited neither the Eiffel Tower nor the Louvre.

_____

Subordinating conjunctions

You use subordinating conjunctions to combine two *clauses,* or parts of a sentence that have both a noun and a verb. The conjunction tells you that the clause after it is *subordinate,* meaning that it's dependent on the *main clause;* the subordinate clause can't stand alone. To correctly use a subordinating conjunction, you have to determine which clause is the main clause and which is the subordinate clause. Then put the subordinating conjunction at the beginning of the subordinate clause and join the two clauses.

> **Je pense que tu peux le faire.** (*I think that you can do it.*)

> **Il veut que je travaille.** (*He wants me to work.*)

In the first example, **tu peux le faire** is the subordinate clause — the idea that you can do it is not a fact, the way it would be if the clause were a complete sentence. The subordinating conjunction **que** tells you that these words are dependent on the main clause **je pense.** Though I think you can do it, it's not a fact — in reality, you may or may not be able to. In the second example, **je travaille** is the subordinate clause — I may or may not work, because the subordinating conjunction **que** is explaining that he wants me to work, but that doesn't necessarily mean I am working or will work.

Que is the most common subordinating conjunction, and it's required in French. In English, you can often drop its equivalent *that:* **Je pense que tu as raison** (*I think [that] you're right*). In many constructions, it's more natural to reword the English with a direct object + infinitive: **Il veut que je travaille** becomes *He wants me to work,* rather than the literal translation *He wants that I work.*

See Table 14-2 for some other common subordinating conjunctions. ***Note:*** The starred conjunctions require the subjunctive (see Chapter 8) in the subordinate clause.

Table 14-2	Subordinating Conjunctions
Conjunction	*Translation*
afin que*	*so that*
ainsi que	*just as, so as*
alors que	*while, whereas*
à moins que*	*unless*
après que	*after, when*

Conjunction	Translation
avant que*	before
bien que*	although
de crainte/peur que*	for fear that
en attendant que*	while, until
jusqu'à ce que*	until
lorsque	when
parce que	because
pendant que	while
pour que*	so that
pourvu que*	provided that
puisque	since, as
quand	when
quoique*	even though
quoi que*	whatever, no matter what
sans que*	without
tandis que	while, whereas

> **Il est parti parce qu'il doit travailler.** (*He left because he has to work.*)

The important information in this sentence is in the main clause **il est parti.** Why did he leave? The subordinating conjunction **parce que** introduces the dependent clause to tell you that **il doit travailler.**

If you get confused between the conjunction **parce que** (*because*) and the expression **à cause de** (*because of, due to*), remember that **parce que** has to go in front of a clause: **J'ai froid parce qu'il neige.** (*I'm cold because it's snowing*). **À cause de** goes in front of a noun: **J'ai froid à cause de la neige.** (*I'm cold due to the snow.*)

> **Je ne lis pas quand j'ai sommeil.** (*I don't read when I'm sleepy.*)

The main clause is **je ne lis pas,** but it's not complete because I do read sometimes. I just don't read when, as the subordinating conjunction **quand** tells you, **j'ai sommeil.**

You can't reverse the clauses joined by subordinating conjunctions, because they either make no sense or the meaning changes. **Tu peux le faire que je pense** (*You can do it that I think*) is nonsense, and **J'ai sommeil quand je ne lis pas** (*I'm sleepy when I don't read*) changes the meaning entirely.

You dropped your notes for the presentation you worked on all week in a puddle, and all your conjunctions got smeared. Fill in the blanks with one of these conjunctions, using each one only once.

afin que	à moins que	après que	~~avant que~~	bien que	
de peur que	parce que	pendant que	pour que	quand	que

Q. _____ je commence mon exposé, avez-vous des questions ?

A. **Avant que** je commence mon exposé, avez-vous des questions ? (*Before I start my presentation, do you have any questions?*)

11. Je donne cet exposé avec PowerPoint _____ tout le monde puisse voir les chiffres.

12. Veuillez ne pas parler _____ j'explique chaque graphique.

13. Dans le premier trimestre, les consommateurs n'ont pas beaucoup acheté, _____ l'économie continue à baisser.

14. Au milieu du deuxième trimestre, _____ l'économie se stabilise normalement, les consommateurs ont continué d'être prudents.

15. À ce point-là, nous avons lancé notre nouvelle campagne publicitaire, _____ les ventes étaient toujours stagnantes.

16. Nous avons aussi changé l'emballage de notre produit _____ il soit plus attirant.

17. _____ nous avons analysé les résultats de ces initiatives, nous avons commencé à offrir un remboursement.

18. Nous en saurons plus _____ le rapport annuel sera publié.

19. Le directeur général pense _____ il va falloir réduire le prix de notre produit.

20. C'est tout, _____ vous ayez besoin d'autres informations.

Grasping Relative Pronouns

Relative pronouns and subordinating conjunctions are somewhat similar because they both link subordinate clauses to main clauses. The difference is that although subordinating conjunctions don't have an antecedent, relative pronouns do. An *antecedent* is a word, phrase, or idea that a pronoun replaces and refers back to. An example of a relative pronoun in English is *who*, as in *I'm not who you think I am*. This section squares away relative pronouns and explains how to correctly use them in your writing and speech.

Sizing up relative pronouns

Relative pronouns join two clauses and become the subject or object of the clause they begin. When you join *I know someone* and *He lives in Tunisia,* you use the relative pronoun *who* to replace the subject of the second sentence: *I know someone who lives in Tunisia.* French is very similar: **Je connais quelqu'un. Il habite en Tunisie** becomes **Je connais quelqu'un qui habite en Tunisie.** Because the relative pronoun replaces the subject of the second sentence, it's the subject of the second clause.

French has five relative pronouns:

- ✔ **qui**
- ✔ **que**
- ✔ **lequel**
- ✔ **dont**
- ✔ **où**

I don't include translations for them here because the definitions depend on context and on how you use them in your sentences. (Note that **qui, que**, and **lequel** are also interrogative pronouns, which you can read about in Chapter 5.) The following sections give you some more direction and help you figure out when you need to use these pronouns.

Using qui

Qui is the relative pronoun that you use to replace the *subject* of a subordinate clause when you join two sentences into one. **Qui** can replace any subject: masculine or feminine, singular or plural, human or inanimate. Qui loosely translates to *who* or *that*.

> **Nous connaissons un boulanger. Il fait du très bon pain. → Nous connaissons un boulanger qui fait du très bon pain.** (*We know a baker. He makes very good bread. → We know a baker who makes very good bread.*)

> **J'ai trouvé des livres. Ils sont très intéressants. → J'ai trouvé des livres qui sont très intéressants.** (*I found some books. They are very interesting. → I found some books that are very interesting.*)

You know that **qui** is the subject of the subordinate clause because it replaces the subject of the verb in the second clause. In the preceding examples, **qui** replaces **il,** the subject of **fait,** and **ils,** the subject of **sont.**

You also use **qui** to replace the indirect object or the *object* of a preposition (that is, the noun or pronoun after a preposition):

> **Voici l'ingénieur. Je travaille avec lui. → Voici l'ingénieur avec qui je travaille.** (*Here is the engineer. I work with him. → Here is the engineer [whom] I work with.*)

> **Connais-tu la fille ? Je lui ai parlé hier. → Connais-tu la fille à qui j'ai parlé hier?** (*Do you know the girl? I talked to her yesterday. → Do you know the girl [whom] I talked to yesterday?*)

You may find it helpful to follow the rule about not ending a sentence with a preposition in English to remember the French word order, as in *Here is the engineer with whom I work* and *Do you know the girl to whom I talked yesterday?* It's a bit stilted, but it's a good reminder of the fact that French word order is stricter; you literally can't end a sentence with a preposition.

In French, relative pronouns are required, but in English, they're sometimes optional, as in *the book that you wrote* or *the book you wrote;* both constructions are acceptable. But in French, you can't say **le livre tu as écrit** — you have to say **le livre que tu as écrit.**

You can use **qui** as an indirect object (*to/for* + someone/something) or object of a preposition only when it refers to a person. If it's a thing, use **lequel**. In addition, you can't use **qui** after the preposition **de** — you have to use **dont.** (You can read more about direct and indirect objects in Chapter 13.)

Using que

Que replaces the *direct object* of the subordinate clause. **Que** loosely translates to *whom, that,* or *which,* and it can replace any direct object: a person or thing of any gender or number. **Que** contracts to **qu'** in front of a vowel or mute *h.*

> **Je mange au restaurant. Mon frère l'a acheté. → Je mange au restaurant que mon frère a acheté.** (*I'm eating at the restaurant. My brother bought it. → I'm eating at the restaurant that my brother bought.*)

> **Nous cherchons la ville. Étienne la visite chaque été. → Nous cherchons la ville qu'Étienne visite chaque été.** (*We're looking for the town. Étienne visits it every summer. → We're looking for the town [that] Étienne visits every summer.*)

> **Je ne connais pas l'homme. Je l'ai vu hier. → Je ne connais pas l'homme que j'ai vu hier.** (*I don't know the man. I saw him yesterday. → I don't know the man [whom] I saw yesterday.*)

Que replaces the direct object in these sentences. You know it's the direct object because it answers the question "who or what is the verb acting on?" What did my brother buy? The restaurant. What are we looking for? The town. Whom did I see? The man.

Using lequel

Lequel is the pronoun you use when the indirect object or object of the preposition of the subordinate clause is not a person. (Remember that when the indirect object or object of the preposition is a person, you use **qui.**) **Lequel** loosely translates to *which.*

> **J'ai acheté un livre. Il y a un billet de loterie dans le livre. → J'ai acheté un livre dans lequel il y a un billet de loterie.** (*I bought a book. There's a lottery ticket in the book. → I bought a book in which there's a lottery ticket.*)

In this example, you replace **dans le livre** (*in the book*) with **dans lequel** (*in which*) and place this phrase at the beginning of the second clause.

> **Gérard travaille pour cette entreprise. Cette entreprise vend des appareils électroménagers. → L'entreprise pour laquelle Gérard travaille vend des appareils électroménagers.** (*Gérard works for this company. This company sells appliances. → The company [that] Gérard works for sells appliances.* or *The company for which Gérard works sells appliances.*)

Here, you replace **pour cette entreprise** (*for this company*) with **pour laquelle** (*for which*).

Unlike the other relative pronouns, **lequel** has different forms for masculine, feminine, singular, and plural. In addition, the masculine singular and both plural forms contract with the prepositions **à** and **de,** just like the definite articles **le** and **les** do (you can read about that in Chapter 12). Take a look at Table 14-3 for the different forms of **lequel.**

Table 14-3	Forms of Lequel		
Form	*No Preposition*	*à*	*de*
Masculine singular	**lequel**	**auquel**	**duquel**
Feminine singular	**laquelle**	**à laquelle**	**de laquelle**
Masculine plural	**lesquels**	**auxquels**	**desquels**
Feminine plural	**lesquelles**	**auxquelles**	**desquelles**

When you say *to think about* in the sense of *to have on one's mind,* you need the French verb **penser** followed by the preposition **à,** so you're going to use a form of **auquel:**

> **Les villes auxquelles je pense sont en Europe.** (*The towns I'm thinking about are in Europe.* or *The towns about which I'm thinking are in Europe.*)

You use **duquel** with prepositional phrases ending in **de.** For example, **à côté de** means *next to.*

> **Le musée à côté duquel il travaille est fermé.** (*The museum he works next to is closed.* or *The museum next to which he works is closed.*)

Using dont

Dont is the relative pronoun that replaces **de** + an object (person or thing). It loosely translates to *about, of whom,* or *what.*

> **Je parle d'un ami. Il habite en Tunisie. → L'ami dont je parle habite en Tunisie.** (*I'm talking about a friend. He lives in Tunisia. → The friend [whom] I'm talking about lives in Tunisia.* or *The friend about whom I'm talking lives in Tunisia.*)

> **Nous rêvons d'une plage. Le sable de cette plage est noir. → Nous rêvons d'une plage dont le sable est noir.** (*We're dreaming about a beach. This beach's sand is black. → We're dreaming about a beach whose sand is black.*)

If the preposition is just **de,** use **dont.** If the preposition is one or more words plus **de,** use the form of **duquel** that corresponds with the gender and number of the noun you're replacing: **à côté de** (*next to*) → **à côté duquel** (*next to which*).

Using où

You use the relative pronoun **où** to refer to a place or to a time. It loosely translates to *where* or *when.*

> **J'habite dans un village. Il est très touristique. → Le village où j'habite est très touristique.** (*I live in a village. It is very touristy. → The village where I live is very touristy.*)

> **C'était le moment où elle est tombée amoureuse de la France.** (*That was the moment when she fell in love with France.*)

Quand is the normal translation of *when* in questions and after verbs — for example, **Je ne sais pas quand il va arriver** (*I don't know when he's going to arrive*). But you can't use it as a relative pronoun to refer back to a time — you have to use **où.**

Fill in the blanks with the correct relative pronoun. When there's a preposition in front of the blank, consider whether it forms a contraction or needs to be replaced; if so, cross out the preposition and write in the correct relative pronoun.

0. La France est le pays à _____ je rêve.

A. La France est le pays à **auquel** je rêve. (*France is the country I dream about.*)

21. J'offre une récompense à la personne _____ trouve mon portefeuille.

22. Voici le restaurant de _____ il nous a parlé.

23. C'est exactement la robe _____ je cherche depuis deux mois !

24. La rue dans _____ il est tombé passe devant le théâtre.

25. C'était le jour _____ j'ai décidé de me divorcer.

26. L'ordinateur _____ nous venons d'acheter ne marche pas.

27. C'est la fille _____ a chanté à la fête.

28. L'hôtel _____ je suis resté la dernière fois est interdit aux chiens.

29. Le parking en face de _____ j'habite est très propre.

30. Les assistants de _____ nous avons besoin doivent travailler à plein temps.

Identifying indefinite relative pronouns

Unlike standard relative pronouns, indefinite relative pronouns don't have a specific antecedent — they refer back to something unknown. When you say, "What I like" or "That's what we think," *what* is an indefinite relative pronoun. It's a sort of dummy subject of the clause.

French has four indefinite relative pronouns:

- **ce qui** (*what*)
- **ce que** (*what*)
- **ce dont** (*about what*)
- **quoi** (*what*)

You see that the English translations for three of the French indefinite pronouns are identical. That's because in French, you need different pronouns depending on how you're using those words (as a subject, direct object, or object of a preposition), whereas in English, you just need *what*. If you're talking about a person, you don't use indefinite relative pronouns in French — you use the non-indefinite relative pronouns **qui** or **que,** as I explain in the preceding section.

Using ce qui

You use **ce qui** as the subject of a relative clause:

> **Ce qui me dérange le plus, c'est la malhonnêteté.** (*What bothers me the most is dishonesty.*)
>
> **C'est ce qui m'inquiète.** (*That's what worries me.*)
>
> **Vois-tu ce qui fait ce bruit ?** (*Do you see what's making that noise?*)

In these examples, you know **ce qui** is the subject because it tells you what is performing the action of the verb.

Note: **Ce qui** always takes the third-person singular (**il**) form of the verb.

Using ce que

Ce que serves as the indefinite direct object of a relative clause:

> **Ce que nous avons, c'est impossible à expliquer.** (*What we have is impossible to explain.*)
>
> **C'est ce que j'aimerais savoir.** (*That's what I'd like to know.*)
>
> **Savez-vous ce que Philippe a acheté ?** (*Do you know what Philippe bought?*)

The direct object is the answer to the question *who* or *what* + whatever the verb is. What is impossible to explain? What we have. What would I like to know? That.

Using ce dont

You use **ce dont** to replace the preposition **de** + its object:

> **Ce dont j'ai envie, c'est une nouvelle voiture.** (*What I want is a new car.*)
>
> **C'est ce dont il parlait.** (*That's what he was talking about.*)
>
> **Sais-tu ce dont elles rêvent ?** (*Do you know what they dream about?*)

Whenever you use a verb that requires **de** (see Chapter 12), the indefinite relative pronoun will be **ce dont. Avoir envie de** (*to want*), **parler de** (*to talk about*), and **rêver de** (*to dream about*) all require **de,** so when you use an indefinite relative pronoun with them, it has to be **ce dont.**

Using quoi

After any preposition except **de,** you use **quoi** in relative clauses:

> **Sur quoi pouvons-nous écrire ?** (*What can we write on?* or *On what can we write?*)
>
> **Je ne sais pas à quoi ils s'intéressent.** (*I don't know what they're interested in.*)

When you use **quoi** with **à** at the beginning of the clause or after the expression **c'est,** you need to add **ce** in front of the preposition.

> **Ce à quoi nous nous attendons, c'est une lettre d'excuses.** (*What we're expecting is a letter of apology.*)
>
> **C'est ce à quoi je m'intéresse.** (*That's what I'm interested in.*)

French verbs often require different prepositions than English verbs do, and it's the French preposition that tells you whether to use **ce dont** or **quoi.** If there's no French preposition, use **ce que** — even if English requires a preposition. Take a look at Chapter 12 to read about verbs with and without prepositions.

Translate these sentences into French, using indefinite relative pronouns.

Q. All I know is that he lied to us.

A. **Tout ce que je sais, c'est qu'il nous a menti.**

31. What will help me is a little support.

_____

32. That's what he's talking about.

_____

33. Do you know what we can sit on?

_____

34. What she wants is an apartment in France.

_____

35. That's what I dream about.

_____

36. All I need is a good job.

_____

37. That's what inspires us.

_____

38. I don't know what's happening.

_____

39. What you need to respond to is your family's appeal.

_____

40. That's what she's looking for.

_____

Answer Key

1 Tu peux/Vous pouvez utiliser un stylo ou un crayon.

2 Veulent-ils de la crème et/ou du sucre ?

3 Je dois travailler, ensuite nous pouvons sortir.

4 Elle est ou courageuse ou folle. / Elle est soit courageuse soit folle.

5 Vas-tu nous aider, ou bien vas-tu partir ? / Allez-vous nous aider, ou bien allez-vous partir ?

6 Nous avons vu et Hélène et Marie.

7 As-tu/Avez-vous trouvé mes clés ou mon portefeuille ?

8 J'aimerais y aller, mais je dois attendre Paul.

9 C'était soit lui soit moi. / C'était ou lui ou moi.

10 Je n'ai visité ni la tour Eiffel ni le Louvre.

11 Je donne cet exposé avec PowerPoint **pour que** tout le monde puisse voir les chiffres. (*I'm giving this presentation in PowerPoint so that everyone can see the figures.*)

12 Veuillez ne pas parler **pendant que** j'explique chaque graphique. (*Please don't speak while I explain each graphic.*)

13 Dans le premier trimestre, les consommateurs n'ont pas beaucoup acheté, **de peur que** l'économie continue à baisser. (*In the first quarter, consumers did not buy much, for fear that the economy would continue to slump.*)

14 Au milieu du deuxième trimestre, **bien que** l'économie se stabilise normalement, les consommateurs ont continué d'être prudents. (*In the middle of the second quarter, even though the economy usually stabilizes, consumers continued to be cautious.*)

15 À ce point-là, nous avons lancé notre nouvelle campagne publicitaire, **parce que** les ventes étaient toujours stagnantes. (*At that point, we launched our new ad campaign, because sales were still stagnant.*)

16 Nous avons aussi changé l'emballage de notre produit **afin qu'**il soit plus attirant. (*We also changed our product's packaging so that it was more eye-catching.*)

17 **Après que** nous avons analysé les résultats de ces initiatives, nous avons commencé à offrir un remboursement. (*After we analyzed the results of these initiatives, we started offering a rebate.*)

18 Nous en saurons plus **quand** le rapport annuel sera publié. (*We will know more when the annual report is published.*)

19 Le directeur général pense **qu'**il va falloir réduire le prix de notre produit. (*The CEO thinks that we're going to have to reduce the price of our product.*)

20 C'est tout, **à moins que** vous ayez besoin d'autres informations. (*That's all, unless you need other information.*)

21 J'offre une récompense à la personne **qui** trouve mon portefeuille. (*I'm offering a reward to the person who finds my wallet.*)

22 Voici le restaurant ~~de~~ **dont** il nous a parlé. (*Here's the restaurant he talked to us about.*)

23 C'est exactement la robe **que** je cherche depuis deux mois ! (*That's exactly the dress I've been looking for for two months!*)

24 La rue dans **laquelle** il est tombé passe devant le théâtre. (*The road in which he fell passes in front of the theater.*)

25 C'était le jour **où** j'ai décidé de me divorcer. (*That was the day I decided to get divorced.*)

26 L'ordinateur **que** nous venons d'acheter ne marche pas. (*The computer we just bought doesn't work.*)

27 C'est la fille **qui** a chanté à la fête. (*That's the girl who sang at the party.*)

28 L'hôtel **où** je suis resté la dernière fois est interdit aux chiens. (*The hotel where I stayed last time doesn't allow dogs.*)

29 Le parking en face ~~de~~ **duquel** j'habite est très propre. (*The parking lot I live across from is very clean.*)

30 Les assistants ~~de~~ **dont** nous avons besoin doivent travailler à plein temps. (*The assistants we need have to work full time.*)

31 **Ce qui va m'aider, c'est un peu de soutien.**

32 **C'est ce dont il parle.**

33 **Sais-tu/Savez-vous sur quoi on peut s'asseoir ?**

34 **Ce qu'elle veut, c'est un appartement en France.**

35 **C'est ce à quoi je rêve.**

36 **Tout ce dont j'ai besoin, c'est un bon emploi.**

37 **C'est ce qui nous inspire.**

38 **Je ne sais pas ce qui se passe.**

39 **Ce à quoi tu dois (vous devez) répondre, c'est l'appel de ta (votre) famille.**

40 **C'est ce qu'elle cherche.**

Part IV

That Was Then, and What Will Be, Will Be: The Past and Future Tenses

The 5th Wave   By Rich Tennant

"...and remember, no more French tongue twisters until you know the language better."

In this part . . .

Talking about the past requires knowledge of several past tenses. The **passé composé** (*compound past*), which I address first in this part, tells you what happened. Later, the **imparfait** (*imperfect*) explains what was happening. You can also read about two additional past tenses: the **plus-que-parfait** (*past perfect* or *pluperfect*), which says that something happened before something else, and the **passé simple** (*simple past*), which is used almost exclusively in writing.

Meanwhile, to look ahead, you need to use the **futur** (*future*) tense. And when talking about something that could or would happen, you need the **conditionnel** (*conditional*). The last two chapters in this part have you covered.

Chapter 15

It's All in the Past: Passé Composé

- -

In This Chapter

▶ Finding past participles

▶ Choosing auxiliary verbs

▶ Using the **passé composé**

- -

When you want to say what happened, you usually need the **passé composé,** but this compound verb conjugation is far from passé. The **passé composé** is actually the most common French past tense. You use it when you want to say that something happened or that something has happened. Like all compound conjugations, the **passé composé** is conjugated with an *auxiliary,* or helping verb, plus the past participle. This chapter explains all about auxiliary verbs; how to find the past participle of regular, stem-changing, spelling-change, and irregular verbs; agreement; and how to use the **passé composé.**

Understanding and Creating the Passé Composé

The **passé composé** is a *compound verb tense,* which means it has two parts:

> ✔ An auxiliary verb, either **avoir** or **être,** which you conjugate in the present tense
>
> ✔ A past participle

The **passé composé** is the French equivalent of both the simple past (*I saw*) and the present perfect (*I have seen*). For the most part, you use the **passé composé** — **j'ai vu** — when you'd use either of those tenses in English. The **passé composé** has an equivalent tense, the **passé simple,** which you use in literature and other formal writing. You can read about the **passé simple** in Chapter 17.

The **passé composé** is just one of several compound tenses, all of which you conjugate with the auxiliary verb and past participle. The choice of auxiliary verb (**avoir** or **être**) is the same for each verb in all the compound tenses — not just the **passé composé** but also the **plus-que-parfait** (*past perfect*), future perfect, conditional perfect, and so on. However, the conjugation of the auxiliary verb changes according to the compound tense: It's in the present for the **passé composé,** the future for the future perfect, the conditional for the conditional perfect, and so on.

This section breaks down the two components of the **passé composé** so you can conjugate this verb tense. For more info about the **plus-que-parfait,** check out Chapter 17.

Choosing your helper: avoir or être

In order to conjugate verbs in the **passé composé,** you first need to know how to conjugate the two auxiliary verbs: **avoir** and **être.** After you conjugate the appropriate one in the present tense (see Chapter 4), you add the appropriate past participle and voilà! The **passé composé.**

The auxiliary you use depends on the verb you're using it with. No need to worry, though. More than 99 percent of French verbs use **avoir,** leaving just the following few intransitive verbs that require **être.** (*Intransitive* means the verbs can't have a direct object, such as *to go.*) The verbs in Table 15-1 are known as **être** verbs.

Table 15-1	Verbs Conjugated with Être in Compound Tenses		
Verb	*Translation*	*Verb*	*Translation*
aller	*to go*	partir	*to leave*
arriver	*to arrive*	passer	*to pass, go by*
descendre	*to descend*	rester	*to stay*
entrer	*to enter*	retourner	*to return*
monter	*to climb*	sortir	*to go out*
mourir	*to die*	tomber	*to fall*
naître	*to be born*	venir	*to come*

Furthermore, most of their derivatives need **être** in the compound tenses as well: **devenir** (*to become*), **rentrer** (*to return home*), and so on.

In addition to **être** verbs, you always conjugate pronominal verbs in the **passé composé** with **être,** such as **Il s'est couché.** (*He went to bed.*)

Être verbs are intransitive (that is, have no direct object). When you use one of these verbs followed directly by a noun, with no preposition, or when it's preceded by a direct-object pronoun (see Chapter 13), the verb is transitive.

When you use **être** verbs transitively, you need to use the auxiliary **avoir:**

>   **Je suis descendu à midi.** (*I went downstairs at noon.*)

>   **J'ai descendu le bébé.** (*I took the baby downstairs.*)

Table 15-2 shows which **être** verbs this transitive/intransitive rule affects and how their meanings differ according to usage.

Table 15-2	Using Être Verbs with and without Direct Objects	
Verb	*Intransitive Meaning (with être)*	*Transitive Meaning (with avoir)*
descendre	*to descend*	*to take down*
monter	*to go up*	*to take up*
passer	*to pass* (by, in front of, behind)	*to spend time, to pass a place* (no preposition)
rentrer	*to return home*	*to take/bring in*
retourner	*to return* (to/from a place)	*to return* (something)
sortir	*to go out*	*to take out*

Decide which auxiliary verb you should use for these verbs, assuming that you're using them intransitively.

Q. descendre

A. être

1. mourir _____

2. courir _____

3. passer _____

4. retourner _____

5. entrer _____

6. finir _____

7. remonter _____

8. déménager _____

9. naître _____

10. aller _____

11. marcher _____

12. rester _____

13. sortir _____

14. dormir _____

15. tomber _____

16. arriver _____

17. avoir _____

18. être _____

19. partir _____

20. devenir _____

Finding past participles

The second part of the **passé composé** is the past participle. In English, most past participles end in *-ed* or *-en: walked, eaten.* In French, the past participle usually ends in **-é, -i,** or **-u,** depending on what kind of verb it is. The following sections show how to form the past participle of regular and irregular verbs.

The past participle isn't only for the **passé composé** and the other compound tenses. You can sometimes use it as an adjective:

Je suis fatigué. (*I'm tired.*)

Nous sommes déçus. (*We're disappointed.*)

J'ai vu un chat mort. (*I saw a dead cat.*)

Past participles of regular verbs

Regular verbs have regular past participles. Each of the three categories of regular verbs has its own past participle formation. To find the past participle of regular **-er** verbs, all you have to do is replace the **-er** ending with **-é.** You pronounce the past participles of **-er** verbs exactly the same as the infinitives.

- **parler** (*to talk*) → **parlé**
- **travailler** (*to work*) → **travaillé**

To create the past participle for regular **-ir** verbs, replace **-ir** with **-i:**

- **choisir** (*to choose*) → **choisi**
- **réussir** (*to succeed*) → **réussi**

Regular verbs that end in **-re** drop the ending and add **-u:**

- **entendre** (*to hear*) → **entendu**
- **vendre** (*to sell*) → **vendu**

Past participles of irregular verbs

Some irregular verbs have regular past participles, some have patterns, and some are completely irregular. You just have to memorize the different rules; with practice, you'll master them in no time. Table 15-3 shows you which patterns to look for.

Table 15-3	Past Participle Verb Patterns	
Verb Type	*Change*	*Examples*
Irregular **-er** verbs		
Stem-changing and spelling-change verbs, as well as **aller**	Follow regular past participles — replace **-er** with **-é**	**appeler** (*to call*) → **appelé** **commencer** (*to begin*) → **commencé** **aller** (*to go*) → **allé**
Irregular **-ir** verbs		
Verbs conjugated like **partir**	Follow regular past participles — change **-ir** to **-i**	**partir** (*to leave*) → **parti** **sortir** (*to go out*) → **sorti** **dormir** (*to sleep*) → **dormi**
Irregular **-ir** verbs conjugated like regular-**er** verbs in the present tense	Drop **-rir** and add **-ert**	**ouvrir** (*to open*) → **ouvert** **offrir** (*to offer*) → **offert** **souffrir** (*to suffer*) → **souffert**
Venir, tenir, and all their derivatives	Replace **-ir** with **-u**	**venir** (*to come*) → **venu** **devenir** (*to become*) → **devenu** **tenir** (*to hold*) → **tenu** **obtenir** (*to obtain*) → **obtenu**
Verbs that end in **-cevoir**	Change **-cevoir** to **-çu**	**apercevoir** (*to glimpse*) → **aperçu** **décevoir** (*to disappoint*) → **déçu** **recevoir** (*to receive*) → **reçu**

Verb Type	Change	Examples
Irregular -re verbs		
Prendre (*to take*) and its derivatives	Past participle of **prendre** is **pris**; its derivatives follow this pattern	**apprendre** (*to learn*) → **appris** **comprendre** (*to understand*) → **compris** **surprendre** (*to surprise*) → **surpris**
Mettre (*to put*) and its derivatives	Past participle of **mettre** is **mis**; its derivatives follow this pattern	**admettre** (*to admit*) → **admis** **permettre** (*to permit*) → **permis** **promettre** (*to promise*) → **promis**
Verbs that end in **-uire**	Drop the **-re** and add **-t**	**conduire** (*to drive*) → **conduit** **construire** (*to build*) → **construit** **produire** (*to produce*) → **produit**
Verbs that end in **-dre** (but not regular **-re** verbs like **vendre**)	Drop **-dre** in favor of **-t**	**craindre** (*to fear*) → **craint** **joindre** (*to join*) → **joint** **peindre** (*to paint*) → **peint**
Verbs ending in **-aître** (except **naître**)	Drop **-aître** and replace it with **-u**	**connaître** (*to know*) → **connu** **paraître** (*to seem*) → **paru** **apparaître** (*to appear*) → **apparu**

See Chapter 4 for lists of verbs that follow each conjugation pattern.

Table 15-4 shows irregular verbs that choose to do their own thing with the past participle.

Table 15-4	Irregular Verbs That Have Uniquely Irregular Past Participles
Irregular -ir Verbs	*Irregular -re Verbs*
avoir (*to have*) → **eu**	**boire** (*to drink*) → **bu**
courir (*to run*) → **couru**	**croire** (*to believe*) → **cru**
devoir (*to have to*) → **dû**	**dire** (*to say*) → **dit**
falloir (*to be necessary*) → **fallu**	**écrire** (*to write*) → **écrit**
mourir (*to die*) → **mort**	**être** (*to be*) → **été**
pouvoir (*to be able*) → **pu**	**faire** (*to do, make*) → **fait**
savoir (*to know*) → **su**	**lire** (*to read*) → **lu**
voir (*to see*) → **vu**	**naître** (*to be born*) → **né**
vouloir (*to want*) → **voulu**	**rire** (*to laugh*) → **ri**
	suivre (*to follow*) → **suivi**
	vivre (*to live*) → **vécu**

Provide the past participle for each of these verbs.

O. manger

A. **mangé** (*eaten*)

21. devenir _____

22. rendre _____

23. vivre _____

24. aller _____

25. repartir _____

26. omettre _____

27. grossir _____

28. avoir _____

29. lire _____

30. être _____

Creating agreement with the passé composé

In addition to the auxiliary verb and past participle, you need to consider a third element when using the **passé composé:** grammatical agreement, particularly in writing. *Agreement* is the addition or changing of certain letters to make one French part of speech agree with another. Just as adjectives and articles agree with their nouns, past participles sometimes have to agree with their subjects or objects.

Agreement with être verbs

When you use a verb that is conjugated with the auxiliary **être** in the **passé composé,** the past participle has to agree with the subject in gender and number. This is similar to the agreement of nouns and adjectives explained in Chapter 2, but there are no irregular agreements. When the subject is feminine, add an **-e.** When it's plural, add an **-s.** When the subject is both feminine and plural, add an **-e** followed by an **-s.** Here are the basics:

✔ When the subject of the verb is masculine, use the plain past participle.

> **Philippe est allé au cinéma.** (*Philippe went to the movies.*)

✔ When it's feminine, add an **-e.**

> **Analise est allée au musée.** (*Analise went to the museum.*)

✔ When it's plural, add an **-s.**

> **Ils sont allés au théâtre.** (*They went to the theater.*)

✔ When it's feminine and plural, add **-es.**

> **Geneviève et Denise sont allées au marché.** (*Geneviève and Denise went to the market.*)

When the subject is a pronoun, such as **je** (*I*) or **tu** (*you*), you still need to think about the gender of the person that pronoun represents. I, Laura, have to write **je suis allée,** but my husband would write **je suis allé.** Don't forget that when you have two or more people or things, if at least one of those people or things is masculine, the agreement will be masculine plural. For instance, consider **Mes sœurs et mon frère sont allés au cinéma hier soir** (*My sisters and brother went to the movies yesterday*). Even though more sisters went than brothers, the past participle is masculine.

Remember that all pronominal verbs require that you use **être** when forming the **passé composé.** Pronominal verbs require agreement with the reflexive pronoun, except when the verb also has a direct object (see Chapter 11 for more on reflexive, reciprocal, and idiomatic pronominal verbs):

> **Elle s'est habillée.** (*She got dressed.*)
>
> **Ils se sont levés très tôt.** (*They got up really early.*)

However, if the sentence contains a direct object, you don't make agreement:

> **Elle s'est lavé les mains.** (*She washed her hands.*)
>
> **Nous nous sommes acheté de la glace.** (*We bought ourselves some ice cream.*)

Agreement with avoir verbs

Unlike **être** verbs, **avoir** verbs never agree with their subjects. The only time **avoir** verbs require agreement is with a *preceding direct object*. This situation may occur when you have a sentence with a relative pronoun (see Chapter 14 for info about relative pronouns):

> **La voiture que j'ai achetée . . .** (*The car that I bought . . .*)
>
> **Plusieurs touristes que nous avons vus . . .** (*Several tourists that we saw . . .*)

There's no agreement when the direct object follows the verb:

> **J'ai acheté une voiture.** (*I bought a car.*)
>
> **Nous avons vu plusieurs touristes.** (*We saw several tourists.*)

Nor is there agreement when an indirect object or object of a preposition precedes the verb:

> **La personne à qui j'ai téléphoné . . .** (*The person I called . . .*)
>
> **Les livres dont nous avons parlé . . .** (*The books we talked about . . .*)

The agreement of the **passé composé** conjugated with **avoir** is particularly tricky when you have an object pronoun in the sentence. You need to determine whether this object pronoun is the direct object, as in **J'ai acheté une voiture. Je l'ai trouvée il y a deux semaines.** (*I bought a car. I found it two weeks ago.*) In the second sentence, **l'** refers to **la voiture,** which is feminine, so **trouvée** has an **-e** to agree with it.

Remember that many French verbs require prepositions, which means they take indirect objects, and sometimes the English translations of those verbs take direct objects. For example, **téléphoner à** takes an indirect object in French, but *to call* takes a direct object in English. See Chapter 12 to read about French verbs that need prepositions.

Putting It All Together

After you know which auxiliary verb to use, the past participle of your verb, and whether you need agreement, you can conjugate the **passé composé.** Just use the present tense of the auxiliary verb, either **avoir** or **être,** followed by the past participle. Take a look at **parler** (*to speak*) in the **passé composé;** it doesn't require agreement.

parler (to speak)	
j'ai **parlé**	nous **avons parlé**
tu **as parlé**	vous **avez parlé**
il/elle/on **a parlé**	ils/elles **ont parlé**
J'ai parlé avec mon frère hier. (*I spoke with my brother yesterday.*)	

Remember that **être** verbs require agreement, which I indicate in parentheses in this **aller** (*to go*) chart.

aller (to go)	
je **suis allé(e)**	nous **sommes allé(e)s**
tu **es allé(e)**	vous **êtes allé(e)(s)**
il/on **est allé**, elle **est allée**	ils **sont allés**, elles **sont allées**
Elle **est allée** en France. (*She went to France.*)	

Pronominal verbs — such as **se lever** (*to get up*) also need agreement — you can read more about them in Chapter 11.

se lever (to get up)	
je me **suis levé(e)**	nous nous **sommes levé(e)s**
tu t'**es levé(e)**	vous vous **êtes levé(e)(s)**
il/on s'**est levé**, elle s'**est levée**	ils se **sont levés**, elles se **sont levées**
Nous **nous sommes levés** très tôt. (*We got up very early.*)	

Conjugate each of these verbs into the **passé composé** for the grammatical person in parentheses.

Q. finir (je)

A. **j'ai fini** (*I finished*)

31. se coucher (tu) _____

32. rentrer (il) _____

33. venir (nous) _____

34. lire (vous) _____

35. s'habiller (elles) _____

36. voyager (je) _____

37. écrire (tu) _____

38. avoir (elle) _____

39. vendre (nous) _____

40. sortir (ils) _____

Using the Passé Composé

To properly use the **passé composé** in a normal sentence, just follow this simple formula:

subject + auxiliary verb + past participle

J'ai pleuré. (*I cried.*)

Ils sont partis. (*They left.*)

Of course, writing and speaking include much more than just simple sentences. You use the **passé composé** to refer to one of three things:

✔ Something that was entirely completed in the past:

Je suis allé à la banque hier. (*I went to the bank yesterday.*)

Est-il arrivé avant la fête ? (*Did he arrive before the party?*)

✔ Something that happened a certain number of times in the past:

J'ai visité la tour Eiffel trois fois. (*I've visited the Eiffel Tower three times.*)

Combien de fois lui as-tu téléphoné ? (*How many times did you call him?*)

✔ A series of actions that occurred one after another in the past:

Je me suis levé, j'ai déjeuné et je suis parti avant 7h00. (*I got up, had breakfast, and left before 7 a.m.*)

Quand nous avons entendu les cris, nous avons téléphoné à la police. (*When we heard the screams, we called the police.*)

You often use the **passé composé** in conjunction with the imperfect. You can read about it in Chapter 16.

The following helps you use the **passé composé** in other situations. When you negate the **passé composé, ne** goes in front of the auxiliary verb, and the second part of the negative structure goes after it. (You can read about negation in Chapter 6.) The only exception is **personne,** which goes after the past participle:

Je n'ai pas pleuré. (*I didn't cry.*)

Je n'ai vu personne. (*I didn't see anyone.*)

When you ask a question with inversion (see Chapter 5), you invert just the subject and auxiliary verb and put the past participle after that:

As-tu mangé ? (*Have you eaten?*)

À qui a-t-il parlé ? (*Whom did he talk to?*)

Any object, adverbial, and reflexive pronouns (which you can read about in Chapter 13) precede the auxiliary verb, **avoir** or **être:**

Je l'ai déjà fait. (*I already did it.*)

Il me l'a donné. (*He gave it to me.*)

When you have negation + pronouns, the pronouns go directly in front of the auxiliary verb, and **ne** precedes them:

Je ne l'ai pas fait. (_I didn't do it._)

Tu ne nous l'a pas montré. (_You didn't show it to us._)

Remember that if a direct-object pronoun precedes the verb, you have to make the past participle agree with it. If **l'** in the above example referred to **une bicyclette** (_bicycle_), you'd say **Tu ne nous l'a pas montrée.**

You're in France, writing a postcard to your best friend. Translate these sentences into French, using the **passé composé** to describe what you did and didn't do.

Q. This morning, I got up at 8 a.m.

A. Ce matin, je me suis levé(e) à 8h00.

Carte Postale

Salut Charles,

41. I had breakfast and then went to Montmartre. _____

_____

42. I saw a lot of artists and bought this postcard. _____

_____

43. They told me to visit Notre Dame. _____

_____

44. I asked for directions twice and I didn't get lost. _____

_____

45. I found an interesting restaurant and ate there several times. _____

_____

Charles Degrate
2b Leevina Trail
New York, NY 12345
USA

Answer Key

1 mourir: **être**

2 courir: **avoir**

3 passer: **être**

4 retourner: **être**

5 entrer: **être**

6 finir: **avoir**

7 remonter: **être**

8 déménager: **avoir**

9 naître: **être**

10 aller: **être**

11 marcher: **avoir**

12 rester: **être**

13 sortir: **être**

14 dormir: **avoir**

15 tomber: **être**

16 arriver: **être**

17 avoir: **avoir**

18 être: **avoir**

19 partir: **être**

20 devenir: **être**

21 **devenu** (*became*)

22 **rendu** (*returned*)

23 **vécu** (*lived*)

24 **allé** (*gone*)

25 **reparti** (*left again*)

26 **omis** (*omitted*)

27 **grossi** (*became fat*)

28 **eu** (*had*)

29 **lu** (*read*)

30 **été** (*been*)

31 **tu t'es couché(e)** (*you went to bed*)

32 **il est rentré** (*he returned home*)

33 **nous sommes venu(e)s** (*we came*)

34 **vous avez lu** (*you read*)

35 **elles se sont habillées** (*they got dressed*)

36 **j'ai voyagé** (*I traveled*)

37 **tu as écrit** (*you wrote*)

38 **elle a eu** (*she had*)

39 **nous avons vendu** (*we sold*)

40 **ils sont sortis** (*they went out*)

Carte Postale

Salut Charles,

41. I had breakfast and then went to Montmartre. *J'ai déjeuné et puis je suis allé(e) à Montmartre.*

42. I saw a lot of artists and bought this postcard. *J'ai vu beaucoup d'artistes et j'ai acheté cette carte postale.*

43. They told me to visit Notre Dame. *Ils m'ont dit de visiter Notre Dame.*

44. I asked for directions twice and I didn't get lost. *J'ai demandé des directions deux fois et je ne me suis pas égaré(e).*

45. I found an interesting restaurant and ate there several times. *J'ai trouvé un restaurant intéressant et j'y ai mangé plusieurs fois.*

Charles Degrate
2b Leevina Trail
New York, NY 12345
USA

Chapter 16

What Was Happening? The Imparfait Tense

*T*he **imparfait** (*imperfect*) tense isn't flawed — just unfinished. Grammatically speaking, *perfect* means complete, and the **imparfait** tells you that an action wasn't completed — it was an ongoing state of being (it was hot, I was hungry) — or that it happened repeatedly (I used to go to the beach every weekend). You often use the **imparfait** in conjunction with the **passé composé** to describe some action (imperfect) that got interrupted by some other action (**passé composé**), as in *I was eating when you called.* (Check out Chapter 15 for more info about the **passé compose.**) This chapter explains how to conjugate regular and irregular verbs in the **imparfait,** how and when to use the **imparfait,** the difference between the **imparfait** and **passé composé,** and how to use them together.

Conjugating the Imparfait

The **imparfait** is the easiest of all the French tenses to conjugate because you conjugate virtually all verbs exactly the same way. You take the present-tense **nous** form of the verb, drop **-ons,** and add the **imparfait** endings: **-ais, -ais, -ait, -ions, -iez,** and **-aient.** These endings are the same for all verbs in the **imparfait.** This section shows how to conjugate all the different verbs — regular, stem-changing, spelling-change, and irregular — to show you how easy this tense is.

Regular verbs

To conjugate regular verbs in the **imparfait,** just find the present-tense **nous** form of the verb, drop **-ons,** and add the **imparfait** endings. The **nous** form of the regular **-er** verb **parler** (*to speak*) is **parlons,** so the stem is **parl-,** and the conjugations for all regular **-er** verbs look like this.

parler (*to speak*)	
je parl**ais**	nous parl**ions**
tu parl**ais**	vous parl**iez**
il/elle/on parl**ait**	ils/elles parl**aient**
Il **parlait** trop vite. (*He was speaking too quickly.*)	

The singular conjugations and third-person plural conjugation all sound identical, but the subject pronoun lets you know who was talking.

Verbs that end in **-ier**, like **étudier**, can look a little strange in the **imparfait**. When you drop **-ons** from the **nous** form **étudions**, you find a stem than ends in **i**: **étudi-**. Because the **nous** and **vous imparfait** endings begin with **i**, you end up with a double **i** in those conjugations.

étudier (*to study*)	
j'étudi**ais**	nous étudi**ions**
tu étudi**ais**	vous étudi**iez**
il/elle/on étudi**ait**	ils/elles étudi**aient**
Nous **étudiions** hier soir. (*We were studying yesterday evening.*)	

The **nous** and **vous** forms of the **imparfait** end in **-ions** and **-iez** for all verbs: **nous parlions** (*we were talking*), **vous fermiez** (*you were closing*). But verbs that end in **-ier** also end in **-ions** and **-iez** in the *present* tense: **nous étudions** (*we study*), **vous skiez** (*you ski*). Therefore, the double **i** is what tells you that **-ier** verbs are in the **imparfait: nous étudiions** (*we were studying*), **vous skiiez** (*you were skiing*).

The **nous** form of the regular **-ir** verb **finir** is **finissons**, so the root for all the **imparfait** conjugations is **finiss-**.

finir (*to finish*)	
je finiss**ais**	nous finiss**ions**
tu finiss**ais**	vous finiss**iez**
il/elle/on finiss**ait**	ils/elles finiss**aient**
Elles **finissaient** leurs études au Canada. (*They were finishing their studies in Canada.*)	

Vendons is the **nous** form of the regular **-re** verb **vendre**, so the root is **vend-**.

vendre (*to sell*)	
je vend**ais**	nous vend**ions**
tu vend**ais**	vous vend**iez**
il/elle/on vend**ait**	ils/elles vend**aient**
Je **vendais** ma voiture. (*I was selling my car.*)	

Stem-changing verbs

The **nous** form of stem-changing verbs does not have a stem change in the present, so the **imparfait** doesn't, either. The **nous** form of **payer** is **payons**, so the stem is **pay-**, and the **nous** form of **acheter** is **achetons,** so the stem is **achet-**.

payer (*to pay*)	
je pay**ais**	nous pay**ions**
tu pay**ais**	vous pay**iez**
il/elle/on pay**ait**	ils/elles pay**aient**
Vous **payiez** trop. (*You were paying too much.*)	

acheter (*to buy*)	
j'achet**ais**	nous achet**ions**
tu achet**ais**	vous achet**iez**
il/elle/on achet**ait**	ils/elles achet**aient**
Tu **achetais** beaucoup de pain. (*You were buying a lot of bread.*)	

Spelling-change verbs

The **nous** form of spelling-change verbs has a spelling change, so you keep that for most of the **imparfait** conjugations. The **nous** form of **commencer** is **commençons,** giving you the stem **commenç-,** and the **nous** form of **manger** is **mangeons,** so the stem is **mange-**.

However, note that the **nous** and **vous imparfait** endings begin with the soft vowel **i,** so you don't need the spelling change in those conjugations. See Chapter 4 for more information about spelling-change verbs.

commencer (*to begin*)	
je commen**çais**	nous commen**cions**
tu commen**çais**	vous commen**ciez**
il/elle/on commen**çait**	ils/elles commen**çaient**
Il **commençait** à lire. (*He was beginning to read.*)	

manger (*to eat*)	
je mang**eais**	nous mang**ions**
tu mang**eais**	vous mang**iez**
il/elle/on mang**eait**	ils/elles mang**eaient**
Nous **mangions** ensemble. (*We were eating together.*)	

Irregular verbs

What's the only irregularity of irregular verbs in the **imparfait?** Well, they're not irregular — you conjugate them just like regular verbs, with the present-tense **nous** form minus **-ons.** Then add the imperfect endings.

aller (*to go*)	
j'all**ais**	nous all**ions**
tu all**ais**	vous all**iez**
il/elle/on all**ait**	ils/elles all**aient**
Ils **allaient** au parc. (*They were going to the park.*)	

venir (*to come*)	
je ven**ais**	nous ven**ions**
tu ven**ais**	vous ven**iez**
il/elle/on ven**ait**	ils/elles ven**aient**
Tu **venais** seul. (*You were coming alone.*)	

écrire (*to write*)	
j'écriv**ais**	nous écriv**ions**
tu écriv**ais**	vous écriv**iez**
il/elle/on écriv**ait**	ils/elles écriv**aient**
Elle **écrivait** une longue lettre. (*She was writing a long letter.*)	

French does have one, single irregular verb that's also irregular in the **imparfait être.** The present-tense **nous** form of **être** is **sommes,** so there's no **-ons** to drop. Instead, you use the stem **ét-** and add the **imparfait** endings to that.

être (*to be*)	
j'ét**ais**	nous ét**ions**
tu ét**ais**	vous ét**iez**
il/elle/on ét**ait**	ils/elles ét**aient**
Vous **étiez** en retard. (*You were late.*)	

Conjugate these verbs in the **imparfait** for the subject in parentheses.

Q. danser (je)

A. **je dansais** (*I was dancing*)

1. choisir (tu) _____

2. rendre (il) _____

3. crier (nous) _____

4. jeter (vous) _____

5. aller (elles) _____

6. nager (je) _____

7. mettre (tu) _____

8. prendre (on) _____

9. pincer (nous) _____

10. bouger (vous) _____

Using the Imparfait

When you're talking about verbs, *perfect* means completed: Perfect tenses include present perfect (completed recently — *he has returned*), past perfect (completed before something else — *he had returned*), future perfect (to be completed in the future — *he will have returned*), and so on. In contrast, the **imparfait** explains that something happened or was happening in the past with no precise beginning or ending. You often translate it as *was/were doing* or *used to do* in English.

You can use the **imparfait** to express a number of things that happened or existed in the past. Here's what to express with the **imparfait:**

✔ Something that happened an unknown number of times, especially habitual actions:

> **Je visitais le Louvre tous les jours.** (*I visited/used to visit the Louvre every day.*)

> **L'année dernière, il lisait régulièrement.** (*Last year, he read regularly.*)

✔ States of being and descriptions:

> **Quand j'étais petit, j'aimais danser.** (*When I was little, I liked/used to like to dance.*)

> **La voiture faisait du bruit.** (*The car was making noise.*)

✔ Actions or states of being with no specific beginning or end:

> **Je regardais la télé pendant le petit déjeuner.** (*I watched/was watching TV during breakfast.*)

> **Nous avions besoin de tomates.** (*We needed tomatoes.*)

✔ Two things that were happening at the same time:

> **Il travaillait et j'étudiais.** (*He was working and I was studying.*)

> **Je lisais pendant que mon frère jouait au tennis.** (*I read while my brother played tennis.*)

✔ Background information and actions/states of being that got interrupted:

> **Travaillais-tu quand je t'ai téléphoné ?** (*Were you working when I called you?*)

> **J'avais faim, donc j'ai acheté un sandwich.** (*I was hungry, so I bought a sandwich.*)

Note that the interruption is expressed with the **passé composé.** See the next section, "Deciding Whether to Use Imparfait or Passé Composé," for more information.

✔ Wishes, suggestions, and conditions after **si** (*if*):

> **Si seulement elle venait avec nous.** (*If only she were coming with us.*)

> **Et si on allait au ciné ce soir ?** (*How about going to the movies tonight?*)

> **Si j'étais riche, je ferais le tour du monde.** (*If I were rich, I would go around the world.*)

In the third example, **je ferais** is the conditional of **faire** (*to do, to make*). See Chapter 19 to read about the conditional.

✔ Time, date, and age:

> **Il était lundi quand . . .** (*It was Monday when . . .*)

> **Tu étais trop jeune.** (*You were too young.*)

> **Il y avait/était une fois . . .** (*Once upon a time . . .*)

Translate these sentences into French, using the **imparfait** as needed.

Q. Were they ready?

A. **Étaient-ils prêts ?**

11. We used to live together.

_____

12. It was hot yesterday.

_____

13. Antoine was singing.

_____

14. Paul and Michel watched a movie every week.

_____

15. If only you had the key.

_____

16. I was sleeping when he arrived.

_____

17. She was very pretty.

_____

18. How about if I help you?

_____

19. He was scared, so he closed his eyes.

_____

20. I wanted to travel.

_____

Deciding Whether to Use the Imparfait or Passé Composé

The **imparfait** and the **passé composé** express the past differently, so only by working together can they can fully express what happened in the past. In order for you to use the right one at the right time, you need to know what each tense describes. Table 16-1 spells out their differences. (You can read more about the **passé composé** in Chapter 15.)

Table 16-1	Functions of the Imparfait and Passé Composé
Uses of the Imparfait	_Uses of the Passé Composé_
What was going on with no indication of when it started or ended	Things that happened with a definite beginning and/or end
Habitual or repeated actions	Single events
Simultaneous actions	Sequential actions
Something that got interrupted	Actions that interrupted something
Background information	Changes in physical or mental states
General descriptions	

Certain terms can help you decide whether to use the **imparfait** or **passé composé**. The following terms are usually used with the **imparfait**:

- **toujours** (*always*)
- **d'habitude, normalement** (*usually*)
- **en général** (*in general*)
- **généralement** (*generally*)
- **souvent** (*often*)
- **parfois, quelquefois** (*sometimes*)
- **de temps en temps** (*from time to time*)
- **chaque semaine, mois, année . . .** (*every week, month, year . . .*)
- **tous les jours, toutes les semaines** (*every day, every week*)
- **le week-end** (*on the weekends*)
- **le lundi, le mardi . . .** (*on Mondays, on Tuesdays*)
- **le matin, le soir** (*in the mornings, in the evenings*)

These terms tell you that you probably should use the **passé composé**:

- **une fois, deux fois, trois fois . . .** (*once, twice, three times . . .*)
- **plusieurs fois** (*several times*)
- **soudainement** (*suddenly*)
- **tout d'un coup** (*all of a sudden*)
- **quand** (*when*)
- **un jour** (*one day*)
- **un week-end** (*one weekend*)
- **lundi, mardi . . .** (*on Monday, on Tuesday*)

In a nutshell, the **imparfait** usually describes the background state of being, and the **passé composé** explains the actions and events. Between the two of them, you get a complete picture of what happened in the past. This section breaks down the different situations in which you have to choose between the **imparfait** and the **passé composé**; it also gives you hints to help you make that decision.

Actions with no end in sight

When you use the **imparfait** to describe an action, you're saying that it had no precise beginning or end:

> **J'écrivais une lettre.** (*I was writing a letter.*)

This action is incomplete, so you use the **imparfait.** You know that at some point I was in the process of writing a letter, but you don't know whether I ever finished it or when I started or stopped. The **passé composé** says that an action did have a specific end. Compare the preceding example to this sentence:

J'ai écrit une lettre. (*I wrote a letter.*)

This has a definite ending — the letter is written. The action is complete, so you use the **passé composé.**

Making a habit of it

When something happened a specific number of times, use the **passé composé.** If it was habitual or repeated, use the **imparfait:**

J'écrivais des lettres le samedi. (*I used to write letters on Saturday.*)

Here, you don't know how many times I wrote letters or how many letters I wrote. This was something I habitually did on Saturdays, so use the **imparfait.** Compare this to

J'ai écrit trois lettres samedi. (*I wrote three letters on Saturday.*)

This action is complete, so you use the **passé composé.** On Saturday, I sat down and wrote three letters. It's done.

The way we were

The **passé composé** indicates a change in someone's or something's state of being; the **imparfait** describes the general state of being of a person or thing:

Étienne avait faim. (*Étienne was hungry.*)

This is just the way Étienne felt — he was hungry, for no particular reason. In this instance, you use the **imparfait.** Compare the preceding example to the next sentence:

Quand il a vu les frites, Étienne a eu faim. (*When he saw the French fries, Étienne was/got/became hungry.*)

Here, Étienne hadn't been hungry, but then he saw those delicious-looking French fries and suddenly was hungry. In this example, you use the **passé composé.**

Two (or more) at a time

When you have two or more actions, the tense you use depends on whether the actions are simultaneous or sequential. You use the **imparfait** to express two or more things that were happening at the same time and the **passé composé** to indicate things that happened one after the other:

Henriette conduisait pendant que Thierry chantait. (*Henriette drove while Thierry sang.*)

Ils sont partis, et puis Viviane a commencé à pleurer. (*They left, and then Viviane started to cry.*)

In the first example, the two actions were occurring at the same time, so you use the **imparfait.** In the second, they left first, and Vivane started to cry afterward. Because these actions are sequential, you use the **passé composé.**

Getting interrupted

The **imparfait** and **passé composé** work together to express something that interrupted something else. The **imparfait** gives you the background info — what was happening when something else (expressed with the **passé composé**) occurred:

> **Je lisais quand quelqu'un a frappé à la porte.** (*I was reading when someone knocked on the door.*)

> **Quand nous sommes arrivés, tout le monde mangeait.** (*When we arrived, everyone was eating.*)

> **Il marchait quand il a trouvé le chien.** (*He was walking when he found the dog.*)

The verbs in the **imparfait** in these three examples tell you what was happening, and the verbs in the **passé composé** tell you what interrupted them.

Your boss needs to you write up a report about this morning's meeting. Conjugate the verbs in parentheses into the French **imparfait** or **passé composé** as required.

Q. La réunion _____ (commencer) à 8h00.

A. La réunion **a commencé** à 8h00. (*The meeting began at 8 a.m.*)

XYZ, Cie.
11, rue de Dai
Paris

Élisabeth (21) _____ (prendre) des notes pendant que Juliette

(22) _____ (donner) son exposé. Elle (23) _____ (demander) s'il y

(24) _____ (avoir) des questions. Thomas (25) _____ (dire) oui —

il (26) _____ (vouloir) plus de détails. Juliette (27) _____ (expliquer)

quelque chose de très compliqué quand Marc (28) _____ (arriver).

Il (29) _____ (porter) des pizzas, et soudainement tout le monde

(30) _____ (avoir) faim.

Answer Key

1 **tu choisissais** (*you were choosing*)

2 **il rendait** (*he was returning*)

3 **nous criions** (*we were screaming*)

4 **vous jetiez** (*you were throwing*)

5 **elles allaient** (*they were going*)

6 **je nageais** (*I was swimming*)

7 **tu mettais** (*you were putting*)

8 **on prenait** (*one was taking*)

9 **nous pincions** (*we were pinching*)

10 **vous bougiez** (*you were moving*)

11 **Nous habitions/vivions ensemble.**

12 **Il faisait chaud hier.**

13 **Antoine chantait.**

14 **Paul et Michel regardaient un film chaque semaine/toutes les semaines.**

15 **Si seulement tu avais/vous aviez la clé.**

16 **Je dormais quand il est arrivé.**

17 **Elle était très jolie.**

18 **Et si je t'aidais/je vous aidais ?**

19 **Il avait peur, donc il a fermé les yeux.**

20 **Je voulais voyager.**

XYZ, Cie.
11, rue de Dai
Paris

Élisabeth (21) **prenait** des notes pendant que Juliette (22) **donnait** son exposé. Elle (23) **a demandé** s'il y (24) **avait** des questions. Thomas (25) **a dit** oui — il (26) **voulait** plus de détails. Juliette (27) **expliquait** quelque chose de très compliqué quand Marc (28) **est arrivé**. Il (29) **portait** des pizzas, et soudainement tout le monde (30) **a eu** faim.

(Élisabeth took notes while Juliette gave her presentation. She asked if there were any questions. Thomas said yes — he wanted more details. Juliette was explaining something very complicated when Marc arrived. He was carrying pizza, and suddenly everyone got hungry.)

Chapter 17

It's All Over! Other Past Tenses

. . . .

In This Chapter

▶ Conjugating and using the **plus-que-parfait** (*past perfect*)

▶ Recognizing the **passé simple** (*simple past*)

. . . .

Although living in the past isn't a good idea, it is important to be able to talk and write about it. How else can you brag about the time you hit the winning home-run or won first prize in that contest? When you write your memoirs, you need to know how to use the different French past tenses.

Besides the **passé composé** and the **imparfait** (see Chapters 15 and 16), French has two other past tenses, although you probably won't use one of them very often. Despite that fact, you still need to be aware of it so you can decipher it when you see it. These two past tenses are

✔ **The plus-que-parfait** (*past perfect,* or *pluperfect*): You use this compound tense for talking about something that happened before something else.

✔ **The passé simple** (*simple past* or *preterite*): This simple tense tells you what happened in the past, but usually only in writing. It's the formal, literary equivalent of the **passé composé,** so unless you're planning to write the Great French Novel, being able to recognize it is the most important thing.

This chapter explains how to conjugate and use the French past perfect and **passé simple.**

Perfecting the Plus-Que-Parfait: What Someone Had Done

The **plus-que-parfait** (*past perfect,* also known as the *pluperfect*) explains something that happened before something else, as in "I *had bought* the tickets before I realized you were busy." You use this tense only when you have two actions that are both in the past and you want to indicate that one came before the other.

In English, you conjugate the past perfect with *had* + past participle; in French, you use the **imparfait** (*imperfect*) of the auxiliary verb (either **avoir** or **être**) plus the past participle. This section walks you through conjugating and using the past perfect.

Conjugating the past perfect

Like the **passé composé,** the **plus-que-parfait** (*past perfect*) is a compound tense, which means you conjugate it with an auxiliary verb — either **avoir** or **être** — plus a past participle. The choice of auxiliary verb depends on the main verb, and the verb–auxiliary verb pairing is the same in all the compound tenses. (See Chapter 15 for more about choosing the correct auxiliary verb, as well as how to create past participles.) In this section, I show you how to piece together the past perfect.

Avoir verbs

Most verbs use **avoir** as the auxiliary verb. For the past perfect, you have to conjugate the auxiliary verb in the imperfect (see Chapter 16), so here's what **avoir** (*to have*) looks like.

auxiliary verb **avoir** (*to have*) in the imperfect	
j'**avais**	nous **avions**
tu **avais**	vous **aviez**
il/elle/on **avait**	ils/elles **avaient**

After you conjugate the auxiliary verb, you just tack on the past participle to get the past perfect. So **parler** (*to speak*), an **avoir** verb (a verb conjugated with **avoir** in the compound tenses), looks like this in the past perfect.

parler (*to speak*)	
j'**avais parlé**	nous **avions parlé**
tu **avais parlé**	vous **aviez parlé**
il/elle/on **avait parlé**	ils/elles **avaient parlé**
J'**avais** déjà **parlé** à Guy quand tu as téléphoné. (*I had already spoken to Guy when you called.*)	

Être verbs

When you want to conjugate a verb in the past perfect and your verb of choice requires **être** (*to be*), you need to conjugate the auxiliary verb **être** in the imperfect.

helping verb **être** (*to be*) in the imperfect	
j'**étais**	nous **étions**
tu **étais**	vous **étiez**
il/elle/on **était**	ils/elles **étaient**

The handful of verbs that use **être** in the **passé composé** also use it in the past perfect. *Note:* The derivatives of these verbs (**devenir** [*to become*], **remonter** [*to climb again*], and so on) also use **être** in the past perfect and other compound tenses:

- ✔ **aller** (*to go*)
- ✔ **arriver** (*to arrive*)
- ✔ **descendre** (*to descend*)
- ✔ **entrer** (*to enter*)
- ✔ **monter** (*to climb*)
- ✔ **mourir** (*to die*)
- ✔ **naître** (*to be born*)

- ✔ **partir** (*to leave*)
- ✔ **passer** (*to pass [by, in front of]*)
- ✔ **rester** (*to stay*)
- ✔ **retourner** (*to return*)
- ✔ **sortir** (*to go out*)
- ✔ **tomber** (*to fall*)
- ✔ **venir** (*to come*)

Verbs conjugated with **être** require agreement in the past perfect: you add an **-e** to the past participle for feminine subjects and an **-s** for plural. Rules of agreement for the past perfect are identical to those for the **passé composé** (see Chapter 15 for more details). Consider the past perfect conjugation of **aller** (*to go*).

aller (*to go*)	
j'**étais allé(e)**	nous **étions allé(e)s**
tu **étais allé(e)**	vous **étiez allé(e)(s)**
il/on **était allé,** elle **était allée**	ils **étaient allés,** elles **étaient allées**
J'**étais allé** à la banque quand tu es arrivé. (*I had gone to the bank when you arrived.*)	

Pronominal verbs also use **être** as their auxiliary verb, and they need to agree with the reflexive pronoun in the past perfect. Note that the reflexive pronoun always changes to match the subject. (Go to Chapter 11 to read about pronominal verbs and reflexive pronouns.) Here's how to conjugate **se lever** (*to get up*) in the past perfect.

se lever (*to get up*)	
je m'**étais levé(e)**	nous nous **étions levé(e)s**
tu t'**étais levé(e)**	vous vous **étiez levé(e)(s)**
il/on s'**était levé,** elle s'**était levée**	ils s'**étaient levés,** elles s'**étaient levées**
Elle s'**était** déjà **levée** quand le réveil a sonné. (*She had already gotten up when the alarm went off.*)	

Conjugate these verbs into the past perfect for the subject in parentheses.

0. téléphoner (je)

A. **j'avais téléphoné** (*I had called*)

1. finir (tu) _____

2. partir (Marianne) _____

3. se coucher (nous) _____

4. descendre (vous) _____

5. vendre (ils) _____

6. écrire (je) _____

7. avoir (tu) _____

8. vouloir (Henri) _____

9. arriver (nous) _____

10. s'habiller (vous) _____

The order of events: Using the past perfect

You use the past perfect to talk about something that happened in the past before something else that happened in the past. The verb referring to the later action is often in the **passé composé** (see Chapter 15 to read about that tense):

> **Je m'étais déjà couché quand il est rentré.** (*I had already gone to bed when he came home.*)

> **Nous avions presque oublié l'incident quand Sandrine est arrivée.** (*We had almost forgotten the incident when Sandrine arrived.*)

> **Pierre m'a téléphoné à midi pour m'inviter à déjeuner, mais j'avais déjà mangé.** (*Pierre called me at noon to invite me to lunch, but I had already eaten.*)

In the last example, the verb referring to the later action is in the imperfect (see Chapter 16 to read about the imperfect as well as how to decide between it and the **passé composé**).

You're keeping a journal of your trip to Switzerland. Fill in the blanks with the past perfect conjugation of the verb in parentheses.

Q. Ce matin, j'ai dû acheter du film, parce que je/j' _____ (oublier) mon appareil numérique.

A. **j'avais oublié** (*This morning I had to buy some film because I'd forgotten my digital camera.*)

Quand nous sommes arrivés à Genève, je/j' (11) _____ (prendre) des douzaines de photos. Nous étions en retard parce que l'autobus (12) _____ (tomber) en panne. En plus, j'ai découvert que l'hôtel (13) _____ (perdre) ma réservation. Je voulais pleurer, mais je/j' (14) _____ (se promettre) de garder mon calme. Mon ami David m'a offert son divan, parce qu'il (15) _____ (louer) une suite.

Waxing Literary: Conjugating the Passé Simple

The **passé simple** is a *literary tense,* which means that it's formal and is used almost exclusively in writing such as literature, poetry, newspapers, textbooks, documents, and so on. The spoken equivalent is the **passé composé,** which you can read about in Chapter 15. Because the **passé simple** is usually written and you're probably not currently writing a French historical novel, it's unlikely that you'll need to know how to conjugate the **passé simple.** However, if you read French books and newspapers, you need to be able to recognize it. You'll probably hear the **passé simple** only in formal discourse such as on the news, in formal speeches, and in announcements.

The **passé simple** is one of the most difficult French verb conjugations because of all its irregularities. However, the tense is easy to recognize as soon as you understand the basic rules. This section helps clarify those rules for the different types of verbs.

Passé simple of -er verbs

To form the **passé simple** of -er verbs, you drop the **-er** and add the following endings: **-ai, -as, -a, -âmes, -âtes,** and **-èrent.** Here's **parler** (*to speak*) in the **passé simple.**

parler (*to speak*)	
je parl**ai**	nous parl**âmes**
tu parl**as**	vous parl**âtes**
il/elle/on parl**a**	ils/elles parl**èrent**
Vous **parlâtes** d'or. (*You spoke words of wisdom.*)	

The irregular **-er** verb **aller** follows the same rules, making it regular in the **passé simple.**

aller (*to go*)	
j'all**ai**	nous all**âmes**
tu all**as**	vous all**âtes**
il/elle/on alla	ils/elles all**èrent**
Nous **allâmes** à l'église. (*We went to church.*)	

Stem-changing verbs are also regular in the **passé simple.** Because there's no stem change in the infinitive, there's no stem change in the **passé simple.** Here's what **acheter** (*to buy*) looks like in this tense.

acheter (*to buy*)	
j'achet**ai**	nous achet**âmes**
tu achet**as**	vous achet**âtes**
il achet**a**	ils achet**èrent**
Il **acheta** une maison. (*He bought a house.*)	

Spelling-change verbs, on the other hand, have the spelling change in all but the third-person plural **passé simple** conjugations. Remember that spelling-change verbs have a spelling change in certain conjugations to maintain the correct pronunciation (see Chapter 4). But because the **passé simple** ending for **ils** begins with the soft vowel **e**, the **ils** conjugation for verbs like **manger** (*to eat*) doesn't need the spelling change.

manger (*to eat*)	
je mange**ai**	nous mange**âmes**
tu mange**as**	vous mange**âtes**
il/elle/on mange**a**	ils/elles mang**èrent**
Elle **mangea** seule. (*She ate alone.*)	

The third-person plural of **commencer** (*to begin*) doesn't need a **ç** because the **è** that follows the **c** keeps that **c** sound soft.

commencer (*to begin*)	
je commenç**ai**	nous commenç**âmes**
tu commenç**as**	vous commenç**âtes**
il commenç**a**	ils commenc**èrent**
Vous **commençâtes** tard. (*You started late.*)	

Passé simple of -ir verbs

To conjugate regular **-ir** verbs, just drop the **-ir** and add the following endings to the root: **-is, -is, -it, -îmes, -îtes**, and **-irent**. Here's an example.

finir (*to finish*)	
je fin**is**	nous fin**îmes**
tu fin**is**	vous fin**îtes**
il/elle/on fin**it**	ils/elles fin**irent**
Il **finit** hier. (*He finished yesterday.*)	

The verbs **s'asseoir** and **voir** have irregular **passé simple** stems but use the regular **-ir** endings. The stem of **s'asseoir** is **s'ass-**, and the stem for **voir** is **v-**.

s'asseoir (*to sit down*)	
je m'ass**is**	nous nous ass**îmes**
tu t'ass**is**	vous vous ass**îtes**
il/elle/on s'ass**it**	ils/elles s'ass**irent**
Ils **s'assirent** immédiatement. (*They sat down immediately.*)	

voir (*to see*)	
je v**is**	nous v**îmes**
tu v**is**	vous v**îtes**
il/elle/on v**it**	ils/elles v**irent**
Je **vis** l'accident. (*I saw the accident.*)	

Most irregular **-ir** verbs that have a past participle that ends in **u** use that participle as their **passé simple** stem. Table 17-1 shows these verbs and their stems. These verbs have irregular **passé simple** endings: Take the past participle and add **-s, -s, -t, -ˆmes, -ˆtes,** and **-rent**.

Table 17-1	Passé Simple Stems Ending in u (-ir Verbs)	
Verb	*Translation*	*Passé Simple Stem*
avoir	*to have*	**eu-**
courir	*to run*	**couru-**
devoir	*to have to*	**du-**
falloir	*to be necessary*	**fallu-**
pleuvoir	*to rain*	**plu-**
pouvoir	*to be able to*	**pu-**
recevoir	*to receive*	**reçu-**
savoir	*to know*	**su-**
valoir	*to be worth*	**valu-**
vouloir	*to want*	**voulu-**

Note that the past participle of **devoir** is actually **dû,** but it loses the circumflex for the **passé simple** conjugations.

Here's what **avoir** (*to have*) looks like in the **passé simple.**

avoir (*to have*)	
j'eu**s**	nous eû**mes**
tu eu**s**	vous eû**tes**
il/elle/on eu**t**	ils/elles eu**rent**
Vous **eûtes** une bonne idée. (*You had a good idea.*)	

The verb **mourir** (*to die*) has the **passé simple** stem **mouru,** and it takes the same endings as irregular **-ir** verbs with past participles ending in **u.**

mourir (*to die*)	
je mouru**s**	nous mourû**mes**
tu mouru**s**	vous mourû**tes**
il/elle/on mouru**t**	ils/elles mouru**rent**
Elle **mourut** hier. (*She died yesterday.*)	

Venir, tenir, and all their derivatives (**devenir** [*to become*], **retenir** [*to retain*], and so on) are irregular in the **passé simple;** they follow this pattern.

venir (*to come*)	
je vin**s**	nous vî**nmes**
tu vin**s**	vous vî**ntes**
il/elle/on vin**t**	ils/elles vin**rent**
Elles **vinrent** trop tard. (*They came too late.*)	

Passé simple of -re verbs

The **passé simple** endings for **-re** verbs are the same as for **-ir** verbs. To form the **passé simple,** drop the **-re** and add the endings to the root: **-is, -is, -it, -îmes, -îtes,** and **-irent.** Take a look at the conjugation of **vendre** (*to sell*).

vendre (*to sell*)	
je vend**is**	nous vend**îmes**
tu vend**is**	vous vend**îtes**
il/elle/on vend**it**	ils/elles vend**irent**
Je **vendis** ma maison. (*I sold my house.*)	

A number of irregular **-re** verbs have irregular **passé simple** stems but use the regular **-re** endings — see Table 17-2.

Table 17-2	Passé Simple Stems for Irregular -re Verbs	
French Verb	*Translation*	*Passé Simple Stem*
conduire	*to drive*	conduis-
craindre	*to fear*	craign-
dire	*to say*	d-
écrire	*to write*	écriv-
faire	*to do, make*	f-
joindre	*to join*	joign-
mettre	*to put*	m-
naître	*to be born*	naqu-
peindre	*to paint*	peign-
prendre	*to take*	pr-
rire	*to laugh*	r-

Check out **faire,** with its irregular stem and regular **-re** verb endings.

faire (*to do, make*)	
je **fis**	nous **fîmes**
tu **fis**	vous **fîtes**
il/elle/on **fit**	ils/elles **firent**
Il **fit** du bon travail. (*He did good work.*)	

Most irregular **-re** verbs that have a past participle ending in **u** use that past participle as their **passé simple** stem. These verbs and their stems are in Table 17-3.

Table 17-3	Passé Simple Stems Ending in u (-re Verbs)	
Verb	*Translation*	*Passé Simple Stem*
boire	*to drink*	bu-
connaître	*to know*	connu-
croire	*to believe*	cru-
lire	*to read*	lu-
vivre	*to live*	vécu-

These verbs use the same **passé simple** endings as **-ir** verbs with stems that end in **u:** Just add **-s, -s, -t, -ˆmes, -ˆtes,** and **-rent.** Check out **croire** (*to believe*).

croire (*to believe*)	
je cru**s**	nous cr**ûmes**
tu cru**s**	vous cr**ûtes**
il/elle/on cru**t**	ils/elles cru**rent**
Il ne le **crut** pas. (*He didn't believe it.*)	

As in other tenses, **être** is irregular in the **passé simple.** It uses the stem **fu-** plus the endings you use for stems that end in **u.**

être (*to be*)	
je fu**s**	nous f**ûmes**
tu fu**s**	vous f**ûtes**
il/elle/on fu**t**	ils/elles fu**rent**
Nous **fûmes** prêts. (*We were ready.*)	

Identify the infinitive for each of these **passé simple** conjugations.

0. je parla

A. **parler** (*to speak*)

16. il sut _____

17. tu vis _____

18. elle tint _____

19. nous lûmes _____

20. elles vécurent _____

21. vous eûtes _____

22. tu bus _____

23. ils furent _____

24. vous rîtes _____

25. je naquis _____

Answer Key

1 **tu avais fini** (*you had finished*)

2 **Marianne était partie** (*Marianne had left*)

3 **nous nous étions couché(e)s** (*we had gone to bed*)

4 **vous étiez descendu(e)(s)** (*you had gone downstairs*)

5 **ils avaient vendu** (*they had sold*)

6 **j'avais écrit** (*I had written*)

7 **tu avais eu** (*you had had*)

8 **Henri avait voulu** (*Henri had wanted*)

9 **nous étions arrivé(e)s** (*we had arrived*)

10 **vous vous étiez habillé(e)(s)** (*you had gotten dressed*)

	Quand nous sommes arrivés à Genève, j' (11) **avais pris** des douzaines de photos.
	Nous étions en retard parce que l'autobus (12) **était tombé** en panne. En plus,
	j'ai découvert que l'hôtel (13) **avait perdu** ma réservation. Je voulais pleurer,
	mais je (14) **m'étais promis(e)** de garder mon calme. Mon ami David m'a offert
	son divan, parce qu'il (15) **avait loué** une suite.
	(*When we arrived in Geneva, I'd taken dozens of pictures. We were late*
	because the bus had broken down. In addition, I discovered that the hotel had
	lost my reservation. I wanted to cry, but I had promised myself to keep my cool.
	My friend David offered me his couch because he had rented a suite.)

16 **savoir** (*to know*)

17 **voir** (*to see*)

18 **tenir** (*to hold*)

19 **lire** (*to read*)

20 **vivre** (*to live*)

21 **avoir** (*to have*)

22 **boire** (*to drink*)

23 **être** (*to be*)

24 **rire** (*to laugh*)

25 **naître** (*to be born*)

Chapter 18

What'll You Do? The Future

*W*hen planning for or dreaming about the future, you need to use the French **futur** (*future*) tense. Whether you're organizing a trip, figuring out a five-year plan, or deciding what to do next Friday night, you'll use the future to explain what's going to happen. The French future tense is easy to conjugate and easy to use. This chapter discusses how to conjugate and use the future tense, as well as some other ways to talk about the future in French.

The Infinitive and Beyond: Conjugating the Futur

Telling the future in French can be a snap (even without a crystal ball). The basic future tense — the **futur simple** — is one of the easiest French verb conjugations because all verbs take the same endings (no matter what the future stem is) and only a few verbs are irregular in the future. For most verbs, you just take the infinitive (and drop the final **-e** on an **-re** verb) and add **-ai, -as, -a, -ons, -ez,** or **-ont.** *Remember:* The future stem for all verbs — regular, stem-changing, spelling-change, and irregular — always ends in **r.**

The future endings for the singular conjugations and the third-person plural are the same as the present-tense conjugations of **avoir** (*to have*). The **nous** and **vous** future endings are the **avoir** conjugations minus **av.**

In French, the future tense is a single verb conjugated for the different grammatical persons, so it's different for each subject: **j'irai, tu iras, il ira,** and so on. In English, the future is the modal verb *will* plus the main verb, and it's the same for all subject pronouns: *I will go, you will go, he will go,* and so on.

This section covers what you need to know when conjugating verbs in the future tense so you're able to correctly say and write what you mean.

Regular and spelling-change verbs

Regular and spelling-change verbs stick with simplicity. Regular **-er** verbs use their infinitive as the future stem, so just add the appropriate ending right on the end of the infinitive: **-ai, -as, -a, -ons, -ez,** or **-ont.**

parler (*to talk*)	
je parler**ai**	nous parler**ons**
tu parler**as**	vous parler**ez**
il/elle/on parler**a**	ils/elles parler**ont**
Je te **parlerai** demain. (*I'll talk to you tomorrow.*)	

Spelling-change verbs like **commencer** (*to begin*) and **manger** (*to eat*) have no spelling change in the future tense. Just take the infinitive and add the appropriate ending: **-ai, -as, -a, -ons, -ez,** or **-ont.**

commencer (*to begin*)	
je commencer**ai**	nous commencer**ons**
tu commencer**as**	vous commencer**ez**
il/elle/on commencer**a**	ils/elles commencer**ont**
Nous **commencerons** dans cinq minutes. (*We'll begin in five minutes.*)	

Regular **-ir** verbs also use their infinitives as the future stem. Just add the appropriate ending: **-ai, -as, -a, -ons, -ez,** or **-ont.**

finir (*to finish*)	
je finir**ai**	nous finir**ons**
tu finir**as**	vous finir**ez**
il/elle/on finir**a**	ils/elles finir**ont**
Ils **finiront** bientôt. (*They'll finish soon.*)	

For regular **-re** verbs, drop the final **-e** from the infinitive before adding the future ending: **-ai, -as, -a, -ons, -ez,** or **-ont.**

vendre (*to sell*)	
je vendr**ai**	nous vendr**ons**
tu vendr**as**	vous vendr**ez**
il/elle/on vendr**a**	ils/elles vendr**ont**
Vendras-tu ta voiture ? (*Will you sell your car?*)	

Conjugate these verbs in the future tense for the subject in parentheses.

Q. marcher (je)

A. **je marcherai** (*I will walk*)

1. choisir (tu) _____

2. manger (Luc) _____

3. rendre (nous) _____

4. vieillir (vous) _____

5. danser (elles) _____

6. annoncer (je) _____

7. pousser (tu) _____

8. remplir (il) _____

9. bouger (nous) _____

10. répondre (vous) _____

Stem-changing verbs

Most stem-changing verbs need the same stem change in the future as they do in the present tense. (See Chapter 4 for conjugations of stem-changing verbs as well as lists of verbs in each category.) The following sections show you how to create the future with the different types of stem-changing verbs.

Verbs with -yer

Verbs that end in **-oyer** and **-uyer** have a required **y**-to-**i** stem change in all the future conjugations. So you take the infinitive, change the **y** to an **i**, and add the future ending **-ai, -as, -a, -ons, -ez,** or **-ont**.

employer (*to use*)	
j'emploierai	nous emploierons
tu emploieras	vous emploierez
il/elle/on emploiera	ils/elles emploieront
Nous **emploierons** notre argent. (*We'll use our money.*)	

However, there are exceptions to this rule. The stem-changing verbs **envoyer** (*to send*) and **renvoyer** (*to fire, to send back*) have irregular future stems: **enverr-** and **renverr-.** Just take these irregular stems and add the appropriate ending.

envoyer (*to send*)	
j'enverrai	nous enverrons
tu enverras	vous enverrez
il/elle/on enverra	ils/elles enverront
Elle **enverra** la lettre. (*She'll send the letter.*)	

Verbs that end in **-ayer** have an optional **y**-to-**i** stem change in the future. There is absolutely no difference between these two conjugations — they are equally acceptable, though you should be consistent. Just use the infinitive **payer** or the stem-changed infinitive **paier** and add the ending **-ai, -as, -a, -ons, -ez,** or **-ont.**

payer (*to pay*)	
je payer**ai**/paier**ai**	nous payer**ons**/paier**ons**
tu payer**as**/paier**as**	vous payer**ez**/paier**ez**
il/elle/on payer**a**/paier**a**	ils/elles payer**ont**/paier**ont**
Je **payerai** demain. (*I'll pay tomorrow.*)	

Verbs with double consonants

Verbs that end in **-eler** need a double **l** in the future, so the future stem for **appeler** is **appeller-**. Just add the ending **-ai, -as, -a, -ons, -ez,** or **-ont.**

appeler (*to call*)	
j'appeller**ai**	nous appeller**ons**
tu appeller**as**	vous appeller**ez**
il/elle/on appeller**a**	ils/elles appeller**ont**
Il **appellera** Marc. (*He'll call Marc.*)	

Verbs that end in **-eter** double the **t** for the future stem, making the future stem for **jeter** (*to throw*) **jetter-,** to which you add the ending **-ai, -as, -a, -ons, -ez,** or **-ont.**

jeter (*to throw*)	
je jetter**ai**	nous jetter**ons**
tu jetter**as**	vous jetter**ez**
il/elle/on jetter**a**	ils/elles jetter**ont**
Ils **jetteront** la balle de tennis. (*They'll throw the tennis ball.*)	

Verbs with accent changes

Verbs that end in **-e*er** (see Chapter 4) need a grave accent on the first **e** for the future stem, so **mener** becomes **mèner-,** and then you add **-ai, -as, -a, -ons, -ez,** or **-ont.**

mener (*to lead*)	
je mèner**ai**	nous mèner**ons**
tu mèner**as**	vous mèner**ez**
il/elle/on mèner**a**	ils/elles mèner**ont**
Je **mènerai** l'enquête. (*I'll lead the investigation.*)	

The only stem-changing verbs that don't have a stem-change in the future are **-é*er** verbs. You keep the acute accent on the first **e,** and just add the future ending to the infinitive to get the future tense.

gérer (_to manage_)	
je gérer**ai**	nous gérer**ons**
tu gérer**as**	vous gérer**ez**
il/elle/on gérer**a**	ils/elles gérer**ont**
Vous **gérerez** la crise. (_You'll handle the crisis._)	

Conjugate these stem-changing verbs in the future tense for the subject in parentheses.

_0._ balayer (nous)

_A._ **nous balayerons** or **nous balaierons** (_we will sweep_)

11. nettoyer (vous) votre chambre. _____

12. renouveler (Charles et Guy) leurs visas. _____

13. rejeter (je) le manuscrit. _____

14. considérer (tu) notre offre. _____

15. essayer (elle) encore demain. _____

16. enlever (nous) les meubles. _____

17. renvoyer (vous) ces deux employés. _____

18. noyer (ils) les champs. _____

19. promener (je) le chien. _____

20. exagérer (tu) ta réussite. _____

Irregular verbs

Irregular verbs can make the future a bit interesting, but everything works out in the end. Many irregular verbs follow the same future conjugation rules as regular verbs, but other irregular verbs have irregular stems. Either way, they all take the same future endings as regular verbs. The following sections point out how to conjugate irregular verbs in the future tense.

Aller

The only irregular **-er** verb, **aller** has an irregular future stem: **ir-.** Start with that stem and add the appropriate ending: **-ai, -as, -a, -ons, -ez,** or **-ont.**

aller (*to go*)	
j'ir**ai**	nous ir**ons**
tu ir**as**	vous ir**ez**
il/elle/on ir**a**	ils/elles ir**ont**
J'**irai** à la banque demain. (*I'll go to the bank tomorrow.*)	

Irregular -ir verbs

Most irregular **-ir** verbs, including **sortir** (*to go out*), **ouvrir** (*to open*), and all verbs conjugated like them (see Chapter 4), use their infinitives as the future stem. No need to change anything. Just add the appropriate ending: **-ai, -as, -a, -ons, -ez,** or **-ont.**

sortir (*to go out*)	
je sortir**ai**	nous sortir**ons**
tu sortir**as**	vous sortir**ez**
il/elle/on sortir**a**	ils/elles sortir**ont**
Nous **sortirons** ce soir. (*We'll go out tonight.*)	

A few irregular **-ir** verbs have irregular future stems. To form the future tense, take the stems in Table 18-1 and add the appropriate ending: **-ai, -as, -a, -ons, -ez,** or **-ont.**

Table 18-1	Irregular Future Stems on -ir Verbs	
Infinitive	*Translation*	*Future Stem*
avoir	*to have*	**aur-**
devoir	*to have to*	**devr-**
mourir	*to die*	**mourr-**
pleuvoir	*to rain*	**pleuvr-**
pouvoir	*to be able to*	**pourr-**
recevoir	*to receive*	**recevr-**
savoir	*to know*	**saur-**
tenir	*to hold*	**tiendr-**
valoir	*to be worth*	**vaudr-**
venir	*to come*	**viendr-**
voir	*to see*	**verr-**
vouloir	*to want*	**voudr-**

For example, here's what **avoir** (*to have*) looks like in the future tense.

avoir (*to have*)	
j'aur**ai**	nous aur**ons**
tu aur**as**	vous aur**ez**
il/elle/on aur**a**	ils/elles aur**ont**
Elle **aura** beaucoup d'argent. (*She'll have a lot of money.*)	

Irregular -re verbs

Most irregular **-re** verbs use their infinitives minus **-e** as their future stem. This set of verbs includes **prendre** (*to take*), **mettre** (*to put*), **craindre** (*to fear*), and all verbs conjugated like them.

prendre (*to take*)	
je prendr**ai**	nous prendr**ons**
tu prendr**as**	vous prendr**ez**
il/elle/on prendr**a**	ils/elles prendr**ont**
Vous **prendrez** des photos. (*You'll take some pictures.*)	

Two irregular **-re** verbs have irregular future stems. The future stem for **être** is **ser-**, and the future stem for **faire** is **fer-.** To form the future, just take the stem and add the appropriate ending: **-ai, -as, -a, -ons, -ez,** or **-ont.**

être (*to be*)	
je ser**ai**	nous ser**ons**
tu ser**as**	vous ser**ez**
il/elle/on ser**a**	ils/elles ser**ont**
Tu **seras** en retard. (*You'll be late.*)	

faire (*to do, make*)	
je fer**ai**	nous fer**ons**
tu fer**as**	vous fer**ez**
il/elle/on fer**a**	ils/elles fer**ont**
Nous **ferons** le lit. (*We'll make the bed.*)	

All future stems are identical to conditional stems; only the endings are different. You can read about the conditional in Chapter 19.

Conjugate these verbs in the future tense for the subject in parentheses.

0. craindre (le chien)

A. **le chien craindra** (*the dog will fear*)

21. mettre (nous) _____

22. aller (vous) _____

23. faire (elles) _____

24. partir (je) _____

25. voir (tu) _____

26. avoir (le restaurant) _____

27. venir (nous) _____

28. dormir (vous) _____

29. savoir (ils) _____

30. être (je) _____

Looking Ahead with the Future Tense

Say you're writing an e-mail to your best friend in Nice and you want to talk about what's going to happen next Sunday, such as the launch of your 80-day trip around the globe. In that case, you use the future tense to let her know whether you'll cross the Atlantic Ocean by boat or hot-air balloon. After you master how to conjugate the future tense (see the previous sections), you can use this tense to illustrate when you're doing something in the future:

> **Je ferai la lessive plus tard.** (*I'll do the laundry later.*)

> **Nous voyagerons en France dans deux semaines.** (*We'll travel to France in two weeks.*)

In French, you also use the future tense after certain conjunctions when they indicate something that is going to happen in the future. Those conjunctions include the following:

- ✔ **après que** (*after*)

- ✔ **aussitôt que** (*as soon as*)

- ✔ **dès que** (*as soon as*)

- ✔ **lorsque** (*when*)

- ✔ **quand** (*when*)

> **Je te téléphonerai quand j'arriverai à l'hôtel.** (*I will call you when I arrive at the hotel.*)

> **Il le fera dès qu'il finira son travail.** (*He'll do it as soon as he finishes his work.*)

You use the present tense after these expressions in English, but in French, the future is required because the action after the expression has not yet occurred.

You can also use the future tense to talk about something that will happen in the future if a certain condition is met. ***Remember:*** The condition after **si** (*if*) has to be in the present tense; you use the future tense only in the main clause.

> **J'irai en France si tu viens avec moi.** (*I will go to France if you come with me.*)

> **Si tu viens chez moi, nous regarderons le film ensemble.** (*If you come to my house, we'll watch the movie together.*)

You can also give polite requests using the future tense — this is more polite than using the imperative, more of a request than a demand. (See Chapter 10 for more information about giving orders in French.)

> **Vous me suivrez, s'il vous plaît.** (*Follow me, please.*)

You're working on your five-year career plan. Fill in the blanks with the correct form of the verb in parentheses.

Q. Cet automne, je _____ (finir) mes études en économie.

A. Cet automne, je **finirai** mes études en économie. (*This fall, I will finish my studies in economics.*)

Plan de carrière (5 ans)
Après que je (31) _____ (recevoir) mon diplôme, je (32) _____ (déménager) en France. Dès que j'y (33) _____ (arriver), je (34) _____ (commencer) à chercher un emploi. Si je le trouve assez rapidement, j' (35) _____ (acheter) un appartement. Si cela prend plus de temps, je (36) _____ (considérer) un autre type de travail. Quoi qui se passe, je (37) _____ (s'habiller) toujours de manière professionnelle. Je (38) _____ (se marier) avec une personne intelligente et intéressante. Nous (39) _____ (avoir) deux enfants. Nous (40) _____ (vivre) à Paris.

Talking about the Near Future in Other Ways

The future tense can have a slightly formal feel to it. If you want to lighten your conversation and make it a tad more informal, you can talk about the future in a couple of other ways, especially if you're discussing something that'll happen soon (like what you'll do to your little brother if he changes the channel *one more time*). This section helps you add a little casualness to your words when referring to the future.

Making the future into a present

In both French and English, you can use the present tense to talk about something that's in the future. When you're going to do something in just a few minutes or in the next few days, the present tense helps bring that event just a little closer. It's slightly less formal than the future.

> **Je vais à la plage demain.** (*I'm going to the beach tomorrow.*)
>
> **Nous partons dans dix minutes.** (*We're leaving in ten minutes.*)

Where there's a will, there's a vais: Using aller to say what's going to happen

You can talk about the near future with the present tense of **aller** (see the table) + the infinitive. This **futur proche** (*near future*) construction is equivalent to *to be going to do something* in English. Like the present tense, the **futur proche** is just slightly informal and tends to be a good choice when what's going to happen is going to happen soon.

aller (*to go*)	
je **vais**	nous **allons**
tu **vas**	vous **allez**
il/elle/on **va**	ils/elles **vont**

> **Il va travailler pendant toute la journée.** (*He's going to work all day.*)
>
> **Alexandre et Laurent vont être déçus.** (*Alexandre and Laurent are going to be disappointed.*)

With pronominal verbs (see Chapter 11), the reflexive pronoun goes in front of the infinitive.

> **Nous allons nous promener sur la plage.** (*We're going to walk on the beach.*)
>
> **Vas-tu t'habiller ?** (*Are you going to get dressed?*)

Object and adverbial pronouns also precede the infinitive:

> **Je vais le faire demain.** (*I'm going to do it tomorrow.*)
>
> **Ils vont en avoir envie.** (*They're going to want some.*)

You can read more about word order with reflexive, object, and adverbial pronouns in Chapter 13.

Answer Key

1. **tu choisiras** (*you will choose*)

2. **Luc mangera** (*Luc will eat*)

3. **nous rendrons** (*we will return*)

4. **vous vieillirez** (*you will get old*)

5. **elles danseront** (*they will dance*)

6. **j'annoncerai** (*I will announce*)

7. **tu pousseras** (*you will push*)

8. **il remplira** (*he will fill*)

9. **nous bougerons** (*we will move*)

10. **vous répondrez** (*you will answer*)

11. **Vous nettoierez votre chambre.** (*You will clean your room.*)

12. **Charles et Guy renouvelleront leurs visas.** (*Charles and Guy will renew their visas.*)

13. **Je rejetterai le manuscrit.** (*I will reject the manuscript.*)

14. **Tu considéreras notre offre.** (*You will consider our offer.*)

15. **Elle essayera/essaiera encore demain.** (*She will try again tomorrow.*)

16. **Nous enlèverons les meubles.** (*We will remove the furniture.*)

17. **Vous renverrez ces deux employés.** (*You will fire these two employees.*)

18. **Ils noieront les champs.** (*They will flood the fields.*)

19. **Je promènerai le chien.** (*I will walk the dog.*)

20. **Tu exagéreras ta réussite.** (*You will exaggerate your success.*)

21. **nous mettrons** (*we will put*)

22. **vous irez** (*you will go*)

23. **Elles feront** (*They will do/make*)

24. **je partirai** (*I will leave*)

25. **tu verras** (*you will see*)

26. **le restaurant aura** (*the restaurant will have*)

27 **nous viendrons** (*we will come*)

28 **vous dormirez** (*you will sleep*)

29 **ils sauront** (*they will know*)

30 **je serai** (*I will be*)

Plan de carriére (5 ans)

Après que je (31) **recevrai** mon diplôme, je (32) **déménagerai** en France. Dès que j'y (33) **arriverai**, je (34) **commencerai** à chercher un emploi. Si je le trouve assez rapidement, j' (35) **achèterai** un appartement. Si cela prend plus de temps, je (36) **considérerai** un autre type de travail. Quoi qui se passe, je (37) **m'habillerai** toujours de manière professionnelle. Je (38) me **marierai** avec une personne intelligente et intéressante. Nous (39) **aurons** deux enfants. Nous (40) **vivrons** à Paris.

(After I receive my diploma, I will move to France. As soon as I arrive, I will start to look for a job. If I find one fairly quickly, I will buy an apartment. If it takes more time, I will consider another type of work. Whatever happens, I will always dress professionally. I will marry an intelligent and interesting person. We will have two kids. We'll live in Paris.)

Chapter 19

What Would You Do? The Conditional Mood

The **conditionnel** (*conditional*) is a verb mood that expresses something that could or would happen, usually depending on whether something else does or does not happen, as in *I could travel around the world if I were rich* or *He would go swimming if he didn't have to work.* It lets you ask people whether they would be happier living somewhere else, and it helps you clarify your relationships so people know whether you'd date someone if he or she were the last person on Earth.

In English, the conditional is a modal verb (*would* or *could*) plus another verb, such as *I would go* or *we would succeed;* in French, it's a verb conjugated with the conditional ending: **j'irais** or **nous réussirions.** This chapter tells you how to conjugate the French conditional mood and explains how to use it.

Setting the Mood with Conditional Conjugations

The present tense of the conditional mood is one of the easiest French verb conjugations because all verbs take the same endings and only a few verbs have irregular conjugations. To conjugate the conditional, just take the infinitive of **-er** and **-ir** verbs, or the infinitive minus **-e** of **-re** verbs, and add the appropriate endings: **-ais, -ais, -ait, -ions, -iez,** and **-aient.** *Note:* The conditional stem for all verbs — regular, stem-changing, spelling-change, and irregular — always ends in **r.** The following sections point out how you conjugate each type of verb in the conditional.

Conditional stems are identical to future stems; only the conjugation endings are different. (You can read about the **futur** [*future*] in Chapter 18.) And the conditional endings match the **imparfait** (*imperfect*) endings (see Chapter 16) — only the stems differ.

Regular and spelling-change verbs

Regular **-er** verbs use their infinitive as the conditional stem, so the regular **-er** verb **parler** looks like this in the conditional.

parler (to talk)	
je parler**ais**	nous parler**ions**
tu parler**ais**	vous parler**iez**
il/elle/on parler**ait**	ils/elles parler**aient**
Je **parlerais** plus lentement. (*I would speak more slowly.*)	

Spelling-change verbs — like **commencer** (*to begin*) and **manger** (*to eat*) — don't quite live up to their name in the conditional: They have no spelling change. The infinitive — which works as the conditional stem — ends in an **r,** so you don't have to change the spelling to preserve the pronunciation as you do in some other conjugations.

commencer (to begin)	
je commencer**ais**	nous commencer**ions**
tu commencer**ais**	vous commencer**iez**
il/elle/on commencer**ait**	ils/elles commencer**aient**
Nous **commencerions** à midi. (*We would begin at noon.*)	

Regular **-ir** verbs also use their infinitives as conditional stems. Just keep the infinitive and add the appropriate endings.

finir (to finish)	
je finir**ais**	nous finir**ions**
tu finir**ais**	vous finir**iez**
il/elle/on finir**ait**	ils/elles finir**aient**
Il **finirait** avant toi. (*He would finish before you.*)	

For regular **-re** verbs, you have to drop the final **e** before adding the conditional endings.

vendre (to sell)	
je vendr**ais**	nous vendr**ions**
tu vendr**ais**	vous vendr**iez**
il/elle/on vendr**ait**	ils/elles vendr**aient**
Elles **vendraient** leur voiture. (*They would sell their car.*)	

Conjugate these verbs into the conditional for the subject in parentheses.

Q. travailler (il)

A. **il travaillerait** (*he would work*)

1. finir (tu) _____

2. bouger (Martine) _____

3. vendre (nous) _____

4. choisir (vous) _____

5. danser (ils) _____

6. lancer (je) _____

7. marcher (tu) _____

8. remplir (mon père) _____

9. manger (nous) _____

10. attendre (vous) _____

Stem-changing verbs

Most stem-changing verbs need the same stem change in the conditional as they do in the present tense. (See Chapter 4 for conjugations of stem-changing verbs as well as lists of verbs in each category.)

Verbs with -yer

Most verbs that end in **-oyer** and **-uyer** have a required **y-to-i** stem change in the conditional. Just change **y** to **i** and add the conditional endings.

employer (*to use*)	
j'emploierais	nous emploierions
tu emploierais	vous emploieriez
il/elle/on emploierait	ils/elles emploieraient
Tu **emploierais** un stylo. (*You would use a pen.*)	

However, the stem-changing verbs **envoyer** (*to send*) and **renvoyer** (*to fire, to send back*) have irregular conditional stems: **enverr-** and **renverr-**.

envoyer (*to send*)	
j'enverrais	nous enverrions
tu enverrais	vous enverriez
il/elle/on enverrait	ils/elles enverraient
Il **enverrait** un chèque. (*He would send a check.*)	

Verbs that end in **-ayer** have an optional **y**-to-**i** stem change in the conditional. So you can either just use the infinitive as your conditional stem or change the **y** to **i** to find your stem. There's absolutely no difference between these two conjugations — they're equally acceptable.

payer (*to pay*)	
je payer**ais**/paier**ais**	nous payer**ions**/paier**ions**
tu payer**ais**/paier**ais**	vous payer**iez**/paier**iez**
il/elle/on payer**ait**/paier**ait**	ils/elles payer**aient**/paier**aient**
Nous **payerions** argent comptant. (*We would pay cash.*)	

Verbs with double consonants

Verbs that end in **-eler** or **-eter** need a double **l** or double **t**, respectively, in the conditional. Take the infinitive, double the **l** or **t** to find your conditional stem, and then add on the conditional endings.

appeler (*to call*)	
j'appeller**ais**	nous appeller**ions**
tu appeller**ais**	vous appeller**iez**
il/elle/on appeller**ait**	ils/elles appeller**aient**
Elle **appellerait** le médecin. (*She would call the doctor.*)	

jeter (*to throw*)	
je jetter**ais**	nous jetter**ions**
tu jetter**ais**	vous jetter**iez**
il/elle/on jetter**ait**	ils/elles jetter**aient**
Vous **jetteriez** la balle. (*You would throw the ball.*)	

Verbs with accent changes

Verbs that end in **-e*er** (see Chapter 4) need a grave accent on the first **e** for the conditional stem; for example, **mener** becomes **mèner-**. After you get the stem, just add the conditional ending you need.

mener (*to lead*)	
je mèner**ais**	nous mèner**ions**
tu mèner**ais**	vous mèner**iez**
il/elle/on mèner**ait**	ils/elles mèner**aient**
Je **mènerais** les enfants. (*I would lead the children.*)	

The only stem-changing verbs that don't have a stem change in the conditional are
-é*er verbs. With these verbs, just keep the infinitive as your stem and add on the
conditional endings.

gérer (to manage)	
je gérer**ais**	nous gérer**ions**
tu gérer**ais**	vous gérer**iez**
il/elle/on gérer**ait**	ils/elles gérer**aient**
Tu **gérerais** le projet. (*You would manage the project.*)	

Conjugate the stem-changing verbs in parentheses into the conditional to complete each
sentence.

0. Il _____ (céder) le pouvoir à son frère.

A. **Il céderait le pouvoir à son frère.** (*He would give up/yield power to his brother.*)

11. Nous _____ (ennuyer) les voisins.

12. Vous _____ (épeler) le prochain mot.

13. Elles _____ (projeter) quelque chose pour les vacances.

14. Je _____ (considérer) ton offre.

15. Tu _____ (balayer) la cuisine.

16. Marc _____ (lever) la main.

17. Nous _____ (envoyer) la lettre.

18. Vous _____ (vouvoyer) les professeurs.

19. Sandrine et Sylvie _____ (amener) la voiture.

20. Je _____ (répéter) la question.

Irregular verbs

Many irregular verbs follow the same conditional conjugation rules as regular verbs,
but other irregular verbs have irregular stems. Either way, they all take the same conditional endings as regular verbs.

Aller

The irregular **-er** verb **aller** has an irregular conditional stem: **ir-**. Take **ir-** and add the
ending you need.

aller (*to go*)	
j'irais	nous irions
tu irais	vous iriez
il/elle/on irait	ils/elles iraient
Nous **irions** à la banque. (*We would go to the bank.*)	

Irregular -ir verbs

Most irregular **-ir** verbs — including **sortir** (*to go out*), **ouvrir** (*to open*), and all verbs conjugated like them (see Chapter 4) — use their infinitives as the conditional stem. Just tack on the conditional endings.

sortir (*to go out*)	
je sortirais	nous sortirions
tu sortirais	vous sortiriez
il/elle/on sortirait	ils/elles sortiraient
Elle **sortirait** ce soir. (*She would go out tonight.*)	

A few irregular **-ir** verbs have irregular conditional stems. Just take these stems, add the appropriate verb ending, and voilà! — the conditional:

- **avoir** (*to have*): **aur-**
- **devoir** (*to have to*): **devr-**
- **mourir** (*to die*): **mourr-**
- **pleuvoir** (*to rain*): **pleuvr-**
- **pouvoir** (*to be able to*): **pourr-**
- **recevoir** (*to receive*): **recevr-**
- **savoir** (*to know*): **saur-**
- **tenir** (*to hold*): **tiendr-**
- **valoir** (*to be worth*): **vaudr-**
- **venir** (*to come*): **viendr-**
- **voir** (*to see*): **verr-**
- **vouloir** (*to want*): **voudr-**

Here's what **avoir** (*to have*) looks like conjugated in the conditional.

avoir (*to have*)	
j'aurais	nous aurions
tu aurais	vous auriez
il/elle/on aurait	ils/elles auraient
Vous **auriez** beaucoup d'argent. (*You would have a lot of money.*)	

Irregular -re verbs

Most irregular **-re** verbs — including **prendre** (*to take*), **mettre** (*to put*), **craindre** (*to fear*), and all verbs conjugated like them — aren't so irregular in the conditional. Like regular **-re** verbs, these verbs use their infinitives minus **e** as their conditional stem.

prendre (*to take*)	
je prend**rais**	nous prend**rions**
tu prend**rais**	vous prend**riez**
il/elle/on prend**rait**	ils/elles prend**raient**
Tu **prendrais** des photos. (*You would take some pictures.*)	

Two irregular **-re** verbs have irregular conditional stems. The conditional stem for **être** is **ser-,** and the conditional stem for **faire** is **fer-.**

être (*to be*)	
je ser**ais**	nous ser**ions**
tu ser**ais**	vous ser**iez**
il/elle/on ser**ait**	ils/elles ser**aient**
Elles **seraient** chez nous. (*They would be at our house.*)	

faire (*to do, make*)	
je fer**ais**	nous fer**ions**
tu fer**ais**	vous fer**iez**
il/elle/on fer**ait**	ils/elles fer**aient**
Nous le **ferions** ensemble. (*We would do it together.*)	

Conjugate these verbs into the conditional for the subject in parentheses.

Q. mettre (je)

A. **je mettrais** (*I would put*)

21. plaindre (tu) _____

22. aller (elle) _____

23. faire (nous) _____

24. partir (vous) _____

25. voir (ils) _____

26. avoir (je) _____

27. venir (tu) _____

28. dormir (René) _____

29. savoir (nous) _____

30. être (vous) _____

Terms and Conditions: When to Use the Conditional

As the name indicates, the conditional mood usually involves a condition — it tells you that something would or could happen only if something else does or does not happen. You use the conditional to express a sense of possibility, or to say that you would do something if something else were to occur.

With si clauses: If only

You use the conditional most commonly with **si** (*if*) clauses, or in *if-then* statements. The conditional actually goes in the *then* clause. Here's how you conjugate each part of the sentence:

- ✔ The **si** clause, which describes the condition, uses the **imparfait** (see Chapter 16).
- ✔ The main clause — the *then* part — uses the conditional.

For example, if a friend asks you to go France with him but you can go only if you find a babysitter, and you think it's unlikely that you'll find one, you'd use the conditional to respond to the invitation:

> **J'irais en France si je trouvais un babysitter.** (*I would go to France if I found a babysitter.*)

Or say you want to buy a car, but whether you can buy a new or used one depends on how much money you earn, and although you're hoping for a raise, you're not sure you'll get it. Here's how you may answer:

> **J'achèterais une voiture neuve si j'obtenais une augmentation de salaire.** (*I would buy a new car if I got a raise.*)

As in English, you can use the French conditional to express something that would happen without a **si**/*if* clause:

> **J'irais en France juste pour voir la tour Eiffel.** (*I would go to France just to see the Eiffel Tower.*)

An if-then statement with the conditional and **imparfait** indicates an unlikely situation. When you talk about something that is likely to occur, you don't use the conditional. Instead, you use the present tense in the **si**/*if* clause and the present or future in the *then* clause. So if you're pretty sure you'll get that raise, you can say this:

> **J'achèterai une voiture neuve si j'obtiens une augmentation de salaire.** (*I will buy a new car if I get a raise.*)

In English, you can sometimes use the conditional after *if*, as in *If you would like to go* or *I don't know if I should go*. You can't do this in French — the French conditional can't follow the word **si** (*if*) — you have to use the present tense instead.

> **Si vous voulez manger avec nous, vous devez vous laver les mains.** (*If you would like to eat with us, you have to wash your hands.*)

> **Je ne sais pas si je dois y aller.** (*I don't know if I should go.*)

In English, you can use *would* in the sense of *used to* in talking about something habitual in the past, as in *When I lived in Paris, I would go to the bakery every day.* You can't use the French conditional here — this construction is equivalent to the French **imparfait: Quand j'habitais à Paris, j'allais à la boulangerie tous les jours.** You can read about the **imparfait** in Chapter 16.

Finish these sentences, using the conditional and whatever else you need to make a complete sentence. I've provided possible responses in the Answer Key.

0. Si j'étais riche, _____

A. Si j'étais riche, **je ferais le tour du monde.** (*If I were rich, I would travel around the world.*)

31. Si je ne devais pas travailler, _____

32. _____ si c'était ton anniversaire.

33. Si nous habitions ensemble, _____

34. Si tu m'écoutais, _____

35. S'il ne pleuvait pas, _____

36. _____ si elles me voyaient ici.

37. Si Marie et Thomas étaient ici, _____

38. Si vous n'étiez pas en retard, _____

39. S'ils avaient un chien, _____

40. _____ si j'habitais au Maroc.

For special verbs: Could, should

The French conditional is most often equivalent to *would* plus a verb in English. However, two French verbs have different English meanings in the conditional:

✔ **Devoir** (*must, to have to*) is equivalent to *should* in the conditional:

> **Je devrais partir avant midi.** (*I should leave before noon.*)

> **Nous devrions manger après le cours.** (*We should eat after the class.*)

✔ **Pouvoir** (*can, to be able to*) is equivalent to *could* in the conditional:

> **Je pourrais le faire pour toi.** (*I could do it for you.*)

> **Pourriez-vous m'aider ?** (*Could you help me?*)

In polite requests: What would you like?

You can use the verbs **vouloir** (*to want*) and **aimer** (*to like*) in the conditional to express polite requests or desires — in the conditional, they both mean *would like:*

Je voudrais manger à treize heures. (*I would like to eat at 1 p.m.*)

Voudriez-vous un appartement au centre-ville ou en banlieue ? (*Would you like an apartment downtown or in the suburbs?*)

J'aimerais bien le voir. (*I would really like to see it.*)

Elle aimerait venir, mais elle est malade. (*She would like to come, but she's sick.*)

Translate these sentences into French.

0. I would like to live in France.

A. **J'aimerais vivre en France.**

41. You should finish it.

_____

42. We could travel together.

_____

43. Do you know if he would like something to eat?

_____

44. They should know the answer.

_____

45. Would you like to try it?

_____

Answer Key

1. **tu finirais** (*you would finish*)

2. **Martine bougerait** (*Martine would move*)

3. **nous vendrions** (*we would sell*)

4. **vous choisiriez** (*you would choose*)

5. **ils danseraient** (*they would dance*)

6. **je lancerais** (*I would throw*)

7. **tu marcherais** (*you would walk*)

8. **mon père remplirait** (*my father would fill*)

9. **nous mangerions** (*we would eat*)

10. **vous attendriez** (*you would wait*)

11. **Nous ennuierions les voisins.** (*We would annoy the neighbors.*)

12. **Vous épelleriez le prochain mot.** (*You would spell the next word.*)

13. **Elles projetteraient quelque chose pour les vacances.** (*They would make plans for vacation.*)

14. **Je considérerais ton offre.** (*I would consider your offer.*)

15. **Tu balaierais la cuisine.** (*You would sweep the kitchen.*)

16. **Marc lèverait la main.** (*Marc would raise his hand.*)

17. **Nous enverrions la lettre.** (*We would send the letter.*)

18. **Vous vouvoieriez les professeurs.** (*You would use "vous" with the teachers.*)

19. **Sandrine et Sylvie amèneraient la voiture.** (*Sandrine and Sylvie would take the car.*)

20. **Je répéterais la question.** (*I would repeat the question.*)

21. **tu plaindrais** (*you would feel sorry for*)

22. **elle irait** (*she would go*)

23. **nous ferions** (*we would do/make*)

24. **vous partiriez** (*you would leave*)

25. **ils verraient** (*they would see*)

26. **j'aurais** (*I would have*)

27 **tu viendrais** (_you would come_)

28 **René dormirait** (_René would sleep_)

29 **nous saurions** (_we would know_)

30 **vous seriez** (_you would be_)

31 Si je ne devais pas travailler, **je vivrais sur une île.** (_If I didn't have to work, I'd live on an island._)

32 **Tu ne serais pas ici** si c'était ton anniversaire. (_You wouldn't be here if it were your birthday._)

33 Si nous habitions ensemble, **nous nous détesterions.** (_If we lived together, we'd hate each other._)

34 Si tu m'écoutais, **tu saurais déjà la réponse.** (_If you listened to me, you would already know the answer._)

35 S'il ne pleuvait pas, **nous irions à la plage.** (_If it weren't raining, we'd go to the beach._)

36 **Elles seraient fâchées** si elles me voyaient ici. (_They'd be mad if they saw me here._)

37 Si Marie et Thomas étaient ici, **ils auraient beaucoup d'idées.** (_If Marie and Thomas were here, they'd have lots of ideas._)

38 Si vous n'étiez pas en retard, **vous auriez assez de temps pour manger.** (_If you weren't late, you'd have enough time to eat._)

39 S'ils avaient un chien, **leur maison serait plus sûre.** (_If they had a dog, their house would be safer._)

40 **J'apprendrais l'arabe** si j'habitais au Maroc. (_I'd learn Arabic if I lived in Morocco._)

41 **Tu devrais/Vous devriez le finir.**

42 **Nous pourrions voyager ensemble.**

43 **Sais-tu/Savez-vous s'il veut quelque chose à manger ?**

44 **Ils devraient savoir la réponse.**

45 **Voudrais-tu/Voudriez-vous l'essayer ?**

Part V
The Part of Tens

In this part . . .

Here I engage in a time-honored *For Dummies* tradition: the tens lists. In this part, you can read about ten common French mistakes and how to avoid them and find out ten ways to start a letter.

Chapter 20

Ten Common French Mistakes and How to Avoid 'Em

*E*veryone makes mistakes, but you can avoid many, if not most, of them by paying extra attention to typical problem areas. This chapter tells you about ten common French pitfalls — and what you can do to avoid falling into the traps.

Translating Word for Word

If you've ever written a paper on a tight deadline, you may have looked up synonyms in a thesaurus and plugged in the first word that sounded good, without bothering to sort out the shades of meaning. In French, trying to do a word-for-word translation can give you a similarly bizarre result — or in thesaurus-speak, "Aspiring to undertake an exact elucidation can bestow on you a comparably grotesque outcome." Yikes!

One of the worst things you can do is translate word for word. Translating French isn't like swapping the discs in your DVD player: Not every word in a sentence has a perfect English equivalent, so you can't always substitute one word for the other. Some French words have more than one English equivalent, and vice versa, and some words have no true equivalent. Besides that, word order is different in the two languages, so you have to keep that in mind when translating as well. When you translate, you have to find a way to express the entire concept, not just the individual words.

For example, the French word **en** is both a pronoun and a preposition. As a pronoun, it usually means *some,* as in **J'en veux** (*I want some*), but as a preposition, it means *in* or *to,* as in **Je vais en France** (*I'm going to France*). You have to think about this difference when translating from French to English to make sure you translate the idea of **en** correctly.

On the other hand, the English word *new* has two French equivalents. In English, when you say, "I bought a new car," there's no way to know whether you bought it from a car showroom or out of the classified ads. It may be brand new, or it may just be new to you — if that distinction is important, you have to add something to your description. In French, that's not necessary, because you can use more-specific words: A brand-new car is **une voiture neuve,** and a car that's just new to you is **une nouvelle voiture.**

French also has entire concepts that fit into a word or phrase, like **chez,** which can mean *at the home of, at the office of, in the mind of,* and more. Idiomatic expressions, too, can cause trouble. **J'ai un petit creux,** which literally translates as *I have a little hollow,* actually means *I'm a little hungry.*

See Chapter 1 for all kinds of tips on using a bilingual dictionary, dealing with synonyms, and understanding idiomatic expressions.

Leaving Out Accents

Accents are very important in French. They have several purposes, and leaving one off in your writing is a spelling mistake at best and a source of confusion at worst. Accents help distinguish between *homographs* — that is, words that are spelled the same but have different meanings. There are hundreds of these words pairs; here are just a few:

- ✔ **cure** (*cure*) — **curé** (*priest*)
- ✔ **jeune** (*young*) — **jeûne** (*fasting*)
- ✔ **mais** (*but*) — **maïs** (*corn*)
- ✔ **ou** (*or*) — **où** (*where*)
- ✔ **parle** (present tense of **parler** [*to talk*]) — **parlé** (past participle of **parler**)
- ✔ **sale** (*dirty*) — **salé** (*salty*)

Some accents also tell you how to pronounce a word. The acute accent on the **e** at the end of a word such as **curé** tells you to pronounce the **e,** whereas you don't pronounce the unaccented **e** at the end of **cure.** (The first means *priest,* and the second means *cure* — two completely different meanings that can confuse the person you're writing to.)

The accent ^ — a *circumflex* — indicates that in Old French, an **s** used to follow that vowel, which makes it easy to see what **hôpital** and **forêt** mean in English.

Technically, you can leave accents off capital letters; however, if you leave them off anywhere else, it's often as bad as using the wrong letter altogether.

Using Too Many Capitals

French uses a lot fewer capital letters than English — many words that have to be capitalized in English can't be capitalized in French. Here are the most important words to watch out for:

- **The personal pronoun *I*:** Don't capitalize the pronoun **je** (*I*) except at the beginning of a sentence.

  > **Je dois partir.** (*I have to leave.*)

  > **Dois-je partir ?** (*Do I have to leave?*)

- **Date words:** Don't capitalize days of the week and months of the year in French unless they're at the beginning of a sentence (see Chapter 3 for the lists).

- **Geographical words:** Although you have to capitalize names of streets, roads, lakes, oceans, and so on in both French and English, in English you also have to capitalize the words *street, road,* and so on when you name a specific one. Not so in French:

  > **15, rue LeBlanc** (*15 LeBlanc Street*)

  > **l'océan Atlantique** (*the Atlantic Ocean*)

- **Languages and nationalities:** Don't capitalize names of languages in French.

  > **Je parle français.** (*I speak French.*)

  > **Il veut apprendre l'allemand.** (*He wants to learn German.*)

  Don't capitalize nationalities used as adjectives:

  > **Il est suisse.** (*He's Swiss.*)

  > **une voiture japonaise** (*a Japanese car*)

  However, you do capitalize nationalities used as nouns:

  > **Je connais deux Français.** (*I know two French people.*)

  > **Il habite avec un Espagnol.** (*He lives with a Spaniard.*)

- **Religions:** Don't capitalize words referring to religion:

  > **le christianisme** (*Christianity*), **chrétien** (*Christian*)

  > **le judaïsme** (*Judaism*), **juif** (*Jewish*)

Not Making Contractions

In English, contractions are optional — you can say *I am* or *I'm* with no difference in meaning (though the contraction is considered less formal than spelling out the two words in their entirety).

In French, contractions are required. When a word like **je** or **le** is followed by a vowel or mute *h,* you have to make a contraction. **Je** + **aime** always contracts to **j'aime** (*I like*), and **le** + **homme** always becomes **l'homme** (*the man*).

These words have to contract when they precede a vowel or mute *h:*

- **ce** (*this*)
- **de** (*of, about*)
- **je** (*I*)
- **le, la** (*the*)

- **ne** (*not*)
- **puisque** (*since*)
- **que** (*that*)
- **se** (*oneself*)

- ✔ **lorsque** (*when*)
- ✔ **me** (*myself*)

- ✔ **si** (*if*)
- ✔ **te** (*yourself*)

Note: **Si** contracts only when it means *if*, and only when it's followed by the letter *i:* **si + il** = **s'il** (*if he*), but **si + elle** = **si elle** (*if she*).

The *h* is always silent in French, but it comes in two varieties. A mute *h* acts like a vowel, so contractions occur as if the *h* weren't there: **l'hôtel** (*the hotel*), **je n'habite pas** (*I don't live*). An aspirate *h* acts like a consonant, so you don't make contractions: **le homard** (*lobster*), **je ne hais pas** (*I don't hate*). When you look up a word in the dictionary, a symbol tells you whether the *h* is mute or aspirate.

Trusting False Friends

French and English share a lot of vocabulary. Some similarly spelled words have the same meanings in both languages, but many have different meanings. These pairs are called *false friends*, and they can cause big problems if you don't double-check the meanings of words before you use them. There's no shortcut to knowing whether a word is a false friend; you just have to get in the habit of looking up words that look similar in French and English and memorizing the ones that have different meanings.

Table 20-1 shows some of the most common and problematic false friends.

Table 20-1		False Friends	
French Word	*True Meaning*	*False Friend*	*Actual French Term for False Friend*
actuellement	*currently*	*actually*	**vraiment, en fait**
assister	*to attend*	*to assist*	**aider**
attendre	*to wait for*	*to attend*	**assister**
un avertissement	*a warning*	*an advertisement*	**une publicité**
blesser	*to wound*	*to bless*	**bénir**
la chair	*flesh*	*the chair*	**la chaise**
un coin	*corner*	*a coin*	**une pièce de monnaie**
un collège	*junior high school*	*college*	**une université**
commander	*to order, request*	*to command*	**ordonner**
un crayon	*a pencil*	*a crayon*	**un pastel**
demander	*to ask for*	*to demand*	**exiger**
une douche	*a shower*	*douche*	**une douche vaginale**
éventuellement	*possibly*	*eventually*	**finalement**
le football	*soccer*	*American football*	**le football américain**

French Word	True Meaning	False Friend	Actual French Term for False Friend
ignorer	*to be unaware of*	*to ignore*	**ne tenir aucun compte de**
une librairie	*a bookstore*	*a library*	**une bibliothèque**
quitter	*to leave*	*to quit*	**démissionner**
un raisin	*a grape*	*a raisin*	**un raisin sec**
rester	*to stay*	*to rest*	**se reposer**
une robe	*a dress*	*a robe*	**un peignoir**
sympathique	*nice*	*sympathetic*	**compatissant**

Not Knowing When to Use Avoir Idiomatically

As I explain in the earlier section on translating word for word, you have to be careful when you translate to and from French. One of the most common French verbs, **avoir**, is one of the biggest culprits in poor translations.

Avoir means *to have,* as in **J'ai deux sœurs** (*I have two sisters*) and **Il n'a pas d'argent** (*He doesn't have any money*). The verb **être** means *to be,* as in **Je suis prêt** (*I'm ready*) and **Il est médecin** (*He's a doctor*). However, in a number of common expressions, **avoir** means *to be.* You have to memorize these idiomatic expressions, because although using **être** in them may seem logical, it's as wrong as can be.

- ✔ **avoir _____ ans** (*to be _____ years old*)
- ✔ **avoir chaud** (*to be hot*)
- ✔ **avoir de la chance** (*to be lucky*)
- ✔ **avoir faim** (*to be hungry*)
- ✔ **avoir froid** (*to be cold*)
- ✔ **avoir honte de** (*to be ashamed of/about*)
- ✔ **avoir la mort dans l'âme** (*to be heartsick*)
- ✔ **avoir le mal de mer** (*to be seasick*)
- ✔ **avoir l'habitude de** (*to be used to, in the habit of*)
- ✔ **avoir mal au cœur** (*to be sick to one's stomach, nauseous*)

  Note that **cœur** literally means *heart,* not *stomach.*
- ✔ **avoir peur de** (*to be afraid of*)
- ✔ **avoir raison** (*to be right*)
- ✔ **avoir soif** (*to be thirsty*)
- ✔ **avoir sommeil** (*to be sleepy*)
- ✔ **avoir tort** (*to be wrong*)

There's no real shortcut to knowing when to use **avoir** idiomatically — you just have to memorize the list. After you use these phrases a few times, it becomes second nature and you don't even think about why you have to say, literally, *I have fear* rather than *I am afraid*.

Misusing Auxiliary Verbs

In the **passé composé** and other compound tenses, you need an *auxiliary,* or *helping,* verb. French has two auxiliary verbs, **avoir** and **être,** and the one you use depends on the main verb you're using it with. Virtually all verbs need **avoir** as the auxiliary, which means that you need to memorize just the short list of verbs that need **être,** plus a couple of rules. You can read more about auxiliary verbs in Chapter 15.

The following verbs, which refer to coming and going (both literally and figuratively) as well as staying, need **être** as their auxiliary (unless you use them with a direct object — see Chapter 15 for details):

- **aller** (*to go*)
- **arriver** (*to arrive*)
- **descendre** (*to descend*)
- **entrer** (*to enter*)
- **monter** (*to climb*)
- **mourir** (*to die*)
- **naître** (*to be born*)
- **partir** (*to leave*)
- **passer** (*to pass*)
- **rester** (*to stay*)
- **retourner** (*to return*)
- **sortir** (*to go out*)
- **tomber** (*to fall*)
- **venir** (*to come*)

Most derivatives of the preceding verbs also need **être: devenir** (*to become*), **revenir** (*to come back*), **parvenir** (*to reach*), and so on. Pronominal verbs (verbs with reflexive pronouns — see Chapter 11) also need **être** in the compound verbs. And that's it — just remember these rules, and you'll never use the wrong auxiliary verb again.

Mixing Up the Passé Composé and the Imparfait

The **passé composé** (*compound past*) and **imparfait** (*imperfect*) are the most common French past tenses, and they work together to give you a complete picture of the past. Because they have distinctly different meanings and uses and because they don't always have perfect English equivalents, some people have a difficult time knowing which tense to use and when.

The **imparfait** describes what was happening and is often — but not always — equivalent to *was/were _____-ing* in English. It explains the following:

✔ Background information and descriptions

✔ Actions that *were happening* with no stated beginning or end

✔ Habitual or repeated actions

✔ Simultaneous actions

✔ Activities that got interrupted

Terms like **toujours** (*always*), **d'habitude** (*usually*), **parfois** (*sometimes*), and **tous les jours** (*every day*) indicate that the imperfect is probably the tense you want to use. (See Chapter 16 to read about how to conjugate and use the **imparfait** as well as more details on distinguishing it from the **passé composé.**)

Meanwhile, the **passé composé** states what happened, and it's usually equivalent to _____-*ed* (any verb in the simple past) in English. It tells you about

✔ Things that *happened* with a definite beginning and/or end

✔ Individual events

✔ Sequential events

✔ Events that interrupted something

✔ Changes in physical or mental states

Expressions like **une fois** (*once*), **tout d'un coup** (*all of a sudden*), **quand** (*when*), and **un jour** (*one day*) indicate that the **passé composé** is likely the correct tense to use. (Chapter 15 explains how to conjugate and use the **passé composé.**)

Misunderstanding the Subjunctive

The subjunctive can be a difficult verb mood to master, largely because there's nothing to relate it to (because the English subjunctive is extremely rare). Many students of the French language either don't use the subjunctive correctly or don't fully understand it. However, the most important thing to remember about the subjunctive is right there in its name: It's *subjective.* When you're doubtful, surprised, delighted, or scared about something that's happening, you're being subjective, and you express this with the subjunctive.

> **Je suis surpris qu'il ne soit pas là.** (*I'm surprised he's not there.*)

> **Nous sommes contents que tu puisses nous aider.** (*We're happy you can help us.*)

When you're giving orders or making suggestions, you're also showing subjectivity, so you also use subjunctive in these instances.

> **J'ordonne que tu le fasses.** (*I order you to do it.*)

> **Il suggère que nous partions à midi.** (*He suggests that we leave at noon.*)

Chapter 8 explains how to conjugate the subjunctive and provides much more detailed information about when to use it and how to avoid it.

Not Knowing the Difference between Tu and Vous

Like many languages, the French language has more than one word for *you*: **tu** and **vous.** Which one you should use depends on your relationship with the person you're talking to. One of the worst mistakes you can make in French is using **tu** when you should be using **vous.** This isn't just a matter of correct grammar; it's about showing the proper respect and distance when talking to another person.

Tu is the singular and familiar *you* — you use it when you're talking to someone you know well, such as a friend or family member, or when talking to a peer or equal — a fellow student, a colleague, or a friend of a friend. It's also standard to use **tu** when talking to children and to animals, and young children often use **tu** with everyone.

> **Marie, tu dois m'aider demain.** (*Marie, you have to help me tomorrow.*)

> **Où vas-tu, Nicolas ?** (*Where are you going, Nicolas?*)

Vous is the plural and formal *you.* When you're talking to more than one person — friends or not — you have to use **vous.** (Purists say English doesn't have an equivalent plural form of *you,* but they've apparently never heard Americans toss a *y'all* or *you guys* in their speech when addressing a group.) In addition, you need **vous** when talking to someone you don't know, such as a new neighbor or a cashier, or someone to whom you want to show respect, such as a doctor, lawyer, or professor. Using **tu** with these people shows a lack of respect and can be very offensive.

> **Monsieur Ricard, pouvez-vous nous expliquer votre décision ?** (*Mr. Ricard, can you explain your decision to us?*)

> **Paul et Thomas, vous serez en retard !** (*Paul and Thomas, you're going to be late!*)

French even has verbs that go with each of these pronouns. **Tutoyer** means *to use **tu** with,* and **vouvoyer** means *to use **vous** with.*

If you really can't decide which word to use, stick with **vous** — the native French speaker will let you know if and when it's okay to use **tu** by saying something like **On peut se tutoyer** (*We can use **tu** with each other*). Until then, you're better off with **vous.**

Chapter 21

Ten Ways to Begin a Letter in French

*W*riting letters in French depends on a few things, and one of the most important is the salutation, or greeting. You need to choose a salutation with the right degree of politeness or closeness, and you also need to consider how much you know about the person or organization you're writing to or e-mailing. Here are ten ways to begin a letter in French, with explanations of when and how to use each one.

Writing letters, especially formal letters, can be tricky. You may want to do an online search for "French business letters" or "writing in French" to find some sample letters that can help you out with formatting and language issues. Remember that if you're writing to people you don't know, you have to use **vous**. And if it's an important letter, like a job application cover letter, definitely ask a native French speaker to proofread it for you. Don't forget to date your letter; see Chapter 3 for details on writing the date in French.

Messieurs (Gentlemen)

Messieurs, which (like all the greetings in this chapter) you follow with a comma, means *gentlemen*. It's a very formal greeting that you use only when writing to an organization at which you don't know anyone. For instance, if you ever decide to write to Switzerland's foreign intelligence agency, the **Service de renseignement stratégique** (*Strategic Intelligence Service*), **Messieurs** may be a good way to start.

Although *gentlemen* may not sound politically correct, in French using this greeting isn't really an issue. The French aren't overly concerned with political correctness; in fact, French job applications and résumés have to include information that would outrage many Americans, including the applicant's gender, age, and marital status, as well as a photograph!

The salutation you use has to be repeated exactly in your closing formula, too, which is much more elaborate than anything you'd write in English:

Je vous prie d'agréer, Messieurs, l'expression de mes salutations distinguées.

Literally, this means *I beg you to accept, gentlemen, the expression of my distinguished greetings,* but it's roughly equivalent to *Sincerely yours.* You can use this closing formula with any of the next six salutations; just remember to replace **Messieurs** with the salutation you're using.

After you've exchanged a letter or two, you can cut out a few words: **Veuillez agréer, Messieurs, mes salutations distinguées.** (Literally, *Please accept, gentlemen, my distinguished greetings.*)

Monsieur, Madame (To Whom It May Concern, Dear Sir or Madam)

Suppose your popsicle stand plans to add **la glace** (*ice cream*) to its menu, and you're trying to decide whether the featured flavor should be chocolate or vanilla. You sell only the best, so you decide to contact a cocoa producer in Côte d'Ivoire and a vanilla producer in Madagascar to get the lowdown on their products. How do you start the letters?

Try **Monsieur, Madame.** It's equivalent to *To whom it may concern* and, like **Messieurs,** is used when you're addressing an organization, not an individual. The inclusion of **Madame** has the advantage over plain old **Messieurs** of being just a bit more politically correct.

You can also use **Monsieur, Madame** when writing a single formal letter to a man and woman, such as a letter to a married couple or to a brother and sister living together.

Monsieur (Dear Sir)

If you're writing to an individual whose name you don't know, such as the head of the publicity department, use **Monsieur,** which is equivalent to *Dear Sir.* Again, this is somewhat politically incorrect, but the French don't worry about that, so you don't necessarily need to, either. If you are worried about it, just use **Monsieur, Madame** instead. When writing to someone you do know but aren't friends with, such as a regular client or a colleague at another branch office, you can use **Cher Monsieur** (*Dear Sir*).

Monsieur . . . (Dear Mr. . . .)

When you write to a man whose name you know but with whom you're not friendly — such as a potential client or the head of human resources (not your arch-nemesis) — use **Monsieur** plus his last name: **Monsieur Marteau, Monsieur de Vine,** and so on. Don't use his first name.

Madame . . . (Dear Mrs. . . .)

When you write to a woman whose name you know but with whom you're not friends, use **Madame** plus her last name: **Madame Coureau, Madame LaSigne,** and so on. Don't use her first name. When writing to someone you do know but aren't friends with, such as a regular client or a colleague at another branch office, you can use **Chère Madame** (*Dear Madam*).

Monsieur le Maire (Mr. Mayor — or Other Title)

In a letter to a man with a title, you should use **Monsieur** plus his title, including a definite article: **Monsieur le Maire, Monsieur le Président,** and so on. Don't include his name (first or last). Of course, if you're writing to a man who shares a title with a number of other men, such as a senator or one of several vice presidents of an organization, you want to put his name on the envelope, to make sure it goes to the right person. It's just the salutation in the letter that should not have his name.

Madame la Directrice (Madam Director — or Other Title)

In a letter to a woman with a title, you should use **Madame** plus her title, including a definite article: **Madame la Directrice, Madame le Ministre,** and so on. Don't include her name (first or last).

Many of the French words for professions, such as **ministre** (*government minister*), are always masculine, even when the person in question is a woman. Therefore, the definite article has to agree with the gender of her title. See Chapter 2 for a list of nouns that are always masculine.

Chers Amis (Dear Friends)

When writing to a group of friends, you can use the group salutation **Chers amis.** If they're all women, use **Chères amies.** You can also add *my* in front — **Mes chers amis, Mes chères amies** (*My dear friends*) — to express additional closeness:

> **Mes chers amis, j'espère que vous pourrez me rejoindre en France.** (*My dear friends, I hope you'll be able to join me in France.*)

At the end of your friendly letter, you can close with one of these:

- **Chaleureusement** (*Warmly, Warm regards*)
- **Amitiés** (*Your friend*)
- **Grosses bises** (*Big kisses*)

  Note that the kisses aren't necessarily considered romantic. It's quite common for platonic male and female friends to end their letters with **bises**.

Cher . . . (Dear . . .)

To address a friend or family member, use **Cher** plus his name for a man and **Chère** plus her name for a woman. You can add *my* in front to express additional closeness: **Mon cher Paul** (*My dear Paul*), **Ma chère Henriette** (*My dear Henriette*).

The choice of masculine or feminine adjective depends on the person you're writing to, not the person who's writing. A man writing to a woman would say **Ma chère . . .**, as would a woman writing to a woman. A woman writing to a man would say **Mon cher . . .**, as would a man writing to a man. See Chapter 9 for more info about adjectives and agreement.

Note: Most English salutations use the word *dear,* but its French equivalent, **cher,** is familiar. You shouldn't use it when writing to someone you don't know. Santa Claus, however, is an exception; you can start your letter to him with **Cher Papa Noël** (*Dear Santa Claus*).

Chéri (Darling)

Ah! In a letter to your beloved, the greeting must express the strength of your love! When you write to a spouse, significant other, or very close family member, you can use **Chéri** (*Darling*) for a man and **Chérie** for a woman. You can also add *my* in front to express additional closeness: **Mon chéri, Ma chérie** (*My darling*).

And just for fun, here are some other terms of endearment, with their literal English meanings:

- **Mon amour** (*My love*)
- **Ma cocotte** (*My hen*)
- **Mon petit chou** (*My little cabbage*)
- **Ma puce** (*My flea*)

Part VI
Appendixes

The 5th Wave   By Rich Tennant

"I'm pretty sure you're supposed to just <u>smell</u> the cork."

In this part . . .

These last pages give you just the facts for when you want to skip over the explanations; just flip open the book, find what you need, and go on your merry way. Use these appendixes to conjugate French verbs (Appendix A), find French translations of English words (Appendix B), and discover what French words mean in English (Appendix C).

Appendix A

Verb Charts

● ●

*U*se these verb charts as a quick-reference guide to conjugations for regular, spelling-change, stem-changing, and irregular verbs. (Chapter 4 shows verbs conjugated in the present tense according to each pattern.)

Note: In this appendix, I list the conjugations in order of the pronouns, from first- to third-person singular and then first- to third-person plural: **je, tu, il/elle/on, nous, vous, ils/elles** (or for the imperative [commands], **tu, nous, vous).**

Regular Verbs

You conjugate regular verbs by taking one of the following stems and adding the appropriate ending from Table A-1:

- ✔ **Present, passé simple:** Infinitive minus **-er, -ir,** or **-re** ending
- ✔ **Imperfect:** Present-tense indicative **nous** form minus **-ons**
- ✔ **Future, conditional:** Infinitive (minus **-e** for **-re** verbs)
- ✔ **Subjunctive:** Present-tense indicative **ils/elles** form minus **-ent**

Table A-1		Regular Verb Endings in Various Tenses				
Subject	*Present* **-er** **-ir** **-re**	*Imperfect*	*Future*	*Conditional*	*Subjunctive*	*Passé Simple* **-er** **-ir** **-re**
je	-e -is -s	-ais	-ai	-ais	-e	-ai -is -is
tu	-es -is -s	-ais	-as	-ais	-es	-as -is -is
il/elle/on	-e -it —	-ait	-a	-ait	-e	-a -it -it

(continued)

Table A-1 *(continued)*

Subject	Present -er -ir -re	Imperfect	Future	Conditional	Subjunctive	Passé Simple -er -ir -re
nous	-ons -issons -ons	-ions	-ons	-ions	-ions	-âmes -îmes -îmes
vous	-ez -issez -ez	-iez	-ez	-iez	-iez	-âtes -îtes -îtes
ils/elles	-ent -issent -ent	-aient	-ont	-aient	-ent	-èrent -irent -irent

-er Verbs

parler (to talk, speak)

Present Participle: parlant

Past Participle: parlé; **Auxiliary Verb:** avoir

Imperative: parle, parlons, parlez

Present: parle, parles, parle, parl**ons**, parl**ez**, parl**ent**

Imperfect: parl**ais**, parl**ais**, parl**ait**, parl**ions**, parl**iez**, parl**aient**

Future: parler**ai**, parler**as**, parler**a**, parler**ons**, parler**ez**, parler**ont**

Conditional: parler**ais**, parler**ais**, parler**ait**, parler**ions**, parler**iez**, parler**aient**

Subjunctive: parle, parle**s**, parle, parl**ions**, parl**iez**, parl**ent**

Passé Simple: parlai, parl**as**, parla, parl**âmes**, parl**âtes**, parl**èrent**

-ir Verbs

finir (to finish)

Present Participle: finissant

Past Participle: fini; **Auxiliary Verb:** avoir

Imperative: finis, finissons, finissez

Present: fin**is**, fin**is**, fin**it**, fin**issons**, fin**issez**, fin**issent**

Imperfect: finiss**ais**, finiss**ais**, finiss**ait**, finiss**ions**, finiss**iez**, finiss**aient**

Future: finir**ai**, finir**as**, finir**a**, finir**ons**, finir**ez**, finir**ont**

Conditional: finir**ais**, finir**ais**, finir**ait**, finir**ions**, finir**iez**, finir**aient**

Subjunctive: finisse, finisse**s**, finisse, finiss**ions**, finiss**iez**, finiss**ent**

Passé Simple: fin**is**, fin**is**, fin**it**, fin**îmes**, fin**îtes**, fin**irent**

-re Verbs

vendre (to sell)

Present Participle: vendant

Past Participle: vendu; **Auxiliary Verb:** avoir

Imperative: vends, vendons, vendez

Present: vend**s**, vend**s**, vend, vend**ons**, vend**ez**, vend**ent**

Imperfect: vend**ais**, vend**ais**, vend**ait**, vend**ions**, vend**iez**, vend**aient**

Future: vendr**ai**, vendr**as**, vendr**a**, vendr**ons**, vendr**ez**, vendr**ont**

Conditional: vendr**ais**, vendr**ais**, vendr**ait**, vendr**ions**, vendr**iez**, vendr**aient**

Subjunctive: vend**e**, vend**es**, vend**e**, vend**ions**, vend**iez**, vend**ent**

Passé Simple: vend**is**, vend**is**, vend**it**, vend**îmes**, vend**îtes**, vend**irent**

Spelling-Change Verbs

-cer Verbs

commencer (to begin)

Present Participle: commençant

Past Participle: commencé; **Auxiliary Verb:** avoir

Imperative: commence, commençons, commencez

Present: commence, commences, commence, commençons, commencez, commencent

Imperfect: commençais, commençais, commençait, commencions, commenciez, commençaient

Future: commencerai, commenceras, commencera, commencerons, commencerez, commenceront

Conditional: commencerais, commencerais, commencerait, commencerions, commenceriez, commenceraient

Subjunctive: commence, commences, commence, commencions, commenciez, commencent

Passé Simple: commençai, commenças, commença, commençâmes, commençâtes, commencèrent

Verbs conjugated like **commencer** — which changes the **c** to **ç** in some conjugations — include **agacer** (*to annoy*), **annoncer** (*to announce*), **avancer** (*to advance*), **effacer** (*to erase*), **lancer** (*to throw*), and **menacer** (*to threaten*)

-ger Verbs

manger (to eat)

Present Participle: mangeant

Past Participle: mangé; **Auxiliary Verb:** avoir

Imperative: mange, mangeons, mangez

Present: mange, manges, mange, mangeons, mangez, mangent

Imperfect: mangeais, mangeais, mangeait, mangions, mangiez, mangeaient

Future: mangerai, mangeras, mangera, mangerons, mangerez, mangeront

Conditional: mangerais, mangerais, mangerait, mangerions, mangeriez, mangeraient

Subjunctive: mange, manges, mange, mangions, mangiez, mangent

Passé Simple: mangeai, mangeas, mangea, mangeâmes, mangeâtes, mangèrent

Similar verbs that sometimes need to put an **e** after the **g** include **bouger** (*to move*), **corriger** (*to correct*), **déménager** (*to move house*), **déranger** (*to disturb*), **diriger** (*to direct*), **exiger** (*to demand*), **juger** (*to judge*), **mélanger** (*to mix*), **nager** (*to swim*), and **voyager** (*to travel*).

Stem-Changing Verbs

-eler Verbs

appeler (to call)

Present Participle: appelant

Past Participle: appelé; **Auxiliary Verb:** avoir

Imperative: appelle, appelons, appelez

Present: appelle, appelles, appelle, appelons, appelez, appellent

Imperfect: appelais, appelais, appelait, appelions, appeliez, appelaient

Future: appellerai, appelleras, appellera, appellerons, appellerez, appelleront

Conditional: appellerais, appellerais, appellerait, appellerions, appelleriez, appelleraient

Subjunctive: appelle, appelles, appelle, appelions, appeliez, appellent

Passé Simple: appelai, appelas, appela, appelâmes, appelâtes, appelèrent

Similar verbs that sometimes double the **l** include **épeler** (*to spell*), **rappeler** (*to call back, recall*), and **renouveler** (*to renew*).

-eter Verbs

jeter (to throw)

Present Participle: jetant

Past Participle: jeté; **Auxiliary Verb:** avoir

Imperative: jette, jetons, jetez

Present: jette, jettes, jette, jetons, jetez, jettent

Imperfect: jetais, jetais, jetait, jetions, jetiez, jetaient

Future: jetterai, jetteras, jettera, jetterons, jetterez, jetteront

Conditional: jetterais, jetterais, jetterait, jetterions, jetteriez, jetteraient

Subjunctive: jette, jettes, jette, jetions, jetiez, jettent

Passé Simple: jetai, jetas, jeta, jetâmes, jetâtes, jetèrent

Hoqueter (*to hiccup*), **projeter** (*to project*), and **rejeter** (*to reject*) are conjugated the same way, doubling the **t** in some conjugations.

-e*er Verbs

acheter (to buy)

Present participle: achetant

Past Participle: acheté; **Auxiliary Verb:** avoir

Imperative: achète, achetons, achetez

Present: achète, achètes, achète, achetons, achetez, achètent

Imperfect: achetais, achetais, achetait, achetions, achetiez, achetaient

Future: achèterai, achèteras, achètera, achèterons, achèterez, achèteront

Conditional: achèterais, achèterais, achèterait, achèterions, achèteriez, achèteraient

Subjunctive: achète, achètes, achète, achetions, achetiez, achètent

Passé Simple: achetai, achetas, acheta, achetâmes, achetâtes, achetèrent

Similar verbs that add a grave accent (**è**) in some conjugations include **amener** (*to take*), **enlever** (*to remove*), **se lever** (*to get up*), **mener** (*to lead*), and **promener** (*to walk*).

-é*er Verbs

gérer (to manage)

Present participle: gérant

Past Participle: géré; **Auxiliary Verb:** avoir

Imperative: gère, gérons, gérez

Present: gère, gères, gère, gérons, gérez, gèrent

Imperfect: gérais, gérais, gérait, gérions, gériez, géraient

Future: gérerai, géreras, gérera, gérerons, gérerez, géreront

Conditional: gérerais, gérerais, gérerait, gérerions, géreriez, géreraient

Subjunctive: gère, gères, gère, gérions, gériez, gèrent

Passé Simple: gérai, géras, géra, gérâmes, gérâtes, gérèrent

Other verbs that change the acute accent (**é**) to a grave accent (**è**) in some conjugations are **compléter** (*to complete*), **espérer** (*to hope*), and **répéter** (*to repeat*).

-yer Verbs

nettoyer (to clean)

Present participle: nettoyant

Past Participle: nettoyé; **Auxiliary Verb:** avoir

Imperative: nettoie, nettoyons, nettoyez

Present: nettoie, nettoies, nettoie, nettoyons, nettoyez, nettoient

Imperfect: nettoyais, nettoyais, nettoyait, nettoyions, nettoyiez, nettoyaient

Future: nettoierai, nettoieras, nettoiera, nettoierons, nettoierez, nettoieront

Conditional: nettoierais, nettoierais, nettoierait, nettoierions, nettoieriez, nettoieraient

Subjunctive: nettoie, nettoies, nettoie, nettoyions, nettoyiez, nettoient

Passé Simple: nettoyai, nettoyas, nettoya, nettoyâmes, nettoyâtes, nettoyèrent

Employer (*to use*), **ennuyer** (*to bore*), and **noyer** (*to drown*) likewise change the **y** to **i** in some conjugations.

Irregular Verbs

aller (to go)

Present Participle: allant

Past Participle: allé; **Auxiliary Verb:** être

Imperative: va, allons, allez

Present: vais, vas, va, allons, allez, vont

Imperfect: allais, allais, allait, allions, alliez, allaient

Future: irai, iras, ira, irons, irez, iront

Conditional: irais, irais, irait, irions, iriez, iraient

Subjunctive: aille, ailles, aille, allions, alliez, aillent

Passé simple: allai, allas, alla, allâmes, allâtes, allèrent

avoir (to have)

Present Participle: ayant

Past Participle: eu; **Auxiliary Verb:** avoir

Imperative: aie, ayons, ayez

Present: ai, as, a, avons, avez, ont

Imperfect: avais, avais, avait, avions, aviez, avaient

Future: aurai, auras, aura, aurons, aurez, auront

Conditional: aurais, aurais, aurait, aurions, auriez, auraient

Subjunctive: aie, aies, ait, ayons, ayez, aient

Passé Simple: eus, eus, eut, eûmes, eûtes, eurent

connaître (to know)

Present Participle: connaissant

Past Participle: connu; **Auxiliary Verb:** avoir

Imperative: connais, connaissons, connaissez

Present: connais, connais, connaît, connaissons, connaissez, connaissent

Imperfect: connaissais, connaissais, connaissait, connaissions, connaissiez, connaissaient

Future: connaîtrai, connaîtras, connaîtra, connaîtrons, connaîtrez, connaîtront

Conditional: connaîtrais, connaîtrais, connaîtrait, connaîtrions, connaîtriez, connaîtraient

Subjunctive: connaisse, connaisses, connaisse, connaissions, connaissiez, connaissent

Passé Simple: connus, connus, connut, connûmes, connûtes, connurent

Other verbs conjugated like **connaître** include **apparaître** (*to appear*), **disparaître** (*to disappear*), **méconnaître** (*to be unaware of*), **paraître** (*to seem*), and **reconnaître** (*to recognize*).

devoir (must, to have to)

Present Participle: devant

Past Participle: dû; **Auxiliary Verb:** avoir

Imperative: dois, devons, devez

Present: dois, dois, doit, devons, devez, doivent

Imperfect: devais, devais, devait, devions, deviez, devaient

Future: devrai, devras, devra, devrons, devrez, devront

Conditional: devrais, devrais, devrait, devrions, devriez, devraient

Subjunctive: doive, doives, doive, devions, deviez, doivent

Passé Simple: dus, dus, dut, dûmes, dûtes, durent

dire (to say, tell)

Present Participle: disant

Past Participle: dit; **Auxiliary Verb:** avoir

Imperative: dis, disons, dites

Present: dis, dis, dit, disons, dites, disent

Imperfect: disais, disais, disait, disions, disiez, disaient

Future: dirai, diras, dira, dirons, direz, diront

Conditional: dirais, dirais, dirait, dirions, diriez, diraient

Subjunctive: dise, dises, dise, disions, disiez, disent

Passé Simple: dis, dis, dit, dîmes, dîtes, dirent

This conjugation pattern is the same for **redire** (*to repeat, to say again*).

être (to be)

Present Participle: étant

Past Participle: été; **Auxiliary Verb:** avoir

Imperative: sois, soyons, soyez

Present: suis, es, est, sommes, êtes, sont

Imperfect: étais, étais, était, étions, étiez, étaient

Future: serai, seras, sera, serons, serez, seront

Conditional: serais, serais, serait, serions, seriez, seraient

Subjunctive: sois, sois, soit, soyons, soyez, soient

Passé Simple: fus, fus, fut, fûmes, fûtes, furent

faire (to do, make)

Present Participle: faisant

Past Participle: fait; **Auxiliary Verb:** avoir

Imperative: fais, faisons, faites

Present: fais, fais, fait, faisons, faites, font

Imperfect: faisais, faisais, faisait, faisions, faisiez, faisaient

Future: ferai, feras, fera, ferons, ferez, feront

Conditional: ferais, ferais, ferait, ferions, feriez, feraient

Subjunctive: fasse, fasses, fasse, fassions, fassiez, fassent

Passé Simple: fis, fis, fit, fîmes, fîtes, firent

Défaire (*to undo, dismantle*), **refaire** (*to do/make again*), and **satisfaire** (*to satisfy*) follow the same pattern.

mettre (to put, to place)

Present Participle: mettant

Past Participle: mis; **Auxiliary Verb:** avoir

Imperative: mets, mettons, mettez

Present: mets, mets, met, mettons, mettez, mettent

Imperfect: mettais, mettais, mettait, mettions, mettiez, mettaient

Future: mettrai, mettras, mettra, mettrons, mettrez, mettront

Conditional: mettrais, mettrais, mettrait, mettrions, mettriez, mettraient

Subjunctive: mette, mettes, mette, mettions, mettiez, mettent

Passé Simple: mis, mis, mit, mîmes, mîtes, mirent

Verbs like **mettre** include **admettre** (*to admit*), **commettre** (*to commit*), **permettre** (*to permit*), **promettre** (*to promise*), and **soumettre** (*to submit*).

offrir (to offer)

Present Participle: offrant

Past Participle: offert; **Auxiliary Verb:** avoir

Imperative: offre, offrons, offrez

Present: offre, offres, offre, offrons, offrez, offrent

Imperfect: offrais, offrais, offrait, offrions, offriez, offraient

Future: offrirai, offriras, offrira, offrirons, offrirez, offriront

Conditional: offrirais, offrirais, offrirait, offririons, offririez, offriraient

Subjunctive: offre, offres, offre, offrions, offriez, offrent

Passé Simple: offris, offris, offrit, offrîmes, offrîtes, offrirent

Verbs like **offrir** include **couvrir** (*to cover*), **découvrir** (*to discover*), **ouvrir** (*to open*), **recouvrir** (*to re-cover, conceal*), and **souffrir** (*to suffer*).

partir (to leave)

Present Participle: partant

Past Participle: parti; **Auxiliary Verb:** être

Imperative: pars, partons, partez

Present: pars, pars, part, partons, partez, partent

Imperfect: partais, partais, partait, partions, partiez, partaient

Future: partirai, partiras, partira, partirons, partirez, partiront

Conditional: partirais, partirais, partirait, partirions, partiriez, partiraient

Subjunctive: parte, partes, parte, partions, partiez, partent

Passé Simple: partis, partis, partit, partîmes, partîtes, partirent

Repartir (*to restart, set off again*) is conjugated the same.

pouvoir (can, to be able to)

Present Participle: pouvant

Past Participle: pu; **Auxiliary Verb:** avoir

Present: peux, peux, peut, pouvons, pouvez, peuvent

Imperfect: pouvais, pouvais, pouvait, pouvions, pouviez, pouvaient

Future: pourrai, pourras, pourra, pourrons, pourrez, pourront

Conditional: pourrais, pourrais, pourrait, pourrions, pourriez, pourraient

Subjunctive: puisse, puisses, puisse, puissions, puissiez, puissent

Passé Simple: pus, pus, put, pûmes, pûtes, purent

prendre (to take)

Present Participle: prenant

Past Participle: pris; **Auxiliary Verb:** avoir

Imperative: prends, prenons, prenez

Present: prends, prends, prend, prenons, prenez, prennent

Imperfect: prenais, prenais, prenait, prenions, preniez, prenaient

Future: prendrai, prendras, prendra, prendrons, prendrez, prendront

Conditional: prendrais, prendrais, prendrait, prendrions, prendriez, prendraient

Subjunctive: prenne, prennes, prenne, prenions, preniez, prennent

Passé Simple: pris, pris, prit, prîmes, prîtes, prirent

Other verbs like **prendre** include **apprendre** (*to learn*), **comprendre** (*to understand*), and **surprendre** (*to surprise*).

savoir (to know)
Present Participle: sachant

Past Participle: su; **Auxiliary Verb:** avoir

Imperative: sache, sachons, sachez

Present: sais, sais, sait, savons, savez, savent

Imperfect: savais, savais, savait, savions, saviez, savaient

Future: saurai, sauras, saura, saurons, saurez, sauront

Conditional: saurais, saurais, saurait, saurions, sauriez, sauraient

Subjunctive: sache, saches, sache, sachions, sachiez, sachent

Passé Simple: sus, sus, sut, sûmes, sûtes, surent

venir (to come)
Present Participle: venant

Past Participle: venu; **Auxiliary Verb:** être

Imperative: viens, venons, venez

Present: viens, viens, vient, venons, venez, viennent

Imperfect: venais, venais, venait, venions, veniez, venaient

Future: viendrai, viendras, viendra, viendrons, viendrez, viendront

Conditional: viendrais, viendrais, viendrait, viendrions, viendriez, viendraient

Subjunctive: vienne, viennes, vienne, venions, veniez, viennent

Passé Simple: vins, vins, vint, vînmes, vîntes, vinrent

Verbs conjugated like **venir** include **advenir** (*to happen*), **devenir** (*to become*), **parvenir** (*to reach, achieve*), **revenir** (*to come back*), and **se souvenir** (*to remember*).

vouloir (to want)
Present Participle: voulant

Past Participle: voulu; **Auxiliary Verb:** avoir

Imperative: veuille, N/A, veuillez

Present: veux, veux, veut, voulons, voulez, veulent

Imperfect: voulais, voulais, voulait, voulions, vouliez, voulaient

Future: voudrai, voudras, voudra, voudrons, voudrez, voudront

Conditional: voudrais, voudrais, voudrait, voudrions, voudriez, voudraient

Subjunctive: veuille, veuilles, veuille, voulions, vouliez, veuillent

Passé Simple: voulus, voulus, voulut, voulûmes, voulûtes, voulurent

Appendix B

English-French Dictionary

*H*ere's some of the French vocabulary used throughout this book, arranged alphabetically by the English translation, to help you when reading or listening to French.

a, an, one: **un** (m.)/**une** (f.)

about, of, from: **de**

above: **dessus**

to advance: **avancer**

after: **après**

again: **encore**

against: **contre**

already: **déjà**

although: **bien que**

always: **toujours**

and: **et**

and/or: **et/ou**

to announce: **annoncer**

to annoy: **ennuyer**

to answer: **répondre**

around: **autour**

to arrange: **arranger**

to arrive: **arriver**

as much/many: **autant**

as soon as: **aussitôt**

at, to, in: **à**

badly: **mal**

to be: **être**

because: **parce que**

before: **avant**

to begin: **commencer**

behind: **derrière**

to believe: **croire**

below: **dessous**

better: **mieux**

to bore: **ennuyer**

to be born: **naître**

both . . . and: **et . . . et**

to bring up, raise: **élever**

to build: **bâtir**

but: **mais**

to buy: **acheter**

by: **par**

to call: **appeler**

to call back, recall: **rappeler**

can, to be able to: **pouvoir**

to celebrate: **célébrer**

certainly: **certainement**

to change: **changer**

to choose: **choisir**

to claim: **prétendre**

to clean: **nettoyer**

to climb: **monter**

to come: **venir**

to complete: **compléter**

to consider: **considérer**

continually: **continuellement**

to correct: **corriger**

currently: **actuellement**

day: **un jour**

to defend: **défendre**

to demand: **exiger**

to denounce: **dénoncer**

to descend: **descendre**

to die: **mourir**

difficult: **dificile**

to direct: **diriger**

to divorce: **divorcer**

to do: **faire**

down: **en bas**

to drink: **boire**

early: **tôt**

to eat: **manger**

either . . . or: **ou . . . ou/soit . . . soit**

to employ: **employer**

enormously: **énormément**

enough: **assez**

to enter: **entrer**

to erase: **effacer**

to establish: **établir**

even though: **quoique**

everywhere: **partout**

expensive: **cher**

to fall: **tomber**

far: **loin**

fat: **gras**

favorite: **préféré**

to fill: **remplir**

finally: **enfin**

to find: **trouver**

to finish: **finir**

flight: **un vol**

fluently: **couramment**

for: **pour**

for a long time: **longtemps**

formal: **formel**

formerly: **autrefois**

fortunately: **heureusement**

to freeze: **geler**

fresh: **frais**

to frighten: **effrayer**

from, about, of: **de**

from/about the: **des** (pl.)/**du** (sing. m.)

to give: **donner**

to give back, return (something): **rendre**

gladly: **volontiers**

to go: **aller**

to go out: **sortir**

to grow: **grandir**

good: **bon**

happy: **heureux**

to hate: **détester**

to have: **avoir**

he, it: **il**

to hear: **entendre**

here: **ici**

to hiccup: **hoqueter**

his, her, its (adj.): **sa** (f.)/**son** (m.)/**ses** (pl.)

his, hers, its (pron.): **le sien** (m. sing.), **la sienne** (f. sing.), **les siens** (m. pl.), **les siennes** (f. pl.)

to hold: **tenir**

to hope: **espérer**

how: **comment**

how much/many: **combien**

I: **je**

immediately: **immédiatement**

in front of: **devant**

in, to (a country): **en**

to influence: **influencer**

inside: **dedans**

intelligently: **intelligemment**

interesting: **intéressant**

just as, so as: **ainsi que**

kind: **gentil**

kindly: **gentiment**

to know: **savoir**

lastly: **dernièrement**

late: **tard**

to lead: **mener**

to leaf through: **feuilleter**

to leave: **partir**

less: **moins**

to lift, raise: **lever**

to like, to love: **aimer**

a little bit: **un peu de**

to live: **vivre**

lively: **vif**

to lodge: **loger**

to look for: **chercher**

to lose: **perdre**

a lot: **beaucoup**

majority: **la plupart de**

to manage: **gérer**

to meet: **réunir**

meeting: **la réunion**

to melt: **fondre**

midnight: **minuit** (m.)

mild: **doux**

mine: **le mien** (m. sing.), **la mienne** (f. sing.), **les miens** (m. pl.), **les miennes** (f. pl.)

to moderate: **modérer**

more than: **plus de/que**

to move: **bouger**

to move house: **déménager**

must, to have to: **devoir**

my: **mon** (m. object)/**ma** (f. object)/**mes** (pl. object)

near: **près**

neither. . . nor: **ne . . . ni . . . ni**

never: **ne . . . jamais**

new: **neuf, nouveau**

newly: **nouvellement**

next: **ensuite**

no: **non**

no one: **ne . . . personne**

none: **ne . . . aucun, ne . . . nul**

noon: **midi**

not: **ne . . . pas**

not always: **ne . . . pas toujours**

not anymore, no more: **ne . . . plus**

not at all: **ne . . . pas du tout**

not yet: **ne . . . pas encore**

now: **maintenant**

nowhere: **ne . . . nulle part**

of, from, about: **de**

often: **souvent**

on: **sur**

on purpose: **exprès**

one, we, they: **on**

only: **ne . . . que**

to open: **ouvrir**

or: **ou**

or else: **ou bien**

our: **notre** (sing.)/**nos** (pl.)

ours: **le nôtre** (m. sing.), **la nôtre** (f. sing.), **les nôtres** (pl.)

outside: **dehors**

to pass: **passer**

to pay: **payer**

to play: **jouer**

politely: **poliment**

to possess: **posséder**

postcard: **la carte postale**

to prefer: **préférer**

pretty: **joli**

to project: **projeter**

to pronounce: **prononcer**

provided that: **pourvu que**

to put: **mettre**

quickly: **vite**

quite a bit: **pas mal de**

quite a few: **bien de**

to rain: **pleuvoir**

rarely: **rarement**

to react: **réagir**

to receive: **recevoir**

recently: **récemment**

to reject: **rejeter**

to remove: **enlever**

to renew: **renouveler**

to repeat: **répéter**

to replace: **remplacer**

to return: **retourner**

sad: **triste**

sadly: **tristement**

to say: **dire**

to see: **voir**

to sell: **vendre**

to send: **envoyer**

serious: **grave**

she, it: **elle**

similar: **pareil**

since: **depuis**

since, as: **puisque**

to sleep: **dormir**

slowly: **lentement**

small: **petit**

so: **donc**

so that: **afin que, pour que**

some: **du** (m.)/**de la** (f.)/**des** (pl.)

sometimes: **parfois, quelquefois**

somewhere: **quelque part**

soon: **bientôt**

to spell: **épeler**

to spend (time): **passer**

squarely: **carrément**

to stay: **rester**

to succeed: **réussir**

sufficiently: **suffisamment**

to suggest: **suggérer**

to sweep: **balayer**

to take: **prendre, amener**

to talk, to speak: **parler**

the: **le** (m.)/**la** (f.)/**les** (pl.)

their: **leur** (sing. object)/**leurs** (pl. object)

theirs: **le leur** (m. sing.), **la leur** (f. sing.), **les leurs** (pl.)

then: **puis**

there: **là**

these: **ces**

they: **ils** (m.)/**elles** (f.)

thin: **mince**

to think: **penser**

this: **ce** (m.)/**cette** (f.)/**cet** (m. before vowel or mute *h*)

to throw: **jeter, lancer**

to travel: **voyager**

to try: **essayer**

to, at, in: **à**

to/at/in the: **au** (m. sing.)/**aux** (pl.)

too much: **trop**

toward: **vers**

truly: **vraiment**

unless: **à moins que**

until: **jusqu'à ce que**

up: **en haut**

to use ***tu:*** **tutoyer**

to use ***vous:*** **vouvoyer**

very: **très**

to wait (for): **attendre**

to walk: **promener**

to want: **vouloir**

to warn: **avertir**

to watch, to look at: **regarder**

we: **nous**

to weigh: **peser**

well: **bien**

what: **quoi**

What time is it?: **Quelle heure est-il ?**

whatever, no matter what: **quoi que**

What's the date?: **Quelle est la date ?**

when: **quand, lorsque**

where: **où**

whereas, while: **tandis que**

which: **quel** (m. sing.), **quelle** (f. sing.), **quels** (m. pl.), **quelles** (f. pl.)

which one: **lequel** (m. sing.), **laquelle** (f. sing.), **lesquels** (m. pl.), **lesquelles** (f. pl.)

while: **pendant que**

while, until: **en attendant que**

while, whereas: **alors que**

who: **qui**

why: **pourquoi**

with: **avec**

without: **sans**

to work: **travailler**

worse: **pire**

to be worth: **valoir**

yes: **oui**

yes (in response to a negation): **si**

you: **tu** (sing. fam.)/**vous** (pl. and/or form.)

your (**tu** form): **ton** (m. object)/**ta** (f. object)/**tes** (pl. object)

your (**vous** form): **votre** (sing. object)/**vos** (pl. object)

yours: **le tien** (sing., fam.)/**le vôtre** (form. and/or pl.)

Appendix C

French-English Dictionary

Here's some of the vocabulary used throughout this book, arranged alphabetically by the French term, to help you when writing or speaking French.

à: *to, at, in*

à moins que: *unless*

acheter: *to buy*

actuellement: *currently*

afin que: *so that*

aimer: *to like, to love*

ainsi que: *just as, so as*

aller: *to go*

alors que: *while, whereas*

amener: *to take*

annoncer: *to announce*

appeler: *to call*

après: *after*

après que: *after, when*

arranger: *to arrange*

arriver: *to arrive*

assez: *enough*

attendre: *to wait (for)*

au (m. sing.): *to, at, in the*

aussitôt: *as soon as*

autant: *as much/many*

automne: *autumn/fall*

autour: *around*

autrefois: *formerly*

aux (pl.): *to/at/in the*

avancer: *to advance*

avant: *before*

avant que: *before*

avec: *with*

avertir: *to warn*

avoir: *to have*

balayer: *to sweep*

bâtir: *to build*

beaucoup: *a lot*

bien: *well*

bien de: *quite a few*

bien que: *although*

bientôt: *soon*

boire: *to drink*

bon: *good*

bouger: *to move*

carrément: *squarely*

la carte postale: *postcard*

ce (m.): *this*

célébrer: *to celebrate*

certainement: *certainly*

ces: *these*

cette (f.): *this*

changer: *to change*

cher: *expensive*

chercher: *to look for*

choisir: *to choose*

combien: *how much/many*

commencer: *to begin*

comment: *how*

compléter: *to complete*

considérer: *to consider*

continuellement: *continually*

contre: *against*

corriger: *to correct*

couramment: *fluently*

croire: *to believe*

de: *of, from, about*

de crainte que: *for fear that*

de la (f. sing.): *some*

de peur que: *for fear that*

dedans: *inside*

défendre: *to defend*

dehors: *outside*

déjà: *already*

demain: *tomorrow*

déménager: *to move house*

dénoncer: *to denounce*

depuis: *since*

dernièrement: *lastly*

derrière: *behind*

des (pl.): *some; from/about the*

descendre: *to descend*

dessous: *below*

dessus: *above*

détester: *to hate*

devant: *in front of*

devoir: *must, to have to*

difficile: *difficult*

dire: *to say*

diriger: *to direct*

divorcer: *to divorce*

donc: *so*

donner: *to give*

dormir: *to sleep*

doux: *mild, soft*

du (m. sing.): *some*

du (m. sing.): *from/about the*

effacer: *to erase*

effrayer: *to frighten*

élever: *to bring up, raise*

elle: *she, it*

elles (f.): *they*

employer: *to employ*

en: *in, to (a country)*

en attendant que: *while, until*

en bas: *down*

en haut: *up*

encore: *again*

enfin: *finally*

enlever: *to remove*

ennuyer: *to bore, annoy*

énormément: *enormously*

ensuite: *next*

entendre: *to hear*

entrer: *to enter*

envoyer: *to send*

épeler: *to spell*

espérer: *to hope*

essayer: *to try*

et: *and*

et . . . et: *both . . . and*

et/ou: *and/or*

établir: *to establish*

être: *to be*

exiger: *to demand*

exprès: *on purpose*

faire: *to do, make*

feuilleter: *to leaf through*

finir: *to finish*

fondre: *to melt*

formel: *formal*

frais: *fresh, cool*

geler: *to freeze*

gentil: *kind*

gentiment: *kindly*

gérer: *to manage*

grandir: *to grow*

gras: *fat*

grave: *serious*

heureusement: *fortunately*

heureux: *happy*

hoqueter: *to hiccup*

ici: *here*

il: *he, it*

ils (m.): *they*

immédiatement: *immediately*

influencer: *to influence*

intelligemment: *intelligently*

intéressant: *interesting*

jamais: *never, ever*

je: *I*

jeter: *to throw*

joli: *pretty*

jouer: *to play*

un jour: *day*

jusqu'à ce que: *until*

la (f.): *the*

là: *there*

lancer: *to throw*
le (m.): *the*
lentement: *slowly*
lequel : *which one*
les (pl.): *the*
leur (sing.): *their*
le leur: *theirs*
leurs (pl.): *their*
lever: *to lift, raise*
loger: *to lodge*
loin: *far*
longtemps: *for a long time*
lorsque: *when*
ma (f.): *my*
maintenant: *now*
mais: *but*
mal: *badly*
manger: *to eat*
mener: *to lead*
mes (pl.): *my*
mettre: *to put*
le mien: *mine*
mieux: *better*
mince: *thin*
modérer: *to moderate*
moins: *less*
mois: *month*
mon (m.): *my*
monter: *to climb*
mourir: *to die*
naître: *to be born*
ne . . . aucun: *none*
ne . . . jamais: *never*
ne . . . ni . . . ni: *neither . . . nor*
ne . . . nul: *none*
ne . . . nulle part: *nowhere*
ne . . . pas: *not*
ne . . . pas du tout: *not at all*
ne . . . pas encore: *not yet*
ne . . . pas toujours: *not always*
ne . . . personne: *no one*
ne . . . plus: *not anymore, no more*
ne . . . que: *only*
nettoyer: *to clean*

neuf, neuve: *new*
non: *no*
nos (pl.): *our*
notre (sing.): *our*
le nôtre: *ours*
nous: *we*
nouveau: *new*
nouvellement: *newly*
on: *one, we, they*
ou: *or*
où: *where*
ou bien: *or else*
ou . . . ou: *either . . . or*
oui: *yes*
ouvrir: *to open*
par: *by*
parce que: *because*
pareil: *similar*
parfois: *sometimes*
parler: *to talk, to speak*
partir: *to leave*
partout: *everywhere*
pas mal de: *quite a bit*
passer: *to spend (time), to pass*
payer: *to pay*
pendant que: *while*
penser: *to think*
perdre: *to lose*
peser: *to weigh*
petit: *small*
un peu de: *a little bit*
pire: *worse*
pleuvoir: *to rain*
la plupart de: *the majority*
plus de: *more than*
poliment: *politely*
posséder: *to possess*
pour: *for*
pour que: *so that*
pourquoi: *why*
pourvu que: *provided that*
pouvoir: *can, to be able to*
préféré: *favorite*
préférer: *to prefer*

premier: *first*
prendre: *to take*
près: *near*
prétendre: *to claim*
projeter: *to project*
promener: *to walk*
prononcer: *to pronounce*
puis: *then*
puisque: *since, as*
quand: *when*
quel: *which*
Quelle est la date ?: *What's the date?*
Quelle heure est-il ?: *What time is it?*
quelque part: *somewhere*
quelquefois: *sometimes*
qui: *who*
quoi: *what*
quoi que: *whatever, no matter what*
quoique: *even though*
rappeler: *to call back, recall*
rarement: *rarely*
réagir: *to react*
récemment: *recently*
recevoir: *to receive*
regarder: *to watch, to look at*
rejeter: *to reject*
remplacer: *to replace*
remplir: *to fill*
rendre: *to give back, return (something)*
renouveler: *to renew*
répéter: *to repeat*
répondre: *to answer*
rester: *to stay*
retourner: *to return*
réunion: *meeting*
réunir: *to meet*
réussir: *to succeed*
sa (f.): *his, her, its*
sans: *without*
savoir: *to know*
secret: *secret*
ses (pl.): *his, her, its*
si: *yes* (in response to a negation)
le sien: *his, hers, its*

soit . . . soit: *either . . . or*
son (m.): *his, her, its*
sortir: *to go out*
souvent: *often*
suffisamment: *sufficiently*
suggérer: *to suggest*
sur: *on*
ta (f.): *your*
tandis que: *while, whereas*
tard: *late*
tenir: *to hold*
tes (pl.): *your*
le tien: *yours*
tomber: *to fall*
ton (m.): *your*
tôt: *early*
toujours: *always*
travailler: *to work*
très: *very*
triste: *sad*
tristement: *sadly*
trop: *too much*
trouver: *to find*
tu (sing. fam.): *you*
tutoyer: *to use **tu***
un (m.)/**une** (f.): *a, an, one*
valoir: *to be worth*
vendre: *to sell*
venir: *to come*
vers: *toward*
vif: *lively*
vite: *quickly*
vivre: *to live*
voir: *to see*
le vol: *flight*
volontiers: *gladly*
vos (pl.): *your*
votre (sing.): *your*
le vôtre: *yours*
vouloir: *to want*
vous (pl. and/or form.): *you*
vouvoyer: *to use **vous***
voyager: *to travel*
vraiment: *truly*

Index

BUSINESS, CAREERS & PERSONAL FINANCE

0-7645-9847-3   0-7645-2431-3

Also available:

- Business Plans Kit For Dummies
  0-7645-9794-9
- Economics For Dummies
  0-7645-5726-2
- Grant Writing For Dummies
  0-7645-8416-2
- Home Buying For Dummies
  0-7645-5331-3
- Managing For Dummies
  0-7645-1771-6
- Marketing For Dummies
  0-7645-5600-2

- Personal Finance For Dummies
  0-7645-2590-5*
- Resumes For Dummies
  0-7645-5471-9
- Selling For Dummies
  0-7645-5363-1
- Six Sigma For Dummies
  0-7645-6798-5
- Small Business Kit For Dummies
  0-7645-5984-2
- Starting an eBay Business For Dummies
  0-7645-6924-4
- Your Dream Career For Dummies
  0-7645-9795-7

HOME & BUSINESS COMPUTER BASICS

0-470-05432-8   0-471-75421-8

Also available:

- Cleaning Windows Vista For Dummies
  0-471-78293-9
- Excel 2007 For Dummies
  0-470-03737-7
- Mac OS X Tiger For Dummies
  0-7645-7675-5
- MacBook For Dummies
  0-470-04859-X
- Macs For Dummies
  0-470-04849-2
- Office 2007 For Dummies
  0-470-00923-3

- Outlook 2007 For Dummies
  0-470-03830-6
- PCs For Dummies
  0-7645-8958-X
- Salesforce.com For Dummies
  0-470-04893-X
- Upgrading & Fixing Laptops For Dummies
  0-7645-8959-8
- Word 2007 For Dummies
  0-470-03658-3
- Quicken 2007 For Dummies
  0-470-04600-7

FOOD, HOME, GARDEN, HOBBIES, MUSIC & PETS

0-7645-8404-9   0-7645-9904-6

Also available:

- Candy Making For Dummies
  0-7645-9734-5
- Card Games For Dummies
  0-7645-9910-0
- Crocheting For Dummies
  0-7645-4151-X
- Dog Training For Dummies
  0-7645-8418-9
- Healthy Carb Cookbook For Dummies
  0-7645-8476-6
- Home Maintenance For Dummies
  0-7645-5215-5

- Horses For Dummies
  0-7645-9797-3
- Jewelry Making & Beading For Dummies
  0-7645-2571-9
- Orchids For Dummies
  0-7645-6759-4
- Puppies For Dummies
  0-7645-5255-4
- Rock Guitar For Dummies
  0-7645-5356-9
- Sewing For Dummies
  0-7645-6847-7
- Singing For Dummies
  0-7645-2475-5

INTERNET & DIGITAL MEDIA

0-470-04529-9   0-470-04894-8

Also available:

- Blogging For Dummies
  0-471-77084-1
- Digital Photography For Dummies
  0-7645-9802-3
- Digital Photography All-in-One Desk Reference For Dummies
  0-470-03743-1
- Digital SLR Cameras and Photography For Dummies
  0-7645-9803-1
- eBay Business All-in-One Desk Reference For Dummies
  0-7645-8438-3
- HDTV For Dummies
  0-470-09673-X

- Home Entertainment PCs For Dummies
  0-470-05523-5
- MySpace For Dummies
  0-470-09529-6
- Search Engine Optimization For Dummies
  0-471-97998-8
- Skype For Dummies
  0-470-04891-3
- The Internet For Dummies
  0-7645-8996-2
- Wiring Your Digital Home For Dummies
  0-471-91830-X

* Separate Canadian edition also available
† Separate U.K. edition also available

Available wherever books are sold. For more information or to order direct: U.S. customers visit www.dummies.com or call 1-877-762-2974.
U.K. customers visit www.wileyeurope.com or call 0800 243407. Canadian customers visit www.wiley.ca or call 1-800-567-4797.

SPORTS, FITNESS, PARENTING, RELIGION & SPIRITUALITY

0-471-76871-5

0-7645-7841-3

Also available:
- Catholicism For Dummies
  0-7645-5391-7
- Exercise Balls For Dummies
  0-7645-5623-1
- Fitness For Dummies
  0-7645-7851-0
- Football For Dummies
  0-7645-3936-1
- Judaism For Dummies
  0-7645-5299-6
- Potty Training For Dummies
  0-7645-5417-4
- Buddhism For Dummies
  0-7645-5359-3

- Pregnancy For Dummies
  0-7645-4483-7 †
- Ten Minute Tone-Ups For Dummies
  0-7645-7207-5
- NASCAR For Dummies
  0-7645-7681-X
- Religion For Dummies
  0-7645-5264-3
- Soccer For Dummies
  0-7645-5229-5
- Women in the Bible For Dummies
  0-7645-8475-8

TRAVEL

Ireland 0-7645-7749-2

New York City 0-7645-6945-7

Also available:
- Alaska For Dummies
  0-7645-7746-8
- Cruise Vacations For Dummies
  0-7645-6941-4
- England For Dummies
  0-7645-4276-1
- Europe For Dummies
  0-7645-7529-5
- Germany For Dummies
  0-7645-7823-5
- Hawaii For Dummies
  0-7645-7402-7

- Italy For Dummies
  0-7645-7386-1
- Las Vegas For Dummies
  0-7645-7382-9
- London For Dummies
  0-7645-4277-X
- Paris For Dummies
  0-7645-7630-5
- RV Vacations For Dummies
  0-7645-4442-X
- Walt Disney World & Orlando
  For Dummies
  0-7645-9660-8

GRAPHICS, DESIGN & WEB DEVELOPMENT

Adobe Creative Suite 2 0-7645-8815-X

Photoshop CS2 0-7645-9571-7

Also available:
- 3D Game Animation For Dummies
  0-7645-8789-7
- AutoCAD 2006 For Dummies
  0-7645-8925-3
- Building a Web Site For Dummies
  0-7645-7144-3
- Creating Web Pages For Dummies
  0-470-08030-2
- Creating Web Pages All-in-One Desk
  Reference For Dummies
  0-7645-4345-8
- Dreamweaver 8 For Dummies
  0-7645-9649-7

- InDesign CS2 For Dummies
  0-7645-9572-5
- Macromedia Flash 8 For Dummies
  0-7645-9691-8
- Photoshop CS2 and Digital
  Photography For Dummies
  0-7645-9580-6
- Photoshop Elements 4 For Dummies
  0-471-77483-9
- Syndicating Web Sites with RSS Feeds
  For Dummies
  0-7645-8848-6
- Yahoo! SiteBuilder For Dummies
  0-7645-9800-7

NETWORKING, SECURITY, PROGRAMMING & DATABASES

Visual Basic 2005 0-7645-7728-X

Wireless Home Networking 0-471-74940-0

Also available:
- Access 2007 For Dummies
  0-470-04612-0
- ASP.NET 2 For Dummies
  0-7645-7907-X
- C# 2005 For Dummies
  0-7645-9704-3
- Hacking For Dummies
  0-470-05235-X
- Hacking Wireless Networks
  For Dummies
  0-7645-9730-2
- Java For Dummies
  0-470-08716-1

- Microsoft SQL Server 2005 For Dummies
  0-7645-7755-7
- Networking All-in-One Desk Reference
  For Dummies
  0-7645-9939-9
- Preventing Identity Theft For Dummies
  0-7645-7336-5
- Telecom For Dummies
  0-471-77085-X
- Visual Studio 2005 All-in-One Desk
  Reference For Dummies
  0-7645-9775-2
- XML For Dummies
  0-7645-8845-1

HEALTH & SELF-HELP

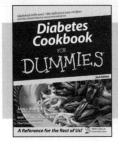

0-7645-8450-2

0-7645-4149-8

Also available:
- Bipolar Disorder For Dummies
  0-7645-8451-0
- Chemotherapy and Radiation
  For Dummies
  0-7645-7832-4
- Controlling Cholesterol For Dummies
  0-7645-5440-9
- Diabetes For Dummies
  0-7645-6820-5* †
- Divorce For Dummies
  0-7645-8417-0 †

- Fibromyalgia For Dummies
  0-7645-5441-7
- Low-Calorie Dieting For Dummies
  0-7645-9905-4
- Meditation For Dummies
  0-471-77774-9
- Osteoporosis For Dummies
  0-7645-7621-6
- Overcoming Anxiety For Dummies
  0-7645-5447-6
- Reiki For Dummies
  0-7645-9907-0
- Stress Management For Dummies
  0-7645-5144-2

EDUCATION, HISTORY, REFERENCE & TEST PREPARATION

0-7645-8381-6

0-7645-9554-7

Also available:
- The ACT For Dummies
  0-7645-9652-7
- Algebra For Dummies
  0-7645-5325-9
- Algebra Workbook For Dummies
  0-7645-8467-7
- Astronomy For Dummies
  0-7645-8465-0
- Calculus For Dummies
  0-7645-2498-4
- Chemistry For Dummies
  0-7645-5430-1
- Forensics For Dummies
  0-7645-5580-4

- Freemasons For Dummies
  0-7645-9796-5
- French For Dummies
  0-7645-5193-0
- Geometry For Dummies
  0-7645-5324-0
- Organic Chemistry I For Dummies
  0-7645-6902-3
- The SAT I For Dummies
  0-7645-7193-1
- Spanish For Dummies
  0-7645-5194-9
- Statistics For Dummies
  0-7645-5423-9

Get smart @ dummies.com®

- **Find a full list of Dummies titles**
- **Look into loads of FREE on-site articles**
- **Sign up for FREE eTips e-mailed to you weekly**
- **See what other products carry the Dummies name**
- **Shop directly from the Dummies bookstore**
- **Enter to win new prizes every month!**

* Separate Canadian edition also available
† Separate U.K. edition also available

Available wherever books are sold. For more information or to order direct: U.S. customers visit www.dummies.com or call 1-877-762-2974.
U.K. customers visit www.wileyeurope.com or call 0800 243407. Canadian customers visit www.wiley.ca or call 1-800-567-4797.

Do More with Dummies

Tickle my ribs!

Grilling FOR DUMMIES

Scrapbooking Basics FOR DUMMIES

12" x 12" kit

Quilting Notions FOR DUMMIES

Sewing Patterns FOR DUMMIES

Cocktail Kit FOR DUMMIES

Poker FOR DUMMIES

Golf FOR DUMMIES

Pilates Workout FOR DUMMIES

'80s Pop Music FOR DUMMIES

'70s Soul Music FOR DUMMIES

Wall & Ceiling Repair Kit FOR DUMMIES

Tarot Deck & Book Set FOR DUMMIES

Sudoku FOR DUMMIES

Texas Hold 'em FOR DUMMIES

**Instructional DVDs • Music Compilations
Games & Novelties • Culinary Kits
Crafts & Sewing Patterns
Home Improvement/DIY Kits • and more!**

WILEY